DESIRE AND DENIAL
IN BYZANTIUM

Society for the Promotion of Byzantine Studies

Publications
6

DESIRE AND DENIAL IN BYZANTIUM

Papers from the Thirty-first Spring Symposium of
Byzantine Studies, University of Sussex,
Brighton, March 1997

Edited by
Liz James

ASHGATE
VARIORUM
Aldershot • Brookfield USA • Singapore • Sydney

Published by Variorum for the Society for the Promotion of Byzantine Studies

Ashgate Publishing Limited
Gower House, Croft Road
Aldershot, Hampshire GU11 3HR
Great Britain

Ashgate Publishing Company
Old Post Road
Brookfield, Vermont 05035–9704
USA

0–86078–788–5

British Library Cataloguing-in-Publication Data

Desire and Denial in Byzantium: Papers from the Thirty-first Spring
Symposium of Byzantine Studies, University of Sussex, Brighton, March 1997.
— (Society for the Promotion of Byzantine Studies: 6)
1. Body, human—Social aspects—Byzantine empire. 2. Love—Social
aspects—Byzantine empire. 3. Byzantine empire—Social life and customs—
Congresses. I. James, Liz. II. Society for the Promotion of Byzantine Studies.
III. Spring Symposium of Byzantine Studies (Thirty-first, 1997, University of
Sussex, Brighton, England)
949.5'02

U.S. Library of Congress Cataloging-in-Publication Data

Desire and Denial in Byzantium: Papers from the Thirty-first Spring
Symposium of Byzantine Studies, University of Sussex, Brighton, March 1997
/ edited by Liz James
    p. cm. – (Publications / Society for the Promotion of Byzantine Studies: 6)
Includes bibliographical references and index.
1. Sex—Byzantine empire—History—Congresses. 2. Sex customs—Byzantine
empire—History—Congresses. 3. Sex in literature—Congresses. 4. Sex in
art—Congresses. I. James, Liz. II. Title. III. Series: Publications (Society for the
Promotion of Byzantine Studies [Great Britain]): 6. IV. Spring Symposium of
Byzantine Studies (Thirty-first, 1997, University of Sussex, Brighton, England)
HQ18.B95S65 1999   98–43403
306.7'09495—dc21   CIP

This volume is printed on acid free paper.

Typeset by   Stanford Desktop Publishing Services, Northampton

Printed and bound in Great Britain by MPG Books Ltd, Bodmin, Cornwall

SOCIETY FOR THE PROMOTION OF BYZANTINE STUDIES – PUBLICATION 6

Contents

v

Acknowledgements

The papers in this volume were presented at the Thirty-first Spring Symposium of Byzantine Studies, held at the University of Sussex in March 1997. As is always the case, not all papers presented at the Symposium appear in the published volume, and I regret that space did not permit the inclusion of more of these communications. Summaries of these appear in volume 24 (1998) of the *Bulletin of British Byzantine Studies*.

I am most grateful to the various foundations and bodies who most generously provided financial support for the Symposium. The A.G. Leventis Foundation, the Hellenic Foundation, the Society for the Promotion of Byzantine Studies and the British Academy provided grants towards the cost of the Symposium. Variorum of Ashgate Publishing Ltd, Aldershot, and the Graduate Research Centre in Cultural and Community Studies of the University of Sussex and the History of Art Subject Group all put up money for the Reception.

Organizing a conference such as this is always more than one person's work. At Sussex, Karen Wraith, Martin Dench, Bev Barstow, Bente Kortegård Bjørnholt, David Felton, Ed Davis all played a major part in keeping the show on the road, as did the assorted members of the student body who ran errands with a hitherto unimagined obedience and efficiency. Without these people, it would have been a nightmare. Dion Smythe and Tony Eastmond were unfailingly helpful and Robin Cormack unfailingly supportive. My thanks to all of these.

In the production of the volume, thanks are due to Ruth Peters at Ashgate Publishing for her hard work, patience and helpfulness (despite Forest), and to Julia Stevenson who had fun with the index.

List of abbreviations

AB	*Analecta Bollandiana*
B	*Byzantion*
BHG	*Bibliotheca hagiographica graeca*, ed. F. Halkin (Brussels, 1957)
BMGS	*Byzantine and Modern Greek Studies*
ByzF	*Byzantinische Forschungen*
BS	*Byzantinoslavica*
BZ	*Byzantinische Zeitschrift*
CahCM	*Cahiers de civilisation médiévale*
CCSG	*Corpus Christianorum, series graeca*
CFHB	Corpus fontium historiae byzantinae
CSHB	Corpus scriptorum historiae byzantinae
CQ	*Classical Quarterly*
DOP	*Dumbarton Oaks Papers*
JÖB	*Jahrbuch der Österreichischen Byzantinistik*
JTS	*Journal of Theological Studies*
JRS	*Journal of Roman Studies*
Lampe	G.W.H.Lampe, *A Patristic Greek Lexicon* (Oxford, 1961–68)
LSJ	H.G.Liddell, R.Scott and H.S.Jones, *A Greek-English Lexicon*
Mansi	G.D.Mansi, *Sacrorum conciliorum nova et amplissima collectio* (Paris and Leipzig, 1901–27)
ODB	*Oxford Dictionary of Byzantium*, ed. A.Kazhdan (Oxford, 1991)
PG	*Patrologiae Cursus Completus, Series Graeca*, ed. J.P. Migne
REB	*Revue des études byzantines*
TM	*Travaux et mémoires*
ZbRad	*Zbornik Radova*

List of plates

Preface

Liz James

Sex, love and the erotic are not terms usually associated with Byzantium and Byzantine studies. Celibacy, virginity and asceticism more readily spring to mind as characteristics of Byzantine society. It was in an attempt to see if there was a balance between these two poles that needed redressing that the theme of desire and denial was adopted for this symposium.

Both desire and denial are problematic terms and it will become apparent that different papers define them in different ways. To paraphrase Freud, the question I began from was: what did the Byzantines want? To answer that, a series of themes were explored: writings about love, both secular and religious; images of sexuality and sensuality; the law; Byzantine attitudes to bodies and to the senses. The book is arranged in five sections. It begins with an examination of different types of text which discuss love and the passions, and from here moves on to the writings of the Church Fathers on different aspects of these topics. The final three sections focus more closely on the actual physical body. They look at different ways in which Christian, especially saintly, bodies were perceived and used; they look at depictions of erotic bodies; they ask how the evidence might offer accounts of 'deviant' bodies. These themes are not comprehensive. What the symposium seems to have revealed is that the question of Byzantine desires is a viable one and one of considerable scope: here, we have only begun to scratch its surface.

Traditionally, symposia volumes have begun with introductions laying out the themes and contents of the book. At this symposium, however, Averil Cameron was asked to sum up the proceedings and here, it is her concluding remarks that set out the case forcefully and eloquently for the further study of desire and denial in Byzantium.

Section I

Love Letters?

1. From Byzantium, with love

Margaret Mullett

My brief is love-letters, and this paper will be concerned, by nature of the subject, with *pothos* rather than with *porneia*,[1] and, by nature of my own interests, with the middle rather than the early Byzantine period. It will concentrate on what went on in the mind, or at least on the page, rather than the body, with what people felt and wrote rather than what they did or were, and with dyads rather than individuals. We shall see that if 'letters mingle soules', their potential is not always exploited or appreciated,[2] and that what constituted *pothos* in the period packs some surprises. I shall not deal with the issue of spiritual love in asceticism. There are three sections: fiction, damned lies, and statistics.

Fiction

If we look in the only theoretical literature on the Byzantine letter which has come down to us, the late antique *Typoi epistolikoi* attributed to Demetrios and the *Epistolimaioi charakteres* attributed to Proklos or Libanios, we have to search for help with love-letters. Demetrios does not list a type at all, and in Proklos-Libanios we find that the *erotike* type (no. 40) is that through which we offer erotic speeches (*logoi*) to our beloveds (feminine). Two examples are given in the *Charakteres*, the first a simple declaration of love which hardly makes use of the epistolarity of the Byzantine letter:

---

[1] These seem the closest Greek approximations to the concept of desire. *Porneia* (LSJ, Lampe) operates at both the wish and deed levels (=lust, fornication), whereas *pothos* (LSJ, Lampe) seems to operate always at a level of feeling (=longing). A. Rousselle, *Porneia: On Desire and the Body in Antiquity* (Oxford, 1988) is an excellent introduction; no equivalent for *pothos* exists.

[2] They can of course be a considerable impediment to bodies, see D. Kennedy, 'The Epistolary Mode and the First of Ovid's Heroides', *CQ*, n.s., 34,2 (1984), 413–22, 144–6 on Richardson's *Pamela*.

> By the Gods, I love, I love your seemly and your lovely shape, and I am not
> ashamed to love it for there is no shame in loving what is seemly. Even if anyone
> were to blame me for being utterly in love, he would on the other hand praise
> me for desiring her who [or the shape which] is good.[3]

It is fairly cool, and were it not for the σῆς μορφῆς we would have been very
unsure that it was addressing the beloved at all; it is very much more
concerned with the lover than the beloved. But we are instantly in the
familiar Greek area of honour and shame in which sexual concerns are
enveloped.[4] The second, found in five manuscripts, is longer and perhaps
more interesting:

> ... My dearest ... soul, as I display the scorching erotic disposition (towards you)
> which is in me, I feel more pride than shame. For I really love you, I love your
> angelic state, I love your prudent and most sweet gaze, I love your quiet
> voice which more sweetly than honey pours from your holy lips, and I prefer
> to throw myself upon your sacred footprints than to luxuriate in imperial
> apartments.[5]

Love again raises the spectre of shame, and the eye contact is virtuous but
the sweetness of eyes, voice and step focus on what makes the beloved
loveable. Yet the repetition, the insistence, ἐρῶ ἐρῶ νὴ τοὺς θεοὺς, of the
first example (no. 40) is repeated here also. Neither of these prescriptions
envisages a developing relationship, or the instrumentality of a letter in the
progress of a passion. What we might categorize as 'before', 'during' and
'after' letters – the letter of seduction (the staple of the eighteenth-century
epistolary novel), letters written during brief separations in the course of
a relationship, and the letters of abandonment and recrimination, the
Heroides type[6] – are each only one facet of the discourse of desire. If we
wish to see this interplay between letters and loving (or lusting)
relationships, we need to look to fiction, to the fictional letter-collections
of late antiquity or to the revived fictional narratives of the twelfth century.

Two major fictional letter-collections have survived, fifty letters in the two
books of Aristainetos dating from the early sixth century, and the eighty-

---

[3] Proklos-Libanios, *Epistolimaioi charakteres*, no. 40, ed. V. Weichert (Leipzig, 1910), 33.

[4] J. Peristiany, ed., *Honour and Shame: The Values of Mediterranean Society* (London, 1965) is
the classic statement, supported by the work of J.K. Campbell, for example, *Honour, Family
and Patronage: A Study of Institutions and Moral Values in a Greek Mountain Community* (Oxford,
1964) and J. du Boulay, for example, *Portrait of a Greek Mountain Village* (Oxford, 1974). For
attempts to move discussion to broader issues of sex and gender, see J. Dubisch, ed., *Gender
and Power in Rural Greece* (Princeton, 1986) and P. Loizos and E. Papataxiarchis, eds, *Contested
Identities: Gender and Kinship in Modern Greece* (Princeton, 1991).

[5] Proklos-Libanios, *Epistolimaioi charakteres*, no. 84, *Exempla in codicibus VatHaFVbMa*,
ed. Weichert, 53.

[6] L.S. Kauffman, *Discourses of Desire: Gender, Genre, and Epistolary Fiction* (Ithaca and
London, 1986).

five letters of Theophylact Simocatta.[7] Both appear to be revival phenomena like the vogue for epigrams and for classicizing historiography, and both have yet to find a sympathetic interpreter, who will look at them in the context of sixth-century erotic epigrams and of contemporary rhetorical practice, and who will also read them against the major fictional collections of the second sophistic, Alkiphron's letters from fishermen, farmers, parasites and *hetairai* and Philostratos's *Epistolai erotikai*.[8] Like these texts, the Byzantine examples are addressed to different persons, some historical, some mythological, some imaginary, women and boys, from men and women. They conjure up a landscape of easy promiscuous sex, of quickly sated passion, of agonistic wooing and world-weary advice, a whole social setting for the interplay of pleasure and longing, cynical, casual, gossipy and concerned. Unlike the 'real' Byzantine letter, they open windows into the populous community of their imagined life rather than portray what Barthes has called the language of an extreme solitude.[9] Though each letter is complete in itself, it depicts a full cast of characters and is set at a particular moment; it casts back and forward in time as the situation demands. Unlike the 'real' Byzantine letter, which concentrates on the relationship between writer and recipient, third persons litter the landscape, urban or rural. The simple declaration of love of Libanios-Proklos is found seldom, sometimes tucked away at the end of a book.[10]

But even if these fictional letters are read in relation to the earlier collections, it seems unlikely that we shall be able to gain as much from this comparison as of late has been achieved in another genre by the reading of the four twelfth-century novels with the five ancient ones.[11] The production and the reception of fictional letters in the new piety of the sixth century conjures up incongruous images of bishops and lawyers flicking through this classicizing pornography[12] before setting off to preach a sermon or try a case of adultery. Yet stranger incongruities existed even earlier: both Brent Shaw and Patricia Cox Miller have commented lately on

---

[7] Aristainetos, *Epp.*, ed. O. Mazal (Stuttgart, 1971); Theophylact Simocatta, *Epp.*, ed. I. Zanetto (Leipzig, 1985).

[8] R. Benner and F.H. Fobes, eds, *Alciphron, Aelian, Philostratus, the Letters* (London and Cambridge MA, 1962).

[9] R. Barthes, *A Lover's Discourse: Fragments*, tr. R. Howard (Harmondsworth, 1979), 1.

[10] Aristainetos, *Ep.* II.21, Habrokomes to his lover Delphis, ed. Mazal, 98–9.

[11] See R. Beaton, *The Medieval Greek Romance*, 2nd edn (London, 1996); S. MacAlister, *Dreams and Suicides: The Greek Novel from Antiquity to the Middle Ages* (London, 1996); M. Alexiou, 'A Critical Reappraisal of Eustathios Makrembolites' *Hysmine and Hysminias*', *BMGS* 3 (1977), 23–43; R. Webb's unpublished work on *Hysmine and Hysminias*, 'Re-writing and Re-reading the Greek Novel: Eustathios Makrembolites and the Metamorphoses of the Text', promises to be the most interesting of all.

[12] On the concept in ancient societies see A. Richlin, *Pornography and Representation in Greece and Rome* (Oxford and New York, 1992).

the habitual pornographic flavour of Jerome's discourses, 'a rhetorical mixture of erotics and outright pornography of which Jerome, a saint, was particularly capable', and in particular on the 'steamy memory' of the erotic dream-content of letter 22 to Eustochium.[13] What, we wonder, are the implications for Jerome's conception of his relationship with her? Occasionally in late antiquity, these two worlds, of a classicizing and bucolic erotic playground and of the popular passion for ascesis now well established in the empire, converge, uncomfortably. In the letters of Procopios of Gaza,[14] there is almost a sense that this erotic playground might sometimes gain a toehold on real life. Procopios's letters are firmly in the tradition of the Byzantine letter, of the real letter, of real problems of communication, of the topoi of presence and absence which make Byzantinists feel at home and are so far from the knowing sophistication of the parasites and prostitutes of the fictional collections. Yet with some correspondents he flirts with the rhetorical and fictional models we have been looking at, and we gain a sense of danger – and emotion.[15]

After this however, we search in vain for this erotic discourse in the Byzantine letter, despite the obvious advantages of the literary form: its monoaxial and dyadic nature, its concentration on emotion, its compressed charge and its illusory intimacy, and the exploitation Byzantine letter-writers made of this quality.[16] This looks like denial indeed. The closest we come to the concentration on love in the fictional letters of the sixth and seventh centuries is in the fictional revival of the eleventh and twelfth centuries.[17] In three of these works, letters of love play a part. Digenes Akrites may have been 'a man's man who lived on the frontier, never met an intellectual, and devoted his life to sex and violence'.[18] But in the *Lay of the Emir*, in Escorial as well as Grottaferrata, letters are prominent, most

[13] B.D. Shaw, 'Body/Power/Identity: the Passions of the Martyrs', *Journal of Early Christian Studies* 4 (1996), 269–312; P. Cox Miller, 'The Blazing Body: Ascetic Desire in Jerome's Letter to Eustochium, *Journal of Early Christian Studies* 1 (1993), 21–45; see also chap. 8, 'Jerome and his Dreams', in Cox Miller, *Dreams in Late Antiquity* (Princeton, 1994), 205–231.

[14] A. Garzya and R.-J. Loenertz, eds, *Procopii Gazaei epistolae et declamationes studia patristica et byzantina*, Studia patristica et byzantina 9 (Ettal, 1963).

[15] *Ep.* 26 to Eusebios, eds Garzya and Loenertz, 18.

[16] On all this see M. Mullett, 'The Classical Tradition and the Byzantine Letter', in M. Mullett and R. Scott, eds, *Byzantium and the Classical Tradition* (Birmingham, 1981), 75–93.

[17] This looks at first sight unpromising ground, in that the casual reader of these works could be forgiven for believing that consensual sex was unknown to Byzantium, though A. Laiou, *Consent and Coercion to Sex and Marriage in Ancient and Medieval Societies* (Washington DC, 1993), 198–217 has made a good case for all the examples of twelfth-century epic and romance as celebrations of virginity; in any case the implications for readership and patronage are serious. See Beaton, *Medieval Greek Romance*, chap. 12, 'Reception', 189–206 and 'Afterword', 224–6, which does not however engage seriously with the gender issue.

[18] P. Magdalino, 'Byzantine Snobbery', in M. Angold, ed., *The Byzantine Aristocracy, IX–XIII Centuries*, BAR International Series 221 (Oxford, 1984), 69.

notably expressing the love of mother for son. In Book I the mother of the *kore* writes (12 lines) to her sons urging them to seek out their sister, and in the next book they reply (6 lines); after the wedding the emir's mother also writes to the emir (full of mourning, accusation and blame, 46 lines). But there are also letters between the lovers: on the emir's journey to visit his mother in Syria, 'every day he sent letters to his love'.[19] The example given is a speedy one-liner (don't weep, I beg you, rather pray), a rather feeble effort compared with the dutiful effusions of maternal epistolary exchange: a reflection perhaps of Komnenian mother-power. But if we turn to the twelfth-century novels proper we can hardly complain of brevity of epistolary discourse.

In Eustathios Makrembolites's *Hysmine and Hysminias*, where the narrative technique is dominated by the discursive levels of dream and first-person narrative, a crucial point in the plot, the reuniting of the lovers at the end of Book IX, is marked with an included letter from the heroine to the hero. Why does Hysmine reveal her presence by letter rather than in a speech to Hysminias? (The obvious answer is because Leukippe in Achilles Tatios's novel[20] does so, but there are more subtle reasons why the parallel is followed.) This move is followed in the next book – in the complication of the plot which makes Rhodope falls in love with Hysminias and uses her slave Hysmine as go-between – by a love-letter from Rhodope to Hysminias.[21] These two letters demand to be read together, as rare examples of inclusion of another genre in this romance, and in the parallelism of their composition. Both, true to the revival mode, use the formal Greek greeting which is no longer found in personal letters of the twelfth century: 'the maiden Hysmine (the maiden Rhodope, daughter of Sostratos) greets Hysminias, the lover'. Both letters then inform Hysminias of something: Hysmine of her rescue by a dolphin from the sea and Rhodope that she has fallen for Hysminias. Both letters, in almost identical phrasing, emphasize the protection of the spring and bow of Artemis for the writer's virginity. Both bow in the direction of a love-letter, Hysmine with an echo of the second example of Proklos-Libanios: 'on your account I dared sea and waves, and on your account tasted bitter death' while Rhodope claims that Hysminias has drenched her whole soul in the spring of Aphrodite and shot her with erotic darts. Despite this both are very contractual, indeed Hysmine actually uses the word *syntheke*; herein lies the difference. Hysmine

---

[19] *Digenis Akrites*, I.70–81, II.7–12, II.52–98, III.38–9, ed. and tr. J. Mavrogordato (Oxford, 1956), 6, 24, 26–30, 46. Elizabeth Jeffrey's new edition, *Digenis Akrites: the Grottaferrata and Escorial versions*, Cambridge Medieval Classics 7 (Cambridge, 1998), reached me too late to incorporate.

[20] Achilles Tatios, *Klitophon and Leukippe*, 5.18, ed. S. Gaselee (London and Cambridge, MA, 1984), 276.

[21] Eustathios Makembolites, *Hysmine and Hysminias*, IX.8, X.2, ed. R. Hercher, *Erotici scriptores graeci* II (Leipzig, 1859), 254.15–26, 263.10–26; ed. F. Conca, *Il romanzo bizantino del XII secolo* (Turin, 1994), 638–40, 652.

reminds Hysminias of their earlier understanding and calls upon him to honour the agreement: she has done her part by preserving her virginity. Rhodope has this card to play but also further transactions: she will exchange her *patris* for his and will surrender her comfortable life and Hysminias's freedom in exchange for his *erotike philia*. A further exchange offers Hysmine's freedom in exchange for the marriage of Hysminias with Rhodope. This contract looks a much better deal than that of Hysmine, and only the power of love, the memory of many erotic graces, can overturn its persuasiveness. The contrast between the delivery of the second letter (six kisses in fifteen lines under cover of a brother-sister relationship[22]) and the reciprocity and symmetry of the contract proposed in the letter is striking. Had the recognition scene been achieved without the first letter the reader would not later be able to compare them and so observe the parallelism of the women's feelings and situations, or the nature of Hysminias's options, or observe so closely the threat to the lovers or see love conquer instrumentality.

The choice here is Hysminias's: here and in *Digenes* we have a male discourse in which the women write; in another novel (not necessarily later)[23] we see what kind of fist a man makes of describing a man writing a love-letter to a secluded girl – and reading it to his comrade. In Niketas Eugenianos's *Drosilla and Charikles*, there is no shortage of literary interest with multiple included genres. Four love-letters, this time from Kleandros, the hero of the sub-plot, to his beloved Kalligone, form an important part of the main plot as a spur to the hero Charikles's own analepsis.[24] The setting is a Parthian prison after the raid of Barzos which split the two couples, and at the beginning of Book II Kleandros attempts to console Charikles with the story of his own wooing. Charikles insists on full documentary detail. The letters are diffuse, bombastic, and unfocused: each begins with a conceit which is quickly forgotten (Charon, the song of the sirens, the moon, Akontios's trick-apple), and Kleandros slips into hyperbolic self-pity, from which he recovers to express his ambition to hold one another beneath one cloak. There is a sense of male bonding in the intervening exchanges: Charikles comments on the ingenuity of the Charon conceit (in fact it warns the reader of the final denouement of the discovery of Kalligone's death), he is advised not to repeat the more sexually frank passages, and by the end has given up asking whether Kalligone had replied to the letter. Kleandros, embarrassed by the lack of response, abandons rhetoric (or

---

[22] *Hysmine and Hysminias*, IX.20, ed. Hercher, 261.14–27; ed. Conca, 648–50.

[23] The relative dating of the twelfth-century novels is by no means decided; see Beaton, *Medieval Greek Romance*, 211–12.

[24] Niketas Eugenianos, *Drosilla and Charikles*, II.144–325, ed. Hercher, II. 453–7; ed. F. Conca, *Nicetas Eugenianus, De Drosilla et Chariclis amoribus*, London Studies in Classical Philology 24 (Amsterdam, 1990), 60–65.

love-lyric?) for an interminable serenade, after which he receives a suspiciously speedy response. We must read, in Eugenianos's highly sophisticated and literary mockery, a privileging of the power of the serenade over the combined forces of four varied and ambitious letters; we remember now that Digenes, rather than communicating by letter, himself speaks directly with the Girl; she in turn sends her nurse to speak, rather than entrusting her feelings to a letter; finally the hero resorts to a lyre in order to achieve her abduction.[25] In this milieu, it would seem, the love-letter as a medium of seduction is not greatly appreciated; it will take the fourteenth-century ingenuity of *Libistros and Rhodamne* to achieve love-letters which are both effective and remembered with affection by the lovers: the secret is the attachment of love-letters to arrows, shot over the battlements and through the windows of the Castle of Silver to succeed in persuading the beloved to a secret meeting, and so to bed.[26]

Now it is clearly dangerous to make assumptions about the way love-letters were viewed simply from the medium of fiction. But we are hard put to it to find examples of real-life letters of the period which can throw this kind of light on Byzantine perceptions of the discourse of desire: the letters of the mother of the emir and the kore, and certainly those of Hysmine and Rhodope have no real-life counterparts. Not that there is any shortage of eleventh- and twelfth-century letters: the problem is that none of them meets any of the definitions of love-letters we have been working with so far. In fictional letters of an earlier period we have found letters to both male and female beloveds by men; in the included letters of twelfth-century fiction we have found letters written by both women and men in lover, married and mother-son relationships. None of these types is clearly visible in 'real' letters of the eleventh and twelfth centuries. It is not hard to find explanations for this, even at a time when changing literary and social circumstances might appear propitious.[27] There are to begin with an

---

[25] Grottaferrata Digenes, IV, 316–18, 320–30, 425–35, ed. Mavrogordato, 92–4, 100.

[26] *Libistros kai Rhodamne*, S70–S990, tr. G. Betts, *Three Medieval Greek Romances,* Garland Library of Medieval Literature 98 (New York and London, 1995), 122–39; for problems of edition of this text see Beaton, *Medieval Greek Romance*, 217; J.A. Lambert, *Le roman de Libistros et Rhodamné publié d'après les manuscrits de Leyde et Madrid avec une introduction, des observations grammaticales et un glossaire*, Verhandelingen der koninklijke Akademie van Wetenschappen, Afteeling Letterkunde 35 (Amsterdam, 1935) is at present, until the publication of Tina Lendari's thesis and Agapitos's integrated edition, the only recourse, but Betts's translation points the way.

[27] See A.E. Laiou, *Mariage, amour et parenté à Byzance aux XIᵉ–XIIIᵉ siècles*, Travaux et Mémoires Monographies 7 (Paris, 1992) on a new interest in sex in the twelfth century. Further, it is at this time, so as A. Kazhdan assures us in, *Change in Byzantine Culture in the Eleventh and Twelfth Centuries* (with A.W. Epstein) (Berkeley, 1985), 197–233, the individual is emerging, and that the revival of the novel, in however small a way, allows the emergence of a romantic hero and heroine to put the ascetic hero, the holy man, in the shade. Desire should then be outpacing denial from our point of view.

enormous number of reasons why in any society love-letters may not survive. Frank and Anita Kermode clearly think of love-letters as central to the genre (as the only letters any of us write in manuscript any more, as the letters which might be kept as a bundle and preserved for sentimental reasons, as – with friendship and business – the reasons for which the vast majority of us exchange letters).[28] But only in a society which gives romantic passion a positive and serious evaluation will writers collect their letters of love with other less frenzied compositions, and even then love-letters may be regarded as belonging to the private sphere, or regarded as ephemeral and instrumental, or as inferior to love-poetry, or as less important than the expression of other relationships. Or embarrassing: 'one feels almost ashamed', says its first editor, of a letter from Nelson to Lady Hamilton, 'at eavesdropping on such intensity of emotion.'[29] In a society like Byzantium where other kinds and objects of love had been privileged from the very beginning[30] and where a very high proportion of literary society was expected and anxious to be celibate, the chances drop considerably, especially in view of the fact that almost all Byzantine letters survive because they have been collected for publication. And in a society where the difficulties of letter-exchange, the dangers of calumny and the public nature of the most private correspondence made restraint an essential feature,[31] the opportunity to read anyone else's love-letters may have been a specially titillating (because rare) voyeuristic attraction of epistolary fiction.

Fiction may play with chronologies, open out the options, validate alternatives, caricature life or allegorize it away – but so may other, less overtly fictional texts, especially autobiographical modes which deal with

---

[28] F. Kermode and A. Kermode, *The Oxford Book of Letters* (Oxford and New York, 1995), xix.

[29] F. Pryor, *The Faber Book of Letters. Letters Written in the English Language 1578–1939* (London and Boston, 1988), xiv.

[30] Thus localizing *eros* in prayer rather than epistolography. See A. M. Cameron, 'Sacred and Profane Love: Thoughts on Byzantine Gender', in L. James, ed., *Women, Men and Eunuchs* (London, 1997), 1–23 for the way in which 'ascetic literature became a literature of eroticism', thus showing the organic relationship of the twin themes of this volume. For the way in which monastic love for God could be expressed in the West in terms of human erotic love, see J. Leclercq, *Monks and Love in Twelfth-Century France* (Oxford, 1979), esp. 49 on John of Mantua's commentary on the *Song of Songs*: 'whenever we wish to speak of love, we are obliged to use the language of love.'

[31] Julian, *Ep.* 29, ed. W.C. Wright, *The Works of the Emperor Julian* III (London and Cambridge, MA., 1923), 100: 'with regard to the letters which he asserts you made public after receiving them from me, it seems ridiculous to bring them into court. For I call the gods to witness I have never written to you or any other man a word which I am not willing to publish for all to see. I have always expressed myself with more dignity and reserve than one observed even on a sacred subject. I call the gods and goddesses to witness that I should not have resented it even if someone had published abroad all that I ever wrote to my wife, so temperate was it in every respect.'

the recreation of self.[32] Fiction in Byzantium may have been not so much a sudden rediscovery in the eleventh century as a subtle colouring of all kinds of writing under the influence of rhetoric[33] in the exploration of possible worlds.[34]

From the point of view of the scholar, one of the advantages of included letters in fiction, or what would develop into the epistolary novel, is that the context is assured, the relationships are spelled out, the instrumentality of a letter, or its failure to turn the plot as desired, is very clear to the reader (though the theorists of epistolarity rejoice in the ambivalence of the form, its exploitation of tension between trust and suspicion, presence and absence, letter and collection).[35] When we deal with real letters, in real collections, we are on our own, and must detect relationships, their history and intensity, as best we may, in the hope that it may lead us to Byzantine expressions of desire in letters. This is what we must now attempt with the 'real' letters of the eleventh and twelfth centuries. And as a point of principle we should proceed by looking at the material which has survived from the period and recording the widest possible range of expressions of desire, of intense emotional longing. Rather than search for something which fits our concept of a love-letter and risk failing to find it, we should seek to identify and interpret whatever discourse of desire may be found there.

Damned lies

From the eleventh and twelfth centuries (depending where we draw the line) we have about twenty major collections (ten letters or more) and as many smaller ones, perhaps fifteen hundred letters in all. Most, apart from three important monastic collections,[36] are published. Ten of the major letter-writers were at some point bishops, six at some point monks. Very few letters

---

[32] See E. Grubgeld, *George Moore and the Autogenous Self: The Autobiography and Fiction* (New York, 1994), especially for letters, chap. 6, 174–99.

[33] G.W. Bowersock, *Fiction as History, Nero to Julian*, Sather Classical Lectures 58 (Berkeley, Los Angeles and London, 1994) opens up all kinds of possibilities.

[34] See R. Ronen, *Possible Worlds in Literary Theory*, Literature, Culture, Theory 7 (Cambridge, 1994), for one way forward.

[35] J. Altman, *Epistolarity; Approaches to a Form* (Columbus, 1982); B. Redford, *The Converse of the Pen: Acts of Intimacy in the Eighteenth-century Familiar Letter* (Chicago and London, 1986).

[36] These are the five letters of Symeon the New Theologian, the forty-three letters of James the Monk and the one hundred and sixty-five letters of Hierotheos the Monk. One of Symeon's letters was published in K. Holl, *Enthusiasmus und Bussgewalt beim griechischen Mönchtum* (Leipzig, 1898), 110–27; the others are reported in N. Tomadakis, *Byzantine Epistolographia* (Athens, 1969), 185 as being edited with French translation by J. Paramelle. An edition of James the Monk by E. Jeffreys is in press with *CCSG*. The collections of Hierotheos were signalled by J. Darrouzès, 'Un receuil épistolaire du XIIe siècle: Académie roumaine cod.gr.508', *REB* 30 (1972), 199–229.

either to[37] or from[38] women or to family members[39] exist. The overwhelming majority of letters are written by men to men in relationships whose nature we must infer from the context. If we compare this body of material with the eleven hundred non-literary letters sent by members of the French nobility between 1700 and 1860 examined by Marie-Claire Grassi[40] we see a very different balance. Only 48 per cent of her letters are man to man, 15.5 per cent are man to woman, 11 per cent woman to woman and 25.5 per cent woman to man. Just as with included letters in twelfth-century Byzantine fiction we sensed a primary reception of a male literary community, so with twelfth-century 'real letters' we must resign ourselves to a similar male–male discourse.

I shall now try to give the flavour of this male–male discourse at its surface level, exploring vocabulary and form and the uses of epistolarity to express emotion. I am not concerned to 'get behind the topoi to the people who formed them';[41] I am interested in the relationships as portrayed in the texts, and the potential of the form to deal with desire.

While each major collection has its own characteristics and vocabulary, and while the discourse of love is restricted to less than 10 per cent of letters, there are certain features in common. Letters are in general short, built on a *metron* which varies from correspondent to correspondent, shorter in the eleventh century, around 400 words, rather longer later, and the emphasis is on the dyadic relationship of writer and recipient. Very few third persons, even fewer historical events appear in these letters. The most intimate of letters are sparkling, witty, darting wordplay, built on the model of a parable or a fable, a pun or a proverb, or framed with classical quotations, or built on a cento of biblical quotations, involving a shared culture often created in the schools of the capital. The correspondent is drawn into the letter with affectionate address, varying from collection to collection, *potheinotate, pampothete, triphilete, tripothete, philtate, thaumasie*. There is talk of love, of dreams, of epic journeys, of the fear of calumny, of the warmth of *philia*, the kindling of desire and the burning of *pothos*. The Aristophanes

---

[37] Female recipients, a handful of imperial women, include Maria the ex-basilissa (one from Theophylact), Eirene Doukaina (one from Michael Italikos, one from Nicholas Kataskepenos, possibly one from Theophylact) and the *sebastokratorissa* Eirene (letters from James the Monk).

[38] There are certainly two letters from groups of nuns in the Hierotheos collection, nos 175 and 176, see Darrouzès, 'Un receuil épistolaire', 225. Alice-Mary Talbot is investigating the extent of female epistolarity throughout the whole Byzantine period with sadly meagre results.

[39] Brother–brother: e.g. Theophylact, *Ep.* 133, ed. P. Gautier, *Théophylacte d'Achrida, Lettres,* CFHB 16,2 (Thessalonike, 1986), 591.

[40] M.C. Grassi, 'Friends and Lovers (or the Codification of Intimacy)', in C.A. Porter, ed., *Men/Women of Letters*, Yale French Studies 71 (New Haven, 1986), 77–92.

[41] B.P. McGuire, *Friendship and Community, the Monastic Experience, 350–1250* (Kalamazoo, 1988), xii.

myth, Empedocles's monsters, *philophiloi* and Zeus *philios* watch over
relationships which are nurtured and nourished with letters of love. Letters
fly to correspondents, cool their longing like dew, sweeten like honey,
console the loss and cure the sickness of separated lovers, are a feast, a gift
from God, the icon of the soul; medical reports were expected in order to
give a truer picture of the soul. Eyes and mouths, kisses and embraces, bring
correspondents together in the mind's eye; cinnamon and sheep's cheese,
furs and fishes remind the other of the sender. Spiritual sons and relatives,
ex-pupils and fellow-sufferers are caught in nets, welcomed with joy to talk
stoma kai stoma and sent off with tears. *Eros, agape, philia* and *pothos*,
especially *pothos*, fill these letters. The intrinsic epistolary precondition of
separation is exploited to the full, even where that separation is the result
of *anachoresis*. Bishops and monks, teachers and bureaucrats cultivated
relationships and polished communications recognizably inhabiting the
same universe but marking individual personality and style. There is an
intensity, a compressed charge, an intimacy, common only to this small
subset, and thus not all of the making of the genre. It is this sense of intense
longing which seems to define for the Byzantines the use of the word
πόθος. These, not the letters of the romances or of fictional collections, are
the true love-letters of the middle Byzantine empire.

It might however be argued that this language of yearning has nothing
to do with either desire or with love-letters, and that what we have been
finding is simply *philia* in the most *philikos* of Byzantine genres.[42] This
might be sustainable if we were certain that a clear demarcation line exists
in Byzantine usage between *philia*[43] and other kinds of love. Greek is very
rich in affective vocabulary, and some texts do try to distinguish among
kinds of love, allotting one word to each kind of love. But there are also
indications – or maybe only straws in the wind – that the vocabulary of love
and friendship in this period in secular writings is rather less clearly
demarcated than we might have imagined, or find delineated in the classic
treatments of *eros* and *agape, philia* and *storge*.[44] One is that in three places

[42] On friendship and the letter see J. Darrouzès, *Épistoliers byzantins du Xᵉ siècle* (Paris, 1960),
and M.E. Mullett, 'Byzantium: A Friendly Society?', *Past and Present* 118 (1987), 3–24.

[43] There is a general consensus that 'the range of *amicitia* is vast', and that of *philia* even more
complicated: P.A. Brunt, 'Amicitia in the Late Roman Republic', *Proceedings of the Cambridge
Philological Society* 191 (1965), 20; A. Kazhdan and G. Constable, *People and Power in Byzantium:
An Introduction to Modern Byzantine Studies* (Washington DC, 1982), 28.

[44] C.S. Lewis, *The Four Loves* (London, 1960) is the clearest, most schematic treatment of a
view which owes a great deal to A. Nygren, *Eros et agape. La notion chrétienne de l'amour et ses
transformations*, 3 vols (Paris, 1951). See C. Osborne, *Eros Unveiled: Plato and the God of Love*
(Oxford, 1994) for corrections of Nygren both on the continuity of Christian concepts of love
with earlier Greek ideas and, by highlighting the considerable patristic debate on different
kinds of love, on his stark contrast between *eros* and *agape*. See also Cameron, 'Sacred and
Profane Love', on Origen's belief that 'the same meaning is conveyed by both'.

in Grottaferrata Digenes there is a description of the role and function of love showing an organic integration of the basic vocabulary rather than a segregation into types of love,[45] and that elsewhere in that text *eros, pothos* and *philia* seem to be used interchangeably, even if 'each keeps its proper rank'.[46] Another indicator is the second example of an *erotike* type of letter in five manuscripts of the *Epistolimaioi charakteres* which I quoted at the beginning of this paper.[47]

This example is clearly to a eunuch, to a boy or to a monk,[48] and is much more in keeping with our twelfth-century letters than the first *erotike* example. It claims to be an example of an eroticized *pneumatikos eros*, an emotion hard to detect in practice in eleventh- and twelfth-century letters.[49] In three of these manuscripts there is a balancing type *pros filon aspastike*,[50] which touches on the role of *agape* in *philia*; its very existence sets up an opposition between the relationships expressed in the two *typoi*, love and friendship. But when these models are compared with real examples from the eleventh and twelfth centuries the distinction crumbles. No eleventh- or twelfth-century writer addresses any correspondent as Ὦ φιλέ, as in the *pros philon aspastike*, whereas they do address people as Ὦ φιλτάτη μοι ψυχή as in the *erotike*.[51] And in the treatment of the *philikos* type in Demetrios the

---

[45] At IV. 4–9, ed. Mavrogordato, 66, the beginning of the story about Digenes proper, the narrator warns the reader,

Straightway let me tell you about *eros*
for he/ it is the root and origin of *agape*,
from which *philia* is born, and then comes *pothos*,
which growing little by little bears such fruit
as constant worries, troubles and cares,
plenty of dangers, separation from parents.

[46] During Digenes's first conversation with the Girl, IV.315–39 and 341–6, ed. Mavrogordato, 94, *eros* is in control, and as master enslaves the mind, like a charioteer the horse: the result is that the lover, the *pothon*, εὐταξίαν οὐκ ἔχει or shame before his relatives or respect for neighbours, but is a shameless slave of *philia*. Then the Girl leans out of the window; in the middle of their conversation, we are again reminded of the anarchic power of these loves, but this time it is *pothos* which attacks the *sophron*, and then the effects are repeated verbatim, IV.525–30, ed. Mavrogordato, 106. I am grateful to Elizabeth Jeffreys for confirming that in translating Grottaferrata Digenes it is impossible to maintain a consistent distinction between these words.

[47] Proklos-Libanios, *Epistolimaioi charakteres*, no. 84, ed. Weichert, 53, tr. above, xxx.

[48] Ἐρῶ τῆς ἀγγελοειδοῦς σου καταστάσεως, ἐρῶ τοῦ εὐλαβοῦς καὶ ἡδυτάτου βλέμματος, ἐρῶ τῆς ἠρεμαίας καὶ γλυκύτερον τοῦ μέλιτος τῶν εὐαγων σου ἐκρεούσης χειλέων φωνῆς ...

[49] This issue needs a study all of its own.

[50] Proklos-Libanios, *Epistolimaioi charakteres*, no. 86, *Exempla in codicibus VatHaF*, ed. Weichert, 53–4.

[51] For example, Michael Italikos, *Ep.* 27 to the imperial *grammatikos*, P. Gautier, ed., *Michel Italikos, Lettres et discours* (Paris, 1972), 181; Michael Psellos, *Ep.* 198 to a friend, E. Kurtz and F. Drexl, eds, *Michaelis Pselli scripta minora* II (Milan, 1941), 223.

author makes a point of saying that not all those who write letters of this type are friends: what he goes on to describe is epistolary acts of patronage.[52] So the language of *eros* may express *philia* and the language of *philia* may conceal a relationship of patronage. The appropriateness of the erotic is certainly not excluded from the emotions and intimacies inscribed in our twelfth-century letters. But we have yet to discuss what these, the transactional content of our intense relationships, actually are.

Students of medieval Latin letters of this period met this problem some time ago: in 1965 Morey and Brooke noted the potentially illusory intimacy of personal letters: 'a kindly, diplomatic and charitable man like Peter the Venerable seems to be on terms of close friendship with everyone in Christendom'.[53] And in 1972 Colin Morris, in comparing troubadour love-lyric with learned letters of the twelfth century, complained that modern readers have sometimes concluded that the monk was in love with his friend and the poet not in love with his lady.[54] There is of course an answer to this conundrum which was suggested by John Boswell in 1980: the monk *was* in love with his friend.[55] Ever since then students of western monasticism and Latin epistolography have been trying to distance themselves from this view, even those who might be forgiven for feeling themselves to be above the debate.[56] When Anselm writes to a friend

> And so it is that because I am not able to have you with me, while I desire you and you me, I love you more not less.
>
> For what is sweeter, what more pleasant, what is a greater consolation for love than love?[57]

is it possible that he meant it, in terms of physical as well as spiritual love? A closer look raises certain problems: one is the promiscuous nature of his eloquent and poetic love-making. This is how he addressed two young relatives he had not yet met:

> My eyes eagerly long to see your faces, most beloved; my arms stretch out to your embraces; my lips long for your kisses; whatever remain of my life desires your company, so that my soul's joy may be full in time to come.[58]

---

[52] Demetrios, *Typoi epistolikoi*, no. 1, ed. Weichert, 2–3.

[53] A. Morey and C. Brooke, *Gilbert Foliot and his Letters* (Cambridge, 1965), 13.

[54] C. Morris, *The Discovery of the Individual, 1050–1200*, Church History Outlines 5 (London, 1972), 96.

[55] J. Boswell, *Christianity, Social Tolerance and Homosexuality. Gay People in Western Europe from the Beginning of the Christian Era to the Fourteenth Century* (Chicago, 1980).

[56] C. White, *Christian Friendship in the Fourth Century* (Cambridge, 1992), 59 in valiant defence of Basil and Gregory, Paulinus and Ausonius; R. W. Southern, *Saint Anselm; A Portrait in a Landscape* (Cambridge, 1990), 148–52 on Anselm; see also the sympathetic fence-sitting of B.P. McGuire, *Brother and Lover: Aelred of Rievaulx* (New York, 1994).

[57] Anselm, *Epp.* 69, 115, ed. F.S. Schmitt, *Anselmi opera omnia* (Edinburgh, 1946), III. 189, 250.

[58] Anselm, *Ep.* 120, ed. Schmitt, *Anselmi opera omnia*, II. 258.

And if we follow through any of the friendships for which he was famous we find that he may have couched them in the language of love, but he seems more interested in the idea than the reality: with Gondulf and with Gilbert Crispin he is accused of coldness and a lack of concern for their feelings, a willingness to abandon them with a homily on *caritas*. This could be a shift of power within a relationship, but it looks far more like the vocabulary of love expressing a reality of acquaintanceship. When I compared his approach with a contemporary Byzantine writer, I decided that Theophylact was more concerned with an *alethinos philos*, but for Anselm what mattered was *verus amor*.[59] This suggestion that Byzantines may have privileged the relationship over the concept is why I want to devote the last part of my paper to the detection of relationship in Byzantine letters with reference to the network I know best, that of Theophylact of Ochrid.

Statistics

I take as my text this cautious advice:

> It will be obvious to thoughtful readers that a considerable problem in conducting an investigation of this kind is presented by the inevitable difficulty of assessing through the alembic of written sources a thousand or more years old the emotions, feelings and desires involved in human emotional relationships. Most English speakers will feel that they can recognise, intuitively, distinctions among feelings that might be characterised loosely as 'erotic', 'friendly', 'fraternal' or 'parental'. In actual fact however such feelings are often confused both by the subject who experiences them and by the person to whom they are directed,

a fortiori, we might add, by over-confident historians. The cautious historian I quote is John Boswell in the brilliant first chapter of his last book, though it did not stop him proceeding by the end of the chapter to a particular interpretation of the word *adelphos* in a particular kind of source.[60] It is a difficult word: we know that non-kin uses the vocabulary of kinship[61] and that in some authors *adelphos* can mean close friend. But it can also be used for co-sons of a spiritual father, co-pupils of a teacher, and regularly, and as standard, for colleagues, particularly episcopal colleagues.[62] I believe we have to proceed systematically, making our criteria as clear as possible, recording always what is said in the sources: to guess at a problematic

---

[59] M. Mullett, *Theophylact of Ochrid. Reading the Letters of a Byzantine Archbishop* (Aldershot, 1997), 123.

[60] J. Boswell, *The Marriage of Likeness. Same-Sex Unions in Pre-Modern Europe* (London, 1995), 3.

[61] E. Gellner, 'Patrons and Clients', in E. Gellner and J. Waterbury, eds, *Patrons and Clients in Mediterranean Societies* (London, 1977), 1.

[62] See Mullett, *Theophylact*, 173–4.

relationship elsewhere attested on the basis of a different kind of source is a recipe for disaster.[63]

The first stage in the detection of relationship is to demonstrate acquaintanceship. With a letter-collection, anyone addressed (in Theophylact's case sixty-three individuals) or referred to (in Theophylact's case forty-six individuals) may be counted an acquaintance; other writings of the subject are then included (in Theophylact's case eight and nine individuals respectively); certain other criteria (succession in post, family membership, reference together in narrative source) are also accepted to indicate acquaintanceship.

The next move is to establish on the basis of criteria like symmetry, duration, directional flow, and *taxis* the relative roles of the participants in the relationship, and then it can be seen whether relations are simplex or multiplex and a final relationship can be decided upon. So in Theophylact's network we can detect one brother, two other family members, fourteen suffragans or other subordinates, eight senior churchmen, five metropolitans or suffragans of other metropolitans, nine patrons, ten clients, eight opponents, six contacts (instrumental friends in the anthropological literature), seven officials, six ex-colleagues, some relatives of ex-colleagues and teachers, forty persons whose role-relation to Theophylact is undefined; thirty of these are candidates for friendship. In this stage forms of address (*despota*, *adelphe*) are used to establish symmetry and role. In contrast Grassi appears to have had no problems in assigning roles to her correspondents: 41 per cent are non-family (lovers, friends); 34 per cent close family (parent/child, sibling, grand-parent/child) and 25 per cent wider family.[64]

The next stage is to group these members in terms of intimacy. This is done by analogy with an anthropological method devised during the late 1960s by Jeremy Boissevain;[65] persons known directly to Theophylact are his first order zone (127); those known to them are his second order zone (40 from personal cell only) and so on. Persons mentioned by him in the letter-collection or in other sources are his nominal zone of the first order network; those whom he addresses without evidence of affect are his effective zone; those where there is some evidence of affect are his intimate zone and of these ten were selected as the closest, his personal cell. This method dovetails well with the intimacy zoning system used by Grassi and deriving from E.T. Hall:[66] intimate, personal, social and public distances.

---

[63] For example, M. Angold, *Church and Society in Byzantium under the Comneni 1081–1261* (Cambridge, 1995), 556–7, acutely observed by Brent Shaw, 'Ritual Brotherhood in Roman and Post-Roman Societies', *Traditio* 52 (1997), 351 note 82. I am grateful to him for showing me his work in draft and sorry not to have been able to use the full symposium, 'Ritual Brotherhood in Ancient and Medieval Europe', ibid., 259–381, in thinking through this paper.

[64] Clearly the 48 per cent of women letter-writers (compared with just over 3 per cent of women in Theophylact's network) increases the possibilities of kin and affine relations here.

[65] J. Boissevain, *Friends of Friends: Networks, Manipulators and Coalitions* (Oxford, 1974).

[66] E.T. Hall, *The Hidden Dimension* (New York, 1966).

But affect is itself a necessary stage of analysis and influences the zoning of the innermost zones above: how do we decide whether someone is a friend or just an acquaintance? There must be some positive evidence; to assume that anyone who is not a relative, a superordinate, a subordinate or any other defined relation must be a friend is to ignore the vast role of affect in many other personal relations in Byzantium, as well as in the theoretical literature.[67] Symmetry is not essential for affect: there is no reason why a close relationship cannot be built up with a patron: indeed he or she may do a better job. (Nor is erotic charge ruled out in an asymmetrical relationship: compare Theophylact's letter to Maria of Alania with accounts of cabinet members' flirting with Margaret Thatcher in her heyday.[68]) Evidence needs to be sifted with and without the forms of address, so as to avoid the danger of circular argument. What we find if we privilege affective forms of address is a few very close relationships, not perhaps enough to construct an ascending scale of affection,[69] but enough to see that Theophylact's relationship with his brother Demetrios is the most valued (and there is some supporting evidence from the period[70]), then with two young officials posted to Bulgaria, then one ex-pupil (others are used as contacts) and a fellow-bishop. Affective vocabulary in Michael Psellos's much larger collection also seems to cluster in the young officials Weiss and Ahrweiler identified as ex-pupils.[71] If we privilege the polish, delicacy and intricacy of the writing we arrive at a very similar result: a group of ex-pupils and young people Theophylact calls his 'sons'. If we were to privilege discussions of *philia* and use of friendship *topoi*[72] we would find a very different short-list;[73] we can almost assume that if Theophylact talks of the law of love it is to someone he wishes to influence. The intimate correspondents who are addressed without forms seem to come in intimacy after those addressed with affective forms and before those addressed

---

[67] Aristotle, *Nicomachaean Ethics*, VIII.vii.1–2, ed. H. Rackham (London and Cambridge MA, 1926), 476–8.

[68] Theophylact, G4, ed. Gautier, 137–41; A. Clark, *Diaries* (London, 1993), e.g. 69.

[69] In the sense that it is used in Homeric scholarship, cf. J.T. Kakrides, *Homeric Researches* (Lund, 1949), 11–42, 44–64, 152–64.

[70] Brother–brother monodies pack a heavier charge of emotion than any other funerary rhetoric in the period; see, for example, the monodies of Christopher of Mitylene on his brother John, Isidore Meles on his brother Constantine, ed. Salaville, *Échos d'Orient* 27 (1921), 402–16; Nikephoros Basilakes on his brother Constantine, in W. Regel, ed., *Fontes rerum Byzantinarum*, II (St Petersburg, 1917), 228–44 and Michael Choniates on his brother Niketas, ed. Lampros, II. 345–66.

[71] G. Weiss, *Oströmische Beamte im Spiegel der Schriften des Michael Psellos*, MiscByzMonac 16 (Munich, 1973), 28–9, 59, and H. Ahrweiler, 'Recherches sur la société byzantine au XIe siècle: nouvelles hierarchies et nouvelles solidarités', *TM* 6 (1976), 99–124 at 109–10.

[72] See my 'Friendship in Byzantium: Genre, Topos and Network', in J. Haseldine, ed., *Friendship in Medieval Europe*, forthcoming.

[73] Here H.-G. Beck, *Byzantinisches erotikon* (Munich, 1986) is no assistance.

with *taxis*-indicators. So forms of address are crucial tools of analysis, but not perhaps in as straightforward a way as one might wish. Grassi found an unwillingness to use the word 'love': the same cannot be said for Theophylact and his contemporaries.

What remains to be detected is erotic charge. Intimacy, affect, *eros* and desire are closely interrelated in this literature and it is very difficult to disentangle them. The evidence for intimacy may be the complexity and level of allusion in the writing (shared allusions, jokes) and also the lack of ceremonial forms of address; the evidence for affect may be direct (use of endearments) or indirect (some kinds of gift-exchange, some kinds of visiting). The evidence of desire I have sketched may be evidence for affect and intimacy, but *pothos* is more an intensification of emotion than an emotion in itself, the result of an intense relationship in separation. I have to confess that in Theophylact's network, or any of the twelfth-century networks, I have failed to detect for certain any specifically sexual erotic charge. Intimacy yes, a delight in and a desire for the other's presence, yes, a light-hearted teasing and flirting with the young, an intense, even romantic love possibly, but I cannot identify anything more – and I do not at this point know what possible criteria I could evolve for a textual relationship of this kind. Objectivity seems at a premium here, for we all carry our own sexuality into the texts that we read, and openness is the greatest desideratum.

But I am equally sure that this search for erotic charge is a valid and necessary process, as necessary as the analysis of symmetry or reciprocity or multiplicity. There are all kinds of reasons why we are reluctant to do it. One is the aspect of tabloid scholarship: does it really serve the aims of scholarship to put two medieval innuendoes together and come up with an affair (as I and others have done with Maria of Alania and Alexios Komnenos,[74] and with Michael III, Basil I and Eudokia Ingerina[75])? Sometimes the texts are clearer, as with that other triangular relationship of Zoe, Constantine and Skleraina.[76] But it is interesting to note that the images of these triangles in the Madrid Skylitzes are far more concerned with *taxis* and validation than with romantic or erotic relationships: the marriage of Basil and Eudokia is sanctioned by the presence of Michael in full regalia; Constantine alone receives the opprobrium of the crowd while Skleraina is shown among, and indistinguishable from, the imperial women.[77] These interpretations deserve record as much as the phrasing

[74] M.E. Mullett, 'The "Disgrace" of the ex-Basilissa Maria', *BS* 45 (1984), 202–10.

[75] C. Mango, 'Eudocia Ingerina, the Normans and the Macedonian Dynasty', *ZbRad* 14–15 (1973), 17–27; Mullett, 'Friendly Society?', 11.

[76] Michael Psellos, *Chronographia*, Constantine IX. 50–61, ed. E. Renauld (Paris, 1967), I. 141–7.

[77] MS. Matritensis gr. fol. 87v (a), eds A. Grabar and M. Manoussacas, *L'illustration du manuscrit de Skylitzes de la bibliothèque nationale de Madrid* (Venice, 1979); fig. 96; fol. 227v, eds Grabar and Manoussacas, fig. 267.

of a chronicler or the more or less salacious imaginations of twentieth-century scholars.

In view of the monotonously male gender profile of Byzantine letter-writers, we may also find ourselves, if we persist in this pursuit of the erotic, engaged in outrageous outing in the medieval world, and we would be wise to be wary of this approach. At its crudest, we learn that Ailred was gay, Anselm was straight – and on these grounds we are asked to rethink all their relationships.[78] Perhaps the rehabilitation of Michael III and Alexander has provided some immunity from homophobic whistle-blowing,[79] but on the basis of Ailred, what about Symeon the New Theologian?[80] Does it make a difference when we have their letters, or when they are hailed as gay icons and sympathetic role-models? (We are unlikely, at any rate with the surviving evidence, to find equivalents in Kecharitomene or Bebaia Elpis to Judith Brown's Renaissance nuns[81] and reach female–female erotic *pothos* in Byzantium).[82] After Foucault[83] (and Goldberg)[84] we find this approach particularly difficult, and are suspicious of attempts to see through misrecognitions of the evidence to a 'real' sexual identity – or even

[78] This whole process, like the assertion in my own 'Friendly society?', 11, note 41, written in 1983, that 'there is no reason to doubt that homosexual relations and relationships existed in Byzantium' now looks remarkably naïve. (The force of that footnote – that what mattered was that friendships, erotic or not, should *function* – still holds.)

[79] P. Karlin-Hayter, 'Études sur les deux histoires du règne de Michel III', *B* 41 (1971), 452–96; 'The Emperor Alexander's Bad Name', *Speculum* 44 (1969), 585–96.

[80] See for example H.J.M. Turner, *St Symeon the New Theologian and Spiritual Fatherhood*, Byzantina Neerlandica 11 (Leiden, 1990), 28–9.

[81] J. Brown, *Immodest Acts* (New York and Oxford, 1986); cf. B.J. Brooten, *Love between Women: Early Christian Responses to Female Homoeroticism* (Chicago, 1996).

[82] There are however clear indications that female homoerotic *porneia* caused some concern in twelfth-century monasteries. See the *typikon* of Phoberou, chap. 58, in A.I. Papadopoulos-Kerameus, ed., *Noctes Petropolitanae* (St Petersburg, 1913), 81.6–11.

[83] On the impact of Foucault on Byzantium see A. M. Cameron, 'Redrawing the Map: Early Christian Territory after Foucault', *JRS* 76 (1986), 266–71; for the influence of Peter Brown on Foucault see *The History of Sexuality*, 2, *The Use of Pleasure*, tr. R. Hurley (Harmondsworth, 1987), 8. The major effect has been to deny a concept of homosexuality until the late nineteenth century; see D.M. Halperin, *One Hundred Years of Homosexuality: and Other Essays on Greek Love* (New York, 1990); D.M. Halperin, J.J. Winkler and F.I. Zeitlin, eds, *Before Sexuality: the Construction of Erotic Experience in the Ancient Greek World* (Princeton, 1990), but see A. Richlin, 'Not before Homosexuality: The Materiality of the *cinaedus* and the Roman Law against Love between Men', *Journal of the History of Sexuality* 3 (1993), 523–73. For antiquity the centrality of the oppositions between active and passive, penetrated and penetrating has been posited instead, see (inventively but incompletely) H.N. Parker, 'The Teratogenic Grid', in J.P. Hallett and M. Skinner, eds, *Roman Sexualities* (Princeton, 1997), 47–65.

[84] J. Goldberg, 'Colin to Hobbinol: Spenser's Familiar Letters', *South Atlantic Quarterly* 88 (1989), 107–26, repr. *Sodometries: Renaissance Texts, Modern Sexualities* (Stanford, 1992), using Foucault's concept of 'a modern deployment of sexuality' to nuance the findings of A. Bray, *Homosexuality in Renaissance England* (London, 1982).

of a 'real' sexual practice.[85] This is why I have posed the problem not in terms of persons or practices but in terms of textual relationships and their erotic charge, not aiming to surprise real Byzantines in *flagrante*, but to catch the echoes of expressed emotion.

It may however be as crass, or insensitive, to fail to ask the question as to answer it too salaciously. We may then be screening out what was there (emending as it were 'burglary' for 'buggery'[86]). There are surely just as many problems with a determined unwillingness to 'be a dirty old man [or woman]' and read sex into romantic or spiritual relationships: Robert Brain's otherwise dazzling command of the anthropological literature[87] suffers from this unwillingness, which seems perverse: how can we know if David fancied (or had sex with) Jonathan? We are certainly not in a position to say that he did not. But a discourse of desire does not automatically mean a real-life passion.[88] With Byzantine texts also we are the prisoners of their generic concerns: in some we may see *porneia*, in others *logismoi*, in yet others *pothos* and the family of loves, each requiring a different *persona*. In crossing these boundaries as well as in other activities of interpretation we risk imposing our own sexuality – or ethical presuppositions – as much as any previous generation of scholars who may have regarded Sappho as a frustrated spinster.[89] So are we reading in? Or are we screening out? As David Lodge might have put it, How far can we go?

The most potent criticisms of Boswell are those[90] which accuse him of being an old-fashioned historian, in that his homoerotic readings in the last book failed to take account of the explosion of research over the last ten or fifteen years into gender studies, queer theory and the history of sex. Byzantine studies is only very slowly beginning to take note. But some of this recent work[91] may help us to revise our own concepts of the erotic and to locate these largely male, close-knit, intimate networks of Byzantine letter-

---

[85] This is a fundamental concern of many contributors to J. Goldberg, ed., *Queering the Renaissance* (Durham and London, 1994). Brooten has to some extent through her use of astrological texts rehabilitated the possibility of a medieval concept of sexual orientation.

[86] E. Pittenger, ' "To serve the queere": Nicholas Udall, Master of Revels', in Goldberg, ed., *Queering the Renaissance*, 165 on William Edgerton's textual solution (in denial) to the puzzles of Udall's trial in the records of the Privy Council.

[87] R. Brain, *Friends and Lovers* (London, 1976), 27–53.

[88] J. Winkler, *The Constraints of Desire; The Anthropology of Sex and Gender in Ancient Greece* (New York and London, 1990), 187 on the practice in late antique rhetoric of hailing the *laudandus* as the rhetor's *eromenos*; on the same page however he suggests that to separate discourse from orientation is quixotic.

[89] Winkler, *Constraints of Desire*, 162.

[90] For example, J. Davidson in *London Review of Books*, 8 February 1996, 17–18.

[91] For example the reception of the work of Eve Kosofsky Sedgwick, especially *Between Men: English Literature and Male Homosocial Desire* (New York, 1985).

writers (and novelists) and their range of emotion and common values somewhere on a spectrum of male homosocial desire, in which *eros*, *agape*, *philia* and *storge* overlap and merge, intensified by *pothos*, in a pattern of multiplex relations we are only slowly beginning to understand.

2. 'Shutting the gates of the soul': spiritual treatises on resisting the passions

Mary B. Cunningham

Spiritual treatises represent a vast genre of literature written by and for ascetics and monks throughout the Byzantine period. This paper, while focusing primarily on the collections of chapters (*kephalaia*) or short sayings compiled by one author, will also include references to related works which do not belong to this category, including the *Apophthegmata Patrum*, collections of 'sayings' compiled from the fifth century onwards, and the seventh-century spiritual treatise known as the *Ladder of Divine Ascent* by John Klimakos. For reasons of space I have chosen to limit myself to works written before the seventh century, although it would be fascinating to pursue the problem of resistance to passions in later texts as well.

Kephalaia, or 'centuries' as they are sometimes called, owing to the fact that many contain one hundred chapters, continued to be written by various authors in the middle and late Byzantine period.[1] Whereas the genre was used only rarely in the Medieval West, it remained extremely popular in Byzantium and the Christian Near East, representing one of the primary vehicles for the transmission of both practical and philosophical monastic teaching. Exactly how such treatises were used, whether they were read aloud in monasteries or circulated for private study, remains unclear. Some assume the form of a letter or reveal in their titles that they were intended for a specific individual; certainly the personal and meditative style of these collections suggests a less public delivery than, for example, monastic or pastoral sermons received.

It is clear from the rich manuscript traditions of spiritual treatises that they were widely used in the Byzantine world, at least in monastic circles.

---

[1] See I. Hausherr, SJ, 'Centuries', *Dictionnaire de Spiritualité* 2, 1 (Paris, 1953), 416–7; E. von Ivanka, 'Κεφάλαια, eine byzantinische Litteraturform und ihre antiken Würzeln', *BZ* 47 (1954), 285–91.

Many have attracted the attention of modern Christians due to the publication of the excellent English translation in four volumes of the *Philokalia*, an eighteenth-century compilation of texts ranging from the fourth century to the end of the fifteenth by St Nikodimos of the Holy Mountain and St Makarios of Corinth.[2] It is worth noting that the *Philokalia* did not represent the first florilegium of this kind, however; while having perhaps as their ancestors the seventh-century *Pandects* by a monk named Antiochos[3] and Anastasios of Sinai's *Questions and Answers*,[4] most Byzantine monastic florilegia were compiled in the eleventh century or later. The *Synagoge* of Paul of Evergetis, compiled between 1049 and 1054,[5] the *Pandects* of Nikon of the Black Mountain[6] and the florilegia of John the Oxite,[7] written later in the eleventh century, are among the most important representatives of this genre.[8] Whereas theologians and lay people with an interest in spiritual texts may have studied treatises on their own or in compilations such as the *Philokalia*, I feel that these genres have been greatly neglected by historians of the Byzantine period. Surely, if hagiography can be viewed as 'invaluable for understanding everyday life and *mentalités*',[9] then so can the texts more explicitly written by and for monks themselves. Spiritual treatises may not contain the sensational accounts of ascetic feats or the lively narratives found in hagiography, but they do provide a vivid picture of the trials and aspirations of people involved in a religious way of life. In some ways the two genres complement each other, one representing the public and the other the internal, monastic view of the eastern Orthodox saint.

In this paper, I would like to examine various aspects of Byzantine spiritual treatises. First, in relation to the theme of 'desire and denial', I will explore how individual writers beginning with Evagrios identify the vice of fornication (*porneia*) and how they suggest it should be resisted. Secondly,

---

[2] G.E.H. Palmer, P. Sherrard and Kallistos Ware, *The Philokalia* I–IV (London, 1979-95) [hereafter *Philokalia*].

[3] *PG* 89, 1415–849.

[4] *PG* 89, 312–824; currently being re-edited by J. Munitiz. See also M. Richard, '"Questions et réponses" d'Anastase le Sinaite', *Bulletin de l'Institut de Recherche et d'Histoire des Textes* 15 (1967–8), 39–56 [= *Opera Minora* III (Turnhout and Louvain, 1977), n. 64)] and J. Munitiz's chapter in this volume.

[5] Makarios of Corinth and Nikodemos Hagiorites, eds, Paul Evergetinos, Εὐεργετινὸς ἤτοι Συναγωγὴ τῶν θεοφθόγγων ῥημάτων καὶ διδασκαλίων τῶν θεοφόρων καὶ ἁγίων πατέρων (Venice, 1783; 7th edn in 4 vols, Athens, 1983) [hereafter *Synagoge*].

[6] This text remains largely unpublished. See K. Ware, 'Prayer and the Sacraments in the *Synagoge*', in M.E. Mullett and A. Kirby, eds, *The Theotokos Evergetis and Eleventh-Century Monasticism*, Belfast Byzantine Texts and Translations 6.1 (Belfast, 1994), 329, notes 10–11.

[7] See M. Richard, 'Florilèges spirituels grecs', *Dictionnaire de Spiritualité* 5 (Paris, 1964), 504–5.

[8] Richard, 'Florilèges spirituels', 499–504.

[9] A.-M. Talbot, ed., *Holy Women of Byzantium. Ten Saints' Lives in English Translation*, Byzantine Saint's Lives in Translation 1 (Washington DC, 1996), viii.

one of the most fascinating aspects of monastic writers' perception of temptation and self-control is their attempt to define the workings of human psychology. Whence do the 'thoughts' (*logismoi*) which represent the temptations sent by the Devil come? Through what parts of the human body do they enter? With which faculties should ascetics resist these temptations? It is these and many other questions which the authors of spiritual treatises attempt to answer. Finally, I would like to look at selected authors' literary treatment of these subjects. The imagery used to describe desire and denial adds considerably to the impact of these texts, as well as revealing much about contemporary views of the human person.

All of the early writers of spiritual treatises identify external sources for the temptations which assail ascetics. Sent by the Devil, the author of evil, these include the demons of gluttony, fornication, vainglory and many others. Evagrios is the first to sort these demons systematically into eight categories: gluttony, fornication, avarice, sadness, anger, *acedia* (despondency), vainglory and pride.[10] Later writers such as Diadochos of Photike, Mark the Monk and John Klimakos also classify the various vices, but often identify different ones or rearrange their order. It is striking, as Peter Brown points out, that gluttony always precedes lust in the list of potential sins.[11] The half-starving ascetic's abstinence from food must have represented a far greater test of self control than did his celibacy. On the other hand, as John Cassian points out, the two disciplines are related 'for no one whose stomach is full can fight mentally against the demon of unchastity'.[12] Most authors concur in identifying the method used by demons to gain access to ascetics' souls as the *logismoi*, or 'thoughts', which assail them as they pray. As Evagrios puts it:

> The devil so passionately envies the man who prays that he employs every device to frustrate that purpose. Thus he does not cease to stir up thoughts of various affairs by means of the memory. He stirs up all the passions by means of the flesh. In this way he hopes to offer some obstacle to that excellent course pursued in prayer on the journey toward God.[13]

The same writer suggests that thoughts inspired by the demons, if allowed by the monk to intrude, produce within him conceptions, or images, of sensory objects. The association of mental images with evil demons is a recurrent theme in spiritual treatises and must be connected with an

---

[10] A. and C. Guillaumont, eds, *Évagre le Pontique. Traité pratique ou le moine* II, SC 171 (Paris, 1971), 506–8 (6).

[11] P. Brown, *The Body and Society. Men, Women and Sexual Renunciation in Early Christianity* (London and Boston, 1988), 218, 220.

[12] *Philokalia* I, 74.

[13] J.E. Bamberger, tr., *Evagrius Ponticus, The Praktikos and Chapters on Prayer*, Cicstercian Studies Series 4 (Kalamazoo, 1981), 62 (46).

iconoclastic tendency in early monastic circles.[14] Evagrios is unequivocal in his identification of imagery with demonic forces and states that God, who is immaterial, must be approached in an immaterial manner.[15] The fifth-century writer Diadochos of Photike, appealing to II Corinthians 11:14, says that 'Paul ... definitely teaches us that everything which appears to the intellect, whether as light or as fire, if it has a shape, is the product of the evil artifice of the enemy. So we should not embark on the ascetic life in the hope of seeing visions clothed with form or shape...'.[16]

While ascetics may keep watch during prayer and increase their resistance to onslaughts of the imagination by fasts and vigils, they remain particularly susceptible to demons when asleep. Evagrios notes that people often experience sensual images during sleep, although those who have achieved a state of complete purity are no longer subject to these passions. John Klimakos, in the seventh century, also refers to the risk of sensual dreams and emissions during the night. The first step in chastity is a refusal to consent to these, presumably by waking oneself up, after which a man may go on to exclude or at least remain unaffected by such dreams. Interestingly, however, sleep may also offer an opportunity to experience the presence of God. As Diadochos puts it:

> The dreams which appear to the soul through God's love are unerring criteria of its health. Such dreams do not change from one shape to another; they do not shock our inward sense, resound with laughter or suddenly become threatening. With great gentleness they approach the soul and fill it with spiritual gladness. As a result, even after the body has woken up, the soul longs to recapture the joy given to it by the dream.[17]

Diadochos thus distinguishes between good and bad, or divine and demonic, dreams. The differences between them allow them to be identified easily by the ascetic: while divinely inspired dreams are peaceful and produce happiness in the soul, those sent by demons tend to be changeable, noisy and full of disturbance. Alchohol or overeating increase the likelihood of experiencing demonic dreams, as well as lustful impulses.[18]

When the ascetic is awake, he may be assailed by demons through his senses or by 'thoughts' occurring within the mind itself. John Klimakos calls this process a 'disturbance' (*pararripismos*) in a vivid passage of his *Ladder of Divine Ascent*:

---

[14] K. Parry, *Depicting the Word. Byzantine Iconophile Thought of the Eighth and Ninth Centuries* (Leiden, 1996), 4, 117.

[15] Bamberger, *Evagrius Ponticus*, 66 (66).

[16] E. des Places, ed., *Diadoque de Photicé, Oeuvres spirituels*, SC 5 bis (Paris, 1955), 108; English translation in *Philokalia* I, 265 (40).

[17] Des Places, *Diadoque de Photicé*, 106 (40); *Philokalia* I, 264 (37).

[18] Des Places, *Diadoque de Photicé* 113 (49); *Philokalia* I, 267, 49–50.

In a moment, without a word being spoken or an image presented, a sudden passionate urge lays hold of the victim. It comes faster than anything in the physical world and is swifter and more indiscernable than any spirit. It makes its appearance in the soul by a simple memory which is unconnected with anything, independent of time and inexpressible, and in some cases comes without the person himself realizing the fact. Someone who has been unable to detect such a subtlety, someone with the gift of mourning, may be able to explain how with the eye alone, with a mere glance, by the touch of a hand, through a song overheard, the soul is led to commit a definite act of unchastity without any notion or evil thought.[19]

This passage suggests that the thought may or may not be linked with impressions received by the senses. Earlier writers are equally ambivalent, but always point to the active role played by the intellect in encouraging such distractions. Evagrios, who always identifies thoughts with their evil geniuses, the demons, describes how the demon of unchastity may inspire 'images of men and women playing with one another' even in the minds of men who have achieved a significant level of dispassion.[20]

Resistance to the demons which invade the intellect may be undertaken in various ways, including increased fasting, vigils, use of the 'Jesus prayer' or even by judicious use of the weapon of anger.[21] Whereas Mark the Monk is clear that thoughts come from outside and that their appearance, when involuntary, does not incur blame on their victims, he stresses the fact that they must immediately be expelled. Allowing the thoughts, or passions, to remain in their minds suggests that monks are in love with their causes, or the actions which inspired the thoughts.[22] According to some writers, however, the battle with the passions may have its own spiritual benefits. A story in the *Apophthegmata* describes one old man (*geron*) asking another, the Abba Joseph, 'What shall I do when the passions approach? Shall I resist their entry or should I allow them to enter?' Abba Joseph answers, 'Allow them to enter and do battle with them.' Later, the first *geron* learns that Joseph gave a different answer to another brother, telling him to cut off the passions before they may even gain entry to his mind. On asking why he gave different answers to each enquirer, Abba Joseph answers that whereas some men are capable of fighting the passions and will benefit by this, others should not attempt the battle owing to their weakness.[23] John Klimakos, on the other hand, warns against entering into an argument with the

---

[19] *PG* 88, 897B–C, in C. Luibheid and N. Russell, trs, *John Climacus, The Ladder of Divine Ascent* (London, 1982), 182–3.

[20] *Philokalia* I, 47.

[21] Des Places, *Diadoque de Photicé*, 121–3 (62); *Philokalia* I, 272.

[22] *De Baptismo*, PG 65, 992C; *Philokalia* I, 135 (122).

[23] *PG* 65, 228D–9A; in B. Ward, tr., *The Sayings of the Desert Fathers. The Alphabetical Collection* (London and Oxford, 1975), 87.

demon of fornication, for 'Nature is on his side and he has the best of the argument'.[24]

Some writers of spiritual treatises undertake detailed analyses of the instinctive and mental processes of desire and denial, thus revealing their views, as it were, of human psychology. The first important point to note is that writers of spiritual treatises from the fourth century onwards employ a precise technical vocabulary which includes words such as *nous* ('intellect'), *dianoia* ('reason'), *kardia* ('heart'), and many others. While writers may differ slightly in their understanding of how these faculties work together, they are for the most part aware of their place in a well-established spiritual tradition. We have already seen how Mark the Monk distinguishes morally between the initial assaults of demons and the thoughts which are allowed to remain in the mind. It is at the stage when a man 'has converse' with a provocation that it becomes a 'thought' (*logismos*) and also may have acquired a form, or image, in his mind. The final step in assenting to sin is when the man decides to act on the thought; Mark tends to regard this as inevitable, the longer the thought is allowed to linger in the mind. It is the job of the intellect or mind (*nous*) to perceive an evil thought and immediately to expel it. The intellect represents man's highest faculty and the means whereby he may come to apprehend God. As Isaiah the Solitary puts it, 'If a monk submits his will to the law of God, then his intellect will govern in accordance with this law all that is subordinate to itself. It will direct as it should all the soul's impulses, especially its incensive power and desire, for these are subordinate to it'.[25] On the other hand, since Adam's fall, when man deliberately turned his back on God, a state of duality has existed in the intellect. Diadochos compares the situation to a man standing out of doors at the break of day, facing east, with the front of his body warmed by the sun while his back remains cold: 'just as the man ... both shivers and yet feels warm at the touch of the sun, so the soul may have both good and evil thoughts simultaneously'.[26] This state of duality explains why the intellect sometimes falls into confusion, thinking both good and evil thoughts at the same time, or feeling tempted towards passion while knowing that this is wrong.

Whereas the fall from grace of Adam and Eve may help symbolically to describe the obvious potential for sin in mankind, many writers stress the responsibility of individuals to overcome this inherited problem. Mark the Monk states categorically that when evil thoughts become active in us we should blame ourselves and not original sin.[27] Monks should also strive to

---

[24] *PG* 88, 884B, in Luibheid and Russell, trs, *John Climacus*, 173.

[25] *Philokalia* I, 28.

[26] Des Places, *Diadoque de Photicé*, 147–8 (88); *Philokalia* I, 287.

[27] *De his qui putant se ex operibus justificari*, *PG* 65, 945D–7A (112).

overcome the condition of duality in the soul. Diadochos takes pains to stress that man is not naturally evil for God made nothing that is not good. Evil begins to exist when a man turns away from God and gives form to what in reality has no existence.[28] Man is not capable of achieving dispassion entirely on his own however; Mark the Monk stresses that divine help is needed. 'Peace is deliverance from the passions', he writes, 'and it is not found except through the action of the Holy Spirit'. What emerges from these treatises is thus not just a picture of a battle taking place on a cosmic level between the forces of good and evil, but rather a sophisticated attempt to explain the different, and often opposing forces, operating within individual human beings and to help monks identify and train the faculties involved in this process. The intellect should act as a responsible caretaker of the heart, protecting it from the attacks of passionate thoughts and, with the help of the Holy Spirit, directing it towards closer union with God. Even when dispassion has been achieved, monks will never be free from the assaults of the appetites which are inherent in man's animal nature, but they should be capable, owing to the intellectual gifts which were also bestowed on them by God, to overcome and even transform these impulses into positive channels.

The metaphors which spiritual writers use to describe the processes of desire and denial in the human person are often memorable. One of the images which is frequently used is that of the fortress or walled city. This represents the monk who has attempted to shut himself away from the world; the doors or gates are his senses and the virtues help to keep watch at these gates. Diadochos writes:

> He who dwells continually in his own heart is detached from the attractions of this world, for he lives in the Spirit and cannot know the desires of the flesh. Such a man henceforward walks up and down within the fortress of the virtues which keep guard at all the gates of his purity. The assaults of the demons are now ineffective against him, even though the arrows of sensual desire reach as far as the doorways of his senses.[29]

Isaac of Nineveh also compares the monk to a city and its doors to the senses, stating that the intellect is able to do battle with those outside the city from the safety of this citadel.[30] The notion that demons mount aggressive assaults on monks, firing arrows or missiles, is reflected in the word used for these attacks, *prosbolai*, which features repeatedly in Mark the Monk's treatises. The initial causes of temptation are clearly shown to come from outside by this vocabulary; fortifications and counter attacks may both be used to repel them.

---

[28] Des Places, *Diadoque de Photicé*, 86 (3).
[29] Des Places, *Diadoque de Photicé*, 117–18 (57).
[30] Isaac of Nineveh, quoted in *Synagoge* IV.5.6.12.

Once the demons have managed to gain entry to the individual soul, however, the imagery becomes descriptive of its resulting state. The inexperienced monk who fails to eradicate the dangerous thoughts which have penetrated into his mind is compared to a calf who, 'running after grass arrives at a precipitous place'.[31] The heart which is deflected from the ascetic way by sensual pleasure becomes difficult to control, like a heavy stone dislodged on steep ground.[32] The idea which underlies all of these metaphors is that once temptation has taken hold, the intellect no longer remains in control. It is a prisoner being dragged about by impassioned thoughts or burned by the fierce heat of evil desire, for as Mark the Monk points out, 'Sin is a blazing fire. The less fuel you give it, the faster it dies down; the more you feed it, the more it burns'.[33]

The ascetic who, on the other hand, has achieved some measure of control over his passions, and who, while still at times assailed by unchaste thoughts, is able to expel them is described by metaphors which evoke images of peace and solitude. Isaac of Nineveh suggests that he is like a heron 'which rejoices and takes delight ... whenever he exiles himself from the inhabited world, and departing into a deserted place, dwells in it.'[34] The Greek Ephrem compares the monk to a cistern of water: when it rains at first the water is disturbed; later it becomes calm. Elsewhere the same writer suggests that he is like a vessel into which new wine has been poured: 'At first it boils as if it were being heated underneath by a very fierce flame so that some of the vessels, unable to withstand the pressure, are shattered by the force. Those which survive, however, having been purged, remain motionless'.[35]

The goal of prayer is not just a state of peace and detachment, however. Diadochos speaks of 'the fire of dispassion'[36] and for many writers, the language of passionate love may be transferred to the feeling which seizes those who are close to God. Isaac of Nineveh describes this as an ardent attraction which causes a man's face to become 'fiery and full of joy, while his body is feverish'.[37] He further compares this feeling to that caused by the bird called a siren:

> If anyone hears the sound of his voice, he is so charmed by it and entirely transported out of himself that he forgets everything which he has in hand through the sweetness of the sound, including his own life, and he falls down dead. The soul which is activated by love experiences the same thing. For

---

[31] *De his qui putant se ex operibus justificari*, PG 65, 940C (67).

[32] *De his qui putant*, PG 65, 940C (66).

[33] *De lege spirituali*, PG 65, 922D (137).

[34] Quoted in *Synagoge* IV.5.6.25.

[35] *Synagoge* IV.6.2.8.

[36] Des Places, *Diadoque de Photicé*, 94 (17).

[37] *Synagoge* IV.4.4.1–2.

whenever the heavenly sweetness falls upon it, revealing to it the mysteries of God, it is so much overcome that forgetting this corporeal life it entirely leaves that behind and longs insatiably for him'.[38]

The language of love may thus be used to express the legitimate longing of the soul for union with God, as well as the snares which the Devil sets for the soul by means of the appetitive passions. It is the gift of discernment which enables an ascetic to distinguish between these seemingly similar, but in fact profoundly opposite impulses; a gift which he only acquires after years of labour and with the help of the Holy Spirit.

In conclusion, I would like to offer a few thoughts which have struck me in the course of my recent work on the genre. First, it is perhaps worth asking what issues are *not* discussed in spiritual treatises and why. As I have demonstrated in this paper, the discussion of desire and denial centres in these texts on the *thoughts (logismoi)* rather than on actual acts of fornication committed by ascetics. Thoughts of passion may certainly lead to actions, as Mark the Monk continually reminds us, but it is primarily in their rôle as distractions from prayer that they are feared. Common sense suggests that for independent ascetics such as the desert fathers, the temptation to sin must frequently have been real as well as imaginary. We know from texts like the *Apophthegmata* that the desert fathers did occasionally transgress, with some ascetics fathering children and others importuning their younger colleagues with homosexual advances.[39] John Klimakos tells us that monks engaged in organized monastic life were also occasionally assailed by temptations of homosexuality or even of sodomy with the monastery's female animals,[40] but the possibility of encountering women by any means other than the imagination in this context was probably remote. Dangers such as these receive on the whole little emphasis, however, and it is reasonable here to ask why. One possible answer concerns the likely audience of these texts and its preoccupations. Whereas spiritual treatises emerged from a spiritual background which had as its ideal a solitary life in the desert, it is likely that they were composed for a larger body of readers who, while aspiring theoretically to that aim, were in fact engaged in the common life of the monastery. In this context, the mental distractions experienced by everyone would feature more importantly than the more unusual temptations which assailed just a few. Secondly, I suggest that as a genre monastic treatises present a deliberately idealized picture. This probably reflects their didactic function and their authors' recognition that both beginners and experienced monks require inspiration rather than cautionary tales as they advance in the spiritual life.

---

[38] *Synagoge* IV.4.11–12.
[39] See Brown, *Body and Society*, 230.
[40] *PG* 88, 697A, 1149B. See also Luibheid and Russell, *John Climacus*, 102, 283.

The intended reader of early Byzantine spiritual treatises is not the remote, miracle-working saint whom we encounter in hagiography. Instead, he is depicted as a fallible, sinful mortal, subject to temptations of many kinds. Most of these temptations appear in the form of 'thoughts', which serve to distract the monk from prayer or even, if allowed to remain in his mind, to divert him from his long-term spiritual goals. While it is thus mental distractions which receive the most emphasis in spiritual treatises, the rigour of monastic discipline should not be minimized. The goal of monks, whether they are engaged in the cenobitic or the solitary life, is to engage in constant prayer and remembrance of God. This discipline may be assisted by the repetition of the short prayers such as the Jesus prayer or by fasting and vigils. While most early Byzantine treatises are thus intended for a monastic and specifically male audience, it is interesting to note that their appeal seems to have widened in the course of their transmission to readers of later periods. Paul of Evergetis's eleventh-century *Synagoge* may have circulated among lay as well as monastic readers.[41] Similarly, the *Philokalia*, while perhaps originally intended for monastics, became in subsequent centuries a source of inspiration for the Greek and Slavic speaking Orthodox laity as well. By means of all these texts, ethical and spiritual ideals which were created in the deserts of Egypt, Palestine and Syria came to represent the core of Orthodox spiritual endeavour, whether this is carried out by genuine anchorites, cenobitic monks or nuns or by lay people living in the world. At the same time, in the face of ideals such as these, it is likely that endeavour will feature more prominently in the spiritual lives of most people than will the attainment of perfection.

[41] See Ware, 'Prayer and the Sacraments', 325. Unpublished preliminary studies of the manuscript tradition undertaken by Barbara Crostini Lappin and Janet Rutherford suggest that the titles in some early manuscripts were adjusted to address a lay audience.

Section II

Do as your Father tells you

3. The sexual and social dangers of *Pornai* in the Septuagint Greek stratum of patristic Christian Greek thought

Kathy L. Gaca

The important distinction between a harlot and a prostitute is clear enough in English, as I will show. The corresponding distinction in early Christian, patristic, and Byzantine Greek writings, however, is not yet well recognized for two reasons. First and foremost, early Christian and patristic scholarship does not yet adequately appreciate the distinctive Septuagint legacy behind the ancient Greek word that corresponds to 'harlot' in English. The word in question is *pornê*. Second, the word *pornê* is also used in pre-Christian and Christian Greek texts to refer to a lower-class prostitute in ancient Greek society, as opposed to the *hetaira* or 'courtesan'. *Pornê* in this sense probably stems from *pernêmi* according to LSJ, and refers to the sale and exportation of captive female slaves for the sex trade in the ancient Mediterranean. In early Christian and patristic scholarship, the use of *pornê* to refer to a prostitute seems the more familiar one. This sense has helped obfuscate how *pornê* in the distinctive Septuagint sense 'harlot' comes strongly into normative play in early Christian, patristic and Byzantine writings. The purpose of my paper is to help clear up this semantic confusion and to explain why the Septuagint conception of *pornê* is morally problematic. Scholars who study women called *pornai* in Christian Greek writings will in turn be better able to judge two points more precisely: what Christian Greek authors mean by calling women *pornai*, and why this term is likely to have a loaded significance that it does not have in pre-Christian Greek writings. I will begin by exploring the difference between a harlot and a prostitute, then I will explicate the Septuagint sense of *pornê*, which corresponds to the term 'harlot' in English.

The Septuagint Pentateuch links *pornai* with sex acts classed as an abomination (Deut 23:18–19). Nowhere, though, does the Septuagint identify the repellent quality of an abomination as the essence of 'the

sexually loose woman' who disobeys biblical rules restricting her sexual
behavior. Numerous readers of the Old Testament, however, make this
association. For example, in Faulkner's novel *Light in August*, the essence
of biblical harlotry is the repellent 'womansign' of disobedient 'womanflesh',
which surfaces especially when women show assertively seductive sexual
behaviour. This idea of female essence dehumanizes women, mainly but
not only the willfully rebellious ones. Consider the nuns mentioned in *Civitas
Dei* 1.26. They took a vow of virginity for God, later faced being raped, and
committed suicide to spare God the harlots they would have become had
they been raped, even though the sexual activity would have been against
their will. Though Augustine regrets their drastic preventive measure, the
Church at the time approved of it. Through pre-emptive suicide the nuns
avoided becoming harlots in the public eye and in the nuns' own
internalized gaze.[1] This dehumanizing self-identification seemed compelling
enough to warrant suicide – better to be dead than Faulkner's 'walking shape
of sluttish bitchery', or so it seems to women who support biblical sexual
rules, such as the nuns.

A harlot in the biblical sense, consequently, is any woman whose sexual
conduct is out of line with the regulations that biblically grounded
communities construct and value as the word of God. These regulations,
insofar as they are based on a Heraclitean flux of biblical exegesis, change
over time and transform in new social settings. Nonetheless they function
consistently to dehumanize women whose sexual contacts do not fit the set
of regulations in place. Even though the dead nuns would have been
harlots against their will if they were raped, they nonetheless would have
had sexual contacts that were out of keeping with an absolute vow of
virginity for God. This would have been an unbearable transgression.

A lush profusion of censoriously pornographic imagery accompanies the
notion of the biblical harlot. Nonetheless, the name 'prostitute' is one of the
few that you will not see written like graffiti on a woman simply because
she has transgressed the sexual regulations in force in any biblically based
community. The reason for this is straightforward, at least in English,
which clearly distinguishes between a harlot and a prostitute. The harlot
is the woman who is deemed to be 'sexually immoral' or 'loose' because
her sexual mores transgress the biblically influenced sexual regulations. This
is true particularly, but not only, if the woman's sexual transgressions are
intentional. In order for a harlot also to be a prostitute, however, she would
have to bring her 'walking shape of sexual defiance' to the marketplace and
earn some material reward from her harlotry. Though it is problematic
whether she makes the material gain for herself or is exploited by pimps,

---

[1] For Augustine's stance in this question, see further J. Rist, *Augustine: Ancient Thought Baptized*
(Cambridge, 1994), 199, 233, 296.

this question is unimportant for the distinction between the terms 'harlot' and 'prostitute' that I am demonstrating. Unless and until money or the like changes hands, in biblical terms the woman is a harlot but not also a prostitute. All prostitutes, however, are also harlots in biblical terms for obvious reasons. Harlotry is the way they make their living.

Though Hellenistic Jewish and Christian Greek writers refer to *pornai* quite frequently, they presuppose far more than they explain. The term is largely a part of the religious jargon that they inherit from the Septuagint and other Jewish writings in Greek. The meaning of this jargon was obvious to them but is now far from obvious today.[2] The most that we can gather about the meaning of *pornai* without investigating its biblical roots is a vague definition: 'sexually immoral women', or the like. The Septuagint, by contrast, is a rich and full source that rewards careful study on the topic of *pornai*. This version of the Old Testament helped provide Hellenistic Jewish and early Christian writers with their presuppositions about how to go about classifying women into religiously grounded sexual types.[3]

The biblical harlot (*pornê*) plays a very important role in the Septuagint's conception of rebelling against God by transgressing his laws. The Septuagint frequently describes apostasy from God with the metaphor of spiritual fornication or *porneia*. In terms of this metaphor, the rebellious members of God's people do not simply defect from God. Rather their defection is also an act of 'fornicating away from, or against' God and his will, even if their transgressions are not themselves sexual. Hence in Numbers, for instance, Israelites who threaten mutiny against Moses commit fornication against God. Sexual activity, however, is the furthest thing from their minds and actions at the time (14:2–3, 26–27, 33). When, however, Israelite male transgressions are genuinely sexual, they occur with women who are by definition harlots or *pornai*, because the women are religious aliens with whom male members of the Lord's people engage in forbidden sexual activity. Some of the women, further, belong to the tribes with whom the Israelites are forbidden to intermingle sexually and in worship. Male members of the Lord's people accordingly commit sexual apostasy if they make love to such women under any circumstances,

---

[2] The New Testament vice lists are a good but extreme case in point, for there the term is used with no elucidation whatsoever. Another good example is the fact that there still is no clear consensus among NT scholars about what Matt 5:32 and 19:9 mean by disallowing divorce except in instances of *porneia*. A wife, however, clearly does not have to engage in literal prostitution to commit *porneia*.

[3] I am not suggesting that the Septuagint text alone did the providing in question, for the transmission of the Old Testament religious ideas had a strong oral basis through homilies and the like. We do not have direct access to the spoken utterances, however, while the Septuagint is available. All references to the Old Testament are to the Septuagint version.

especially in a religiously mixed marriage.[4] The standing of women who are aliens and not members of the officially forbidden tribes remains somewhat more ambiguous. Nonetheless male Israelites clearly fornicate away from God by making love to the women if the women draw them into religiously alien worship. The collective group of religiously alien women are consequently labelled as 'harlots [*pornai*]' since male members of the Lord's people 'fornicate [*porneuein*]' against his will with them.[5] Though the men are the sinners in this case, not the women, the women are vilified. The other group of biblical harlots are female members of the Lord's people who disobey his will by engaging in sexual activity and other religious practices forbidden to them.[6] They are 'harlots [*pornai*]' because they themselves 'fornicate [*porneuein*]' against God's will. The biblical notions of harlotry and spiritual fornication thus link together religiously alien women and female apostates among God's people in an unusual sisterhood. Women are harlots if they engage in sexual or other ritual interactions with male members of the Lord's people but are not themselves bona fide vessels of absolute devotion to the Lord. The Septuagint conception of harlots therefore refers to and stigmatizes religiously alien or alienated women. The idea is consequently not reducible to sexually promiscuous women, let alone to prostitutes.[7]

The Septuagint metaphor of spiritual fornication nonetheless suggests in a misleading and harmful way that all biblical harlots are sexually

---

[4] Exod 34:15–16, 3 Kgdms 11:1, Ezek 16:27–29, Tob 4:12. On implicit and explicit warnings to male members of the Lord's people that the ways of religiously alien women lead them to apostasy, see, for example, Num 25:1–5, Prov 5:1–23, 7:1–27. On blaming alien women for making male members of the Lord's people deviate from their path, see 3 Kgdms 11:1–13, 16:31, 18:19, 4 Kgdms 9:22, Prov 5:1–23, 7:1–27, 2 Esdr 10:10–17, cf. 1 Esdr 8:65–7, Ezek 16:27–9. Such women are biblical harlots, 4 Kgdms 9:22, Hos 1:2.

[5] On *pornai*, see Gen 34:31, 38:15, 38:24 (but Tamar is a *pornê* only from Judah's perspective at this point in the narrative, cf. 38:26), Lev 21:7, 21:14, Deut 23:18, Judg 11:1–3, 3 Kgdms 20:19, 22:38, Prov 5:1–3, 6:26, 7:5–27, 29:3, Jer 5:7, Ep Jer 11. On the similar designation of women as female agents of *porneia*, see 4 Kgdms 9:22, Hos 1:2. See also P. Bird, 'To Play the Harlot', in P. Day, ed., *Gender and Difference in Ancient Israel* (Minneapolis, MN, 1989), 76–80; F. A. Andersen and D. N. Freedman, *Hosea* (New York, 1980), 157–63.

[6] For castigation of apostate female members of the Lord's people, see Hos 4:13, Isa 3:16–25, Jer 51:24–30, esp. 28, Ezek 23:48, Sir 23:22–7.

[7] True prostitutes comprise only a small portion of biblical harlots, on which see Andersen and Freedman, *Hosea*, 160 and S. Légasse, 'Jésus et les prostituées', *Revue Theologique de Louvain* 7 (1976), 137–9. The popular conception that Jesus associated with prostitutes is consequently open to question. The NT claim is that Jesus associated with harlots (*pornai*, Matt 21:31, Luke 15:30, Heb 11:31, Jas 2:25). The term *pornai* might be better taken in the biblical sense of the Septuagint insofar as the Septuagint translations are the formative text behind the NT. If so, then the NT claim is that Jesus associated with religiously alien and alienated women and taught them to follow his conception of the way of the Lord, not merely that he aimed to leave brothels with fewer employees by converting some prostitutes.

seductive, promiscuous, and hence that they are a wilful sexual danger to the Lord's people. Some Septuagint passages reinforce this suggestion. The harlots wink, make seductive movements with their feet, and boldly look men in the eye.[8] This impression is deceptive in two respects. First, biblical harlots are not even necessarily involved in extra-marital sexual activity. For example, Jezebel is no less a biblical harlot than Hosea's adulterous wife Gomer even though Jezebel is sexually faithful to her husband Ahab.[9] Her harlotry is that she leads him and the Lord's people into religiously alien worship and attacks the Yahwists. Second, even if some harlots are involved in fornication, many of them are victims of rape. When soldiers of the Lord's people take religiously alien women as captive wives, then the soldiers commit sexual apostasy and the female prisoners of war are their victims.[10] Similarly, when religiously alien warriors take female members of the Lord's people into sexual servitude as prisoners of war, then the women are victims of rape committed by their male captors.[11] The biblical impression that the harlot is a seductress consequently stigmatizes the harlot sexually even if the prohibited act in which she is involved is not sexual or involves a man's sexual transgression against her. Raped nuns would be a good example of the latter instance.

The strong sexual overtones that envelop the figure of the biblical harlot strongly contribute to the semantic confusion about *pornai* that I highlighted at the beginning of this paper. Religiously alien or alienated women are obviously not all prostitutes. Nonetheless, from a Septuagint-influenced

---

[8] On these seductive bodily gestures by harlots, see Prov 5:1–23, 6:25, 7:1–27, Isa 3:16, Ezek 16:25–9, Sir 26:9.

[9] 4 Kgdms 9:22, Hos 1:2–3.

[10] Deut 21:11–14 permits the taking of female prisoners of war as captive wives. Despite this permission, a female prisoner taken as a captive wife does not say of her own volition, like Ruth, 'your people will be my people and your God will be my God'. Rather she is informed through physical degradation that she is her captor's and his God is hers. Women in this position consequently remain religiously alien at heart and the marriage is fornication against the Lord's will. Further, female prisoners taken as captive wives would presumably have come from the peoples with whom marriage is absolutely forbidden. The biblical mandate is for the Israelites to conquer and annihilate these peoples, and certainly not to marry them (Exod 34:11, 15–16). Israelite soldiers nonetheless saved and kept at least some of the women (Num 31:9–18). The militaristic custom of taking female prisoners of war into sexual servitude therefore conflicts with the biblical rule against marrying religious aliens on two grounds: the wives are forbidden aliens by definition, and even if some of them are not in this class, they nonetheless remain religious aliens at heart. On physical degradation as a sign of enslavement, see O. Patterson, *Slavery and Social Death: A Comparative Study* (1982), 7–8; on the degradation implied by Deut 21:11–14, see S. Thistlethwaite, '"You May Enjoy the Spoil of Your Enemies": Rape as a Biblical Metaphor for War', *Semeia* 61 (1993), 59-75, esp. 65; and on the relationship between taking women captive and the social and sexual subordination of women in general, see G. Lerner, *The Creation of Patriarchy* (1986), 76–100.

[11] See, for example, Joel 4:3.

perspective, women who are not vessels of complete devotion to God are by definition *pornai*. This label arises from the way in which the metaphor of spiritual fornication works to label foreign or internally rebellious women as a sexually alienating danger. Women who are alien to God's people are thus stereotyped in ways that make them all seem part of a disreputable and defiling sex trade. This stereotype serves to deter male members of God's people from leaving their people and joining in marriage or more casual liaisons with women who are religious outsiders. Similarly, female members of God's people are encouraged by the negative imagery surrounding *pornai* to keep their eyes downcast, never to wink, flirt, play footsie or engage in even more overt seductive practices. Otherwise they are at risk of losing their stature as vessels of devotion and will become one of those *pornai*. Consequently, when we encounter *pornai* in our early Christian, patristic and Byzantine studies, we must not simply assume that these *pornai* are prostitutes, even though a few of them may be. If we make such a quick assumption, we are likely to take a complex biblical metaphor literally. The problem, however, is much deeper than getting a matter of poetics wrong. The biblical metaphor of spiritual fornication (*porneia*) has sexually dehumanized religiously alien and alienated women as harlots or whores (*pornai*) and such labels have helped deter women from acting on their own sexual cognisance. Since patristic writers play a key role in the formative Christian branch of this process, we need to give very careful attention to the symbolism that frames their *pornai*.

4. Manly women and womanly men: the *subintroductae* and John Chrysostom

Aideen Hartney

The rhetoric of early Christianity is often very negative in its attitudes to females and femininity, attracting a great deal of attention in the last number of years under the broader heading of gender studies. It is, however, only very recently that discussions of such gender-related topics have also begun to incorporate questions regarding males and masculinity. What is slowly becoming understood is that the proscriptions issued in this rhetoric against women and certain aspects of their behaviour can be read in two ways. The anti-female discourse prevalent in the third and fourth centuries AD does of course indicate a deep suspicion and distrust of the sex. However, such rhetoric also highlights the expectations placed on the opposite sex, including those who constructed the discourse itself. Thus we find the system of patriarchy demanding certain modes of behaviour from those on both sides of the power divide, so that even the upholders of the system are as constrained by their own rules as those they aim to constrain.

This irony is especially evident in two closely connected treatises of St John Chrysostom, the prolific author and renowned preacher of the late fourth century church. In his tracts composed on the *subintroductae* we can trace quite clearly what this author considered to be the appropriate modes of behaviour for each of the sexes.[1] The *subintroductae* were those young women professing to live lives of dedicated celibacy, who had decided either to move in with, or to bring into their own homes, male ascetics. This practice of *syneisaktism* seems to have been growing increasingly popular at this time in the history of Christianity, and not surprisingly proved to be a rich source of scandal. Prohibitions are found in most of the Church Councils convened across the Empire between the second and fifth centuries

---

[1] *Adversus eos qui apud se habent subintroductas virgines (Adv. eos)* and *Quod regulares feminae viris cohabitare non debeant (Quod reg.)*, tr. E. A. Clark, *Jerome, Chrysostom and Friends* (New York, 1979).

AD.[2] No one is quite sure why ascetic couples should have chosen to cohabit in such a manner, although a number of possibilities exist. The woman may have claimed the need for male protection against the dangers of urban living; the man may have desired a form of housekeeper; some couples even claimed that by exposing themselves to such intense temptation they mortified the body to a greater extent than in more normal forms of asceticism, and would thus be deserving of a greater heavenly reward. I am, however, more inclined to believe that *syneisaktism* existed primarily for practical reasons. The practice of asceticism was as yet a relatively disorganized phenomenon, especially where women were concerned. Departure to the desert in isolation was not always possible or safe for a woman, and communities of male ascetics were by no means eager to introduce a female into their midst, since they had left the cities to avoid such fleshy temptations in the first place.[3] Some women simply remained in the family home as virgin daughters, practising their own ascetic regime in private, while some of the leading lights of female asceticism, Macrina or Paula, for example, established the first female monastic communities by means of having many of their family and attendants adopt this mode of life at the same time. However, such groups were still rare at this time, and were often very dependent on the wealth of the foundress. For those women lacking such independent financial support, and sometimes even without the approval of their families, the practice of asceticism within the family or within the city was not always so straightforward.[4] Accordingly, if a woman could establish her own ascetic household, with the financial backing of a male celibate, as well as the greater security a masculine

---

[2] See for example *Canon XIX* of the Council of Ancyra, AD 314, and *Canon III* of the Council of Nicaea, AD 325, which says: 'The great Synod has stringently forbidden any bishop, presbyter, deacon or any one of the clergy whatever, to have a *subintroducta* dwelling with him, except only a mother, or sister, or aunt, or such persons only as are beyond all suspicion.' E. Clark, 'John Chrysostom and the *Subintroductae*', *Church History* 46 (1977), 171–85, gives a general review of prohibitions of syneisaktism in ecclesiastical circles.

[3] Only women who so altered their appearance as to seem like men or even eunuchs were accepted into such monastic groups, since they were not perceived as a threat to the virtue of their neighbours. They were extreme examples, and their 'success' was such that their sex was only discovered after their deaths. See E. Patlagean, *Structure Sociale, famille, chrétienté à Byzance IVe–XIe siècle*, (Aldershot, 1981), and G. Clark, *Women in Late Antiquity* (Oxford, 1993), 129. Paradoxically, cross-dressing by ascetics was also expressly forbidden in Church law. See the Council of Gangra AD 325–81, *Canon XIII*: 'If any woman, under pretence of asceticism, shall change her apparel and, instead of a woman's accustomed clothing, shall put on that of a man, let her be anathema.'

[4] A. Yarbrough, 'Christianization in the Fourth Century: The Example of Roman Women', *Church History* 45 (1976), 154, alludes to a growing pattern of opposition to young women taking vows of celibacy on the part of their families and more particularly, their fathers. St Ambrose, *On Virgins* I.65–6, approvingly records the tale of a young girl who clung to a church altar in defence of her vows of virginity which were angrily opposed by her legal guardian.

presence would offer, the problem might well appear to have been solved.[5] A 'spiritual marriage' such as this, left both members of the partnership free to pursue their devotion to God, unpressured by family, friends, or the worries of surviving in such a harsh environment as the desert. Another important possibility to consider is that such living arrangements, with the emphasis on spiritual devotion to God, opened up previously unexplored opportunities for men and women to enjoy intellectual friendships on an equal basis, something which had once been dismissed as impossible.[6] But whatever advantages were perceived by the ascetics involved to lie in the arrangement, the Church Fathers were unanimous in their disapproval.

The Latin author, St Jerome, also denounced the practice of *syneisaktism* with reference to is prevalence in the Western Empire:

> A brother leaves his virgin sister; a virgin scorning her unmarried brother seeks a stranger to take his place. Both alike pretend to have but one object: they are seeking spiritual consolation among strangers: but their real aim is to indulge at home in carnal intercourse.[7]

What clearly emerges from this letter is the reason for Jerome's disapproval of such cohabitation, and it provides a useful contrast to the opinion of Chrysostom. Jerome is entirely convinced that such living arrangements can only give rise to sexual misconduct, maliciously pointing to those 'virgins' who had been betrayed by their swollen bellies, or the pitter patter of tiny feet behind them.[8] John Chrysostom however, writing only a few years apart from Jerome, and using many of the same rhetorical topoi does not seem to be particularly concerned with such matters. He does mention that there is a regular procession of midwives to such virgins' houses in order to obtain physical proof of their maintained celibacy, and he bemoans the fact that there is even cause for such suspicions as to their virtue to arise.[9] Nevertheless, he professes to believe the claim of the male ascetics that they preserve their housemates inviolate.[10] Having said as much, he remains at a loss to discover why a man would voluntarily enter into such an advanced form of torture, where he constantly looks but cannot touch, unless it be from some perverted and repressed form of sexual desire. One by one he dismisses all reasons for such living arrangements presented by a

---

[5] See S. Elm, *Virgins of God: The Making of Asceticism in Late Antiquity* (Oxford, 1996), 51.

[6] For an advocate of this theory, see M. Alexandre's 'Early Christian Women', in P. Schmitt Pantel, ed., *A History of Women vol. 1 – From Ancient Goddesses to Christian Saints* (Harvard, 1992), 415.

[7] Jerome, *Letter* 22.14 to Eustochium.

[8] Jerome, *Letter* 22.13.

[9] *Quod reg.* 2 in Clark, *Jerome, Chrysostom*, 213. See Clark, *Women in Late Antiquity*, for a discussion of the validity of such 'virginity tests'.

[10] *Adv. eos* 1, in Clark, *Jerome, Chrysostom*, 164–5.

hypothetical ascetic debating the issue with him. It cannot be for the need of domestic help – a man is stronger and better able to care for another man than a woman; nor can it be in order to protect the helpless and destitute female – there are plenty far worse off than this particularly good-looking example; and the possibility that it be purely for the enjoyment of a spiritual and intellectual relationship is not even entered into, since Chrysostom was unequivocal in his opinion that the mind of a woman was unfit for such equal interaction with that of a male. In this he argues nothing new, since female inferiority was an accepted fact by most authors, philosophers and legislators throughout antiquity. Here we are simply given a Christianized version of the same theme. What Chrysostom does detect as happening within these supposedly celibate houses, however, and what he deems particularly disturbing, is an insidious assault on the appropriate boundaries of conduct between the sexes. These *subintroductae* are not behaving as proper women should, while the male ascetics are forgetting the masculine behaviour which is befitting to them.

This belief arises from the opinion of Chrysostom that the women in fact *force* the men into cohabiting with them. He speaks of their seductive glances, their swaying walk, and their carefully managed appearance, all amounting to the invitation of a prostitute; 'Come! Let us roll up together in love.'[11] Chrysostom's extended comparison of these virgins with prostitutes and harlots is very telling. A prostitute does not remain within the normal feminine sphere of the household. Instead she plies her trade in the public streets and marketplace, thus entering the previously male dominated space of commerce and politics. As such she is no longer a 'proper' woman. It was not unusual to compare errant females with harlots, as can be seen in the Old Testament. In the Book of Proverbs, Folly is described in the same terms as a prostitute soliciting for business in the main thoroughfare, and as such is presented as a deviant female:

> The woman Folly is loud; she is undisciplined and without knowledge. She sits at the door of her house, on a seat at the highest point of the city, calling out to those who pass by, who go straight on their way. 'Let all who are simple come in here!' she says to those who lack judgement. 'Stolen water is sweet; food eaten in secret is delicious!'[12]

Similarly, Chrysostom's wayward virgins have begun to transgress the established boundaries of their sex by actively enticing men to forget their vows of celibacy and to live with them in this 'spiritual' marriage. The fact that it is the women who are issuing the invitations in this case again illustrates the reversal of roles, since a proposal of something so akin to marriage would more properly come from the male. It is this absence of

---

[11] *Quod reg.* 1, in Clark, *Jerome, Chrysostom*, 210–11.
[12] Proverbs 9.13–17.

properly feminine submission that outrages Chrysostom far more than any suspicions of sexual impropriety:

> It is a great disgrace when the upper assumes the position of the lower so that the head is below, the body is above. If this dislocation is shameful in marriage, how much more so is the union of which we are speaking, in which it is something dreadful not only insofar as it is a transgression of the divine law, but because it creates an extremely bad reputation for both the woman and the man. If cohabitation is shameful, it is doubtless much more so when the man living with the woman is enslaved.[13]

This rebuke is contained in the treatise ostensibly aimed at the female celibates, largely because Chrysostom feels certain that it is the women who are responsible for seducing the men and causing them to fall into such sinful ways. Eve is alive and well in every woman. However, it would be a mistake to think that John was targeting only the women in his tirade. For if the female gains the ascendancy in any relationship between the sexes, it must imply that the male has allowed himself to be transposed, failing to exercise his natural authority. Chrysostom speaks angrily of those men who even take pride in the fact that they now function as unofficial slaves to their housemates:

> In church they bring unspeakable disgrace upon themselves, as if no place should remain ignorant of their arrogance and ignoble slavery. Even in this holy and formidable spot, they proclaim their lack of self-restraint to everyone, and what is still worse, they show off about things which ought to make them blush. The men receive the women at the door, strutting as if they had been transformed into eunuchs, and when everyone is looking, they guide them in with enormous pride. Nor do they slink away, but go so far as to glory in their performance. Even at that most awesome hour of the mysteries, they are much occupied with waiting on the virgins' pleasure, providing many of the spectators with occasion for offence.[14]

Just as those virgins failing to observe the correct mode of behaviour for their sex are compared to prostitutes, so these men, erring in a similar fashion, are likened to eunuchs, the implication being that they have become emasculated through their own fawning and sycophantic actions. But Chrysostom may also have employed this comparison secure in the knowledge that eunuchs were generally reviled by the rest of society, while the stereotypes portrayed them as being both corrupt and sexually depraved.[15] For a man to take orders from a female, as these self-proclaimed 'eunuchs' did, stands as a direct contravention of the divine order, since God

---

[13] *Quod reg.* 7, in Clark, *Jerome, Chrysostom*, 231.

[14] *Adv. eos* 10, in Clark, *Jerome, Chrysostom*, 194.

[15] See S. Tougher 'Byzantine Eunuchs: An Overview (with special reference to their creation and origin)', in L. James, ed., *Women, Men and Eunuchs: Gender in Byzantium* (London, 1997), 168–84.

had assigned woman to the domestic sphere, leaving the civic arena in the charge of the male.[16] Now however, the man can be seen to take an unseemly interest in affairs normally the preserve of the female. Living in such close contact with a woman and her attendants leads a man to become effeminate. He can be seen rushing about the marketplace, calling at the silversmith's to inquire if his 'mistress's' mirror is ready, then the perfume maker, followed by the linen merchant and umbrella maker.[17] This catalogue of trifling errands illustrates two things which annoy Chrysostom. The first, and most obvious, is his disgust that supposedly dedicated virgins should themselves care so much for worldly frippery of which the only function was to serve their physical beauty. He is however also enraged at the willing manner in which the men have submitted their authority to mere women, and frivolous women at that. This I believe, is the point to each of the subsequent vivid pictures of the practical problems involved in cohabitation between the sexes; men colliding with maid servants in every corner of the house, being surprised while still undressed, walking into a room of gossiping women each evening where the conversation suddenly stops and the tittering begins. A living arrangement in which a man abnegates his natural superiority to this extent can only lead to such turmoil as is depicted in these tableaux. And as the women are portrayed as progressively more silly and foolish, so much worse does the error of the male become, since he is now beneath even the worst examples of weak female nature. Through their actions, the men Chrysostom describes have called into question their very masculinity, since they have allowed the women to

> ...render them softer, more hot-headed, shameful, mindless, irascible, insolent, importunate, ignoble, crude, servile, niggardly, reckless, nonsensical, and, to sum it up, the women take all their corrupting feminine customs and stamp them into the souls of these men.[18]

The men are compared to shorn and tamed lions, again to eunuchs, and in a passage reminiscent of Hector's rebuke to Paris, to armed warriors who withdraw from battle in order to sit down at the spindle with a group of chattering women.[19] Chrysostom continually speaks of these misguided men as being afflicted with a kind of drunkenness and of the need for them to come to their senses. The implication of this is that they have displaced their powers of rational thought and intelligent behaviour, and thus their masculinity. The exercise of reason and the constant pursuit of intellectual

---

[16] *Quod reg.* 7, in Clark, *Jerome, Chrysostom*, 228; see also *Homily XXXIV.5 on 1 Corinthians*, *PG* 61.290–1 for similar sentiments.

[17] *Adv. eos* 9-10, in Clark, *Jerome, Chrysostom*, 192–3.

[18] *Adv. eos* 11, in Clark, *Jerome, Chrysostom*, 197.

[19] *Adv.eos* 11, in Clark, *Jerome, Chrysostom*, 196–7.

improvement were generally perceived both as a masculine preserve and the means by which masculinity could be proven. 'Maleness' was not a state to be taken for granted, nor simply a matter of external appearance, but rather an internal disposition which had to be constantly worked at in order to maintain it. Self-discipline and the application of reason were the processes by which perfect masculinity could be achieved, while the enactment of these processes was itself deemed possible only for men.[20] A natural extension of this logic was the form of praise lavished on those women who met with the approval of their religious authorities. Such females were described as having transcended the natural boundaries of their sex and become manly in their virtue and courage. By implication therefore, those men who chose to behave with a lack of reason were in effect reversing the process and emasculating themselves, forfeiting their position of superiority within the human race.

As well as inveighing against inappropriate behaviour between the sexes therefore, Chrysostom has also sent a clear message to his readership that intellectual ability was an indication of masculinity. He himself continues to illustrate this point in his own text. Once trained by the orator Libanios, his mode of writing is a perfect example of the rhetorical style prized so highly in Roman society. Not only was good rhetoric the mark of an educated man, it was a tribute to his very masculinity. When it came to oratory this was not least because of the sheer physical effort involved in speaking eloquently and effectively in public.[21] Given the fact that Chrysostom himself is said to have been a physically unprepossessing man, his highly charged rhetoric may well have served to forestall any doubts as to his own masculinity as he dominated his audience by means of his power over words, while at the same time offering an exemplum for them to follow. His dramatic mode of presentation may also have been an attempt on his part to win more attention for his urgings than unadorned prose would have done. John's descriptions of what might occur in these ascetic households, and the enticing appearances of the women involved, are titillating in the extreme, bringing to life in full colour before his audience all the scandalous activities he wishes to condemn. Thus he makes the female virgins into the objects of his audience's gaze.[22] Perhaps this was a ploy to gain and hold their attention, presenting his moral

---

[20] This was not a view confined to Christian thinkers. M. Satlow '"Try to Be a Man": The Rabbinic Construction of Masculinity', *Harvard Theological Review* 89, 1 (1996), 19–40, discusses its prevalence in both Jewish and Stoic traditions.

[21] M. Gleason, *Making Men: Sophists and Self-Presentation in Ancient Rome* (Princeton, 1995).

[22] See B. Leyerle, 'John Chrysostom on the Gaze', *Journal of Early Christian Studies* 1,2 (1993), 159–74, for a fuller discussion of this process. I am also indebted to Professor Leyerle for allowing me to read an advance draft of her forthcoming book *Displays of Holiness: John Chrysostom's Attack on Spiritual Marriage*, which deals at length with these texts.

exhortations in a format at least as attractive as the more secular distractions, such as the theatre or real life prostitutes, available to those he was trying to reach. Chrysostom hopes that in this way the desires of his readers will be contained and diffused within the words of his text, rather than in an environment more dangerous for their immortal souls.

Chrysostom's opinion of women remains bleak throughout both of these treatises, dismissing these false virgins as at best foolish and vain, and at worst temptresses and the causes of man's downfall. And it is this bitter invective which remains so memorable after reading the texts. However, it is important to remember that he is equally disgusted by those men who were weak enough to allow the women to practice their feminine wiles on them, since this represented a disregard for their appropriate place at the top of the hierarchy of the sexes. This behaviour is all the more offensive since it was carried out in the full view of the public gaze, thus calling the Church body as a whole into disrepute:

> This is why we have won the reputation everywhere for ourselves of being gluttons, flatterers, and above all slaves of women, because we have dashed to the ground all the nobility given us from above and exchanged it for earthly servility and shabbiness.[23]

Chrysostom's wish throughout his texts is to re-emphasize the boundaries between the sexes, both biologically and behaviourally, with men and women fulfilling their divinely appointed functions, and being seen to do so by all onlookers. Any quest for equality of interaction between the sexes must therefore be abandoned until the afterlife, he claims, where the corporeal body is put aside and gender divisions cease to have significance. Until then the rules laid down in these treatises, and which echoed age-old philosophical opinions, must be adhered to. However, the frantic note we can often detect creeping into Chrysostom's voice, especially in some of his more lurid descriptions of the scandalous actions of the cohabiting ascetics, might suggest that he felt himself to be fighting a losing battle. We can almost hear him echo the cry of Xerxes centuries before when confronted with a warlike Artemisia: 'My men are becoming women, and my women men'.[24]

---

[23] *Adv. eos* 7, in Clark, *Jerome, Chrysostom*, 180–1. It is interesting to note that we have no information regarding the possible practice of syneisaktism in the desert or in rural areas. It is always depicted as occurring in urban centres, and thereby all the more serious a sin on account of its public nature.

[24] Herodotus, *Histories* VIII.88.

5. Anastasios of Sinai's teaching on body and soul

Joseph A. Munitiz

Who ever heard of Anastasios of Sinai? This question needs to be asked not so much of today's readers (many of whom no doubt will have heard something of the author and his works[1]), but of the people who lived in the centuries that we now recognize as those of the middle and late Byzantine Empire: in this case from early in the eighth century, which is as near as we can get to the year in which Anastasios died, down to the fall of Constantinople in the middle of the fifteenth century. The question arises because if he was a relatively unknown or highly abstruse writer, then his influence must have been minimal and his importance very secondary. However there is sufficient evidence for us to be fairly certain that his name at least was quite well known, and several works circulated that were attributed to him. Thus we have not only the *Hodegos*, a sort of layman's theological *vademecum*, but some half-dozen sermons, various collections of stories, and perhaps most characteristic of all a collection of *Questions and Answers* that appear and reappear in very many manuscripts and in somewhat different versions. For the purpose of this chapter I shall be quoting from the new edition of the original collection that I am preparing, but with references where possible to the published text.[2] So far we have at our disposal good editions of only about one third of all his works.

From the evidence of the manuscripts, which are very numerous, Anastasios must have been well known, yet there remains a puzzle. As far as I can see, later professional theologians rarely cite him: he is not, for

---

[1] For his works, see *Clavis Patrum Graecorum* 3, ed. M. Geerard (Turnhout, 1979), nos 7745–81; among the recent secondary literature, see J. Haldon, 'The Works of Anastasius of Sinai: A Key Source for the History of East Mediterranean Society and Belief', in A. Cameron and L. Conrad, eds, *The Early Medieval East: Problems in the Literary Source Materials* (Princeton, 1992), 107–47.

[2] The number in the original collection (*CPG* 7746) first, then in brackets the number in *PG* 89.

example, mentioned by Photios.[3] On the other hand, the *Dioptra*, a popular
work which consists of a dialogue between the Soul and the Flesh on the
Day of Judgement, composed by Philip the Solitary (in the eleventh century)
does include references to him and in very laudatory terms.[4] Similarly,
Anastasios himself rarely cites other patristic authors or professional
theologians (the most obvious would have been Maximos the Confessor),
though we know from the *Hodegos* that Anastasios is not averse to inventing
a few quotations and attributing them to well-known names to give prestige
to his own opinions (these false quotations can be tracked down in the
excellent edition of the *Hodegos* by Karl-Heinz Uthemann[5]). In the *Questions
and Answers*, Pseudo-Dionysios is quoted once,[6] Clement of Alexandria is
mentioned, but the words attributed to him cannot be found.[7] Nearly all
that we know about Anastasios has to be gleaned from hints that he lets
drop himself, such as that he wrote far away from books, that he took part
in disputes with the monophysites in Alexandria,[8] that he also composed
tracts against the monthelites,[9] that he had some experience of Cyprus[10] and
that he had been to the Dead Sea.[11] His name suggests some link with Sinai,
and the likelihood that he was higoumenos of the monastery seems strong.
He was certainly familiar with the Arab occupation of Palestine, and was
well informed about the ravages they had committed.

The picture that emerges is that of a monk who became well known in
his own day, not so much as a professional theologian but rather as an
apologist for the Chalcedonian faith and as an adviser, who could be
consulted by letter and who could be relied upon to preach and write in a
clear, rather homely style; so a man of common sense and good judgement,
and essentially a religious man with pastoral preoccupations. The advantage
of such a writer is that he is more likely to bring us close to the thought world
of ordinary people. The *Questions and Answers* are clearly made up of
genuine questions that had been submitted to Anastasios, probably over

---

[3] So far no iconographic representation of Anastasios is known to me. The detailed study
of the illustrations provided for Anastasios' *Hodegos* (A.D. Kartsonis, *Anastasis: The Making
of an Image*, [Princeton, 1986], chap. 3) does not deal with this aspect. There is a commemoration
of Anastasios of Sinai, with a reference to his extreme old age, in the *Synaxarium*, see H.
Delehaye, ed., *Propylaeum ad Acta Sanctorum Novembris* (Brussels, 1902), cols 617–18 (April 21),
but I have not come across other hagiographic material.
[4] S. Lauriotes, ed., *O ATHOΣ* 1,1, (1920), 9–264, esp. 128–30, 169. For a bibliography, cf. *ODB*
2, 1652 (s.v. Philip Monotropos).
[5] *CCSG* 8 (1981), 448.
[6] Qu. 42 (=100 ter).
[7] Qu. 28 (=96).
[8] *Hodegos*, chap. X.
[9] Some are included in K.-H. Uthemann's edition of the sermons *de creatione* (*CCSG* 12 [1985]).
[10] Qu. 26 (=94).
[11] Qu. 28 (=96).

several years. His answers were sent back and were intended to be made
public, read out in church to groups of interested Christians. The group I
have in mind would be some of the 'private religious foundations', for which
evidence has been found in the Egyptian papyri.[12] Anastasios remarks at
one point that a particular answer may not be suitable for public reading
as it refers to sexual matters.[13]

The non-professional character of Anastasios' teaching on body and
soul soon becomes apparent, and it will probably be most helpful to begin
with what he has to say about the body, and then pass on to the soul. On
the body, perhaps the most striking trait of Anastasios' teaching is that it
presents no problems for him. He simply accepts it in all its mundane,
corporeal reality. He will mention how the body emerges from the dark
cavern of the womb (Qu. 22 [=92]), and will also talk in very matter-of-fact
language about its eventual dissolution (Qu. 22 [=92], Qu. 28 [=96]). Where
his teaching becomes more distinctive is in his repeated reference to the four
elements that make up the body: the hot and the cold, the dry and the wet;
fire and air, earth and water. This 'theory' of the four elements is presented
as something that will not be generally known, or at least as if the
implications of the theory have not been sufficiently worked out. With this
theory as his key,[14] Anastasios attempts to explain how the resurrection of
bodies is possible,[15] why people differ in character (Qu. 27 [=95]), why some
people seem to die 'untimely' deaths (Qu. 28 [=96]), and why some women
are sterile while others are not:

> In many parts of Holy Scripture we find the human body referred to with the
> word 'earth'. Now just as earth which has been moderately watered is fruitful,
> and the earth which receives much water is barren, the same often happens
> with the female womb and the male seed.... It is very difficult for prostitutes
> to conceive. Here also is the reason why in different areas rich people, who live
> in plenty, desire to have children, but do not, whereas the poor people are often
> very fertile. The physical part, which because of want has grown thirsty and
> dry, like parched soil, at once absorbs the moisture of the seed that falls on it,
> as happens also to those destitute and impoverished people among us, the
> desert-wandering Arabs, who barely have enough bread, but who have a super-
> abundance of children. (Qu. 81 [=127])

---

[12] J. P. Thomas, *Private Religious Foundations in the Byzantine Empire*, Dumbarton Oaks
Studies 24 (Washington, 1987), esp. chap. 3 'Private Religious Foundations in Egypt from the
Evidence of the Papyri', which covers the fifth to eighth centuries.

[13] Qu. 81 (=127).

[14] He also refers to the importance of climate and diet as part of this overall theory, see Qu.
26 (=94) and Qu. 28 (=96), and racial remarks are quite commonplace, e.g. Qu. 35 (partly
included in ed. Qu. 8), and Qu. 41 (the reference to the Armenians has been omitted in ed.
Qu. 100 bis).

[15] Qu. 22 (=92).

The substructure of this answer is the theory that two of the elements are the dry and the wet (earth and water) and that they interact, but it is apparent how some other, commonplace but questionable, platitudes have been added.

What does Anastasios have to say about sex as such? His teaching in this area has the same factual and practical character found in all his treatment of the body. Firstly, he is clearly aware of the strength of the sexual drive: this appears when he mentions the predicament of a husband who returns from a journey and wishes to receive communion the following morning, but is counselled to abstain from sexual relations with his wife out of respect for the sacrament. Anastasios takes the line that such a man deserves to be pardoned if he copulates with his wife (Qu. 67 [=115]). Even more interesting, when at one point he wishes to evoke how much we owe to Christ, and how strong should be our devotion and love for him, he writes:

> Let us long for the Lord as we might long for the company of prostitutes! Very often a man will squander all his fortune out of desire for a woman, just to get his foul pleasure. (Qu. 91 [=135])

the implication being that religious men should be prepared to make equal sacrifices. But while Anastasios recognizes the strength of the sexual drive, he is adamant in his condemnation of any improper use of sex.[16] Highest in his list of condemnations comes any active homosexual relationship: he is talking about different classes of sin:

> the forgiveness of somebody who falls, but regrets and laments the sin, is different from that of the person who sins and remains indifferent. And the punishment of the one who uses his body in accordance with nature is one thing, whereas quite different and much more painful than for any other sin is the punishment of someone who gives up acts in accordance with nature and turns to the destruction of the Sodomites, something that even the brute beasts never do.... He who sins against nature kills the soul along with the body. (Qu. 35[17])

Of course it is not surprising that he should write in this vein, and one could hardly have expected anything else in that time and place. What is surprising however is the pastoral sensitivity with regard to carnal sins and bodily weakness which does appear in some of the answers. Two examples:

> I myself have seen men, one hundred years old, who were powerless and shaking all over, but they could not free themselves from their carnal sin because of long habit. On that occasion, when certain professional doctors were

---

[16] Various points are discussed in Qu. 25 and Qu. 35 (both adapted in ed. Qu. 8), Qu. 73 (adapted in ed. Qu. 10), polygamy in Qu. 37 (=99) and Qu. 100 (=139), and adultery in Qu. 77 (=124). The problem of forced prostitution comes up in Qu. 76 (=123).

[17] Qu. 8 in *PG*, which also includes what was Qu. 38 in the original collection.

asked about them, they gave the following reply: 'The conduits and arteries by which the semen is excreted become relaxed and porous after many years of sexual intercourse and habit; as a result the body no longer has the strength to restrain and impede nor to control itself, but a sort of seminal flux is brought on through the feebleness of old age and of habit, so the body is dragged quite involuntarily towards the sin to which it has grown accustomed.' (Qu. 33[18])

This sympathy and understanding for the frailties of old age is very Anastasian. The other example concerns legitimate sexual acts or involuntary emissions of seed: can one just wash oneself and then go to church? The answer is the following:

For a Christian the true way of washing is with one's own tears. You see there are two liquids that flow from the body, one of which can sanctify and the other frequently defiles, viz., tears and semen. The spiritual way of washing is with tears. However ordinary water has come into being to help us purify our bodies. So those who lack the spiritual bath, which purifies the soul, should at least wash their flesh with water, and then certainly partake straight away of the holy mysteries, because thus they will avoid any sort of contempt. (Qu. 38 [=98bis])

Notice how he would prefer his Christians to have easy access to 'tears of compunction', but realizes that this may not be the case; with good pastoral sense he tells them just to wash and get off to church.

There is much more in Anastasios' teaching concerning the body, but this brief account will have to suffice as an introduction. I turn now to his teaching concerning the soul. And here it is at once even more obvious that we are dealing with a non-professional. It is clear for example that he has not read Plato, nor, as far as I can see, Aristotle. In other words he is not working with the model of the soul as a sort of person somehow imprisoned in a body and longing to get out; nor on the other hand is he preoccupied (or even familiar) with hylomorphic theories. Equally absent from his bookshelf seems to be Nemesios of Emesa (who was influenced by Plato), whom one might expect him to have consulted, and indeed other patristic authors, like Basil or the other Cappadocians. The book which he has read very thoroughly is the Bible, and he is very preoccupied that whatever he says about the soul should be in harmony with that essential source. On the other hand, he has clearly dabbled in medicine,[19] and there are times when he feels a certain tension between these two interests: thus at one point he is trying to explain why the visions that people claim to have of dead saints cannot really be of the 'souls' of these saints:

---

[18] Again a text which was not included in the Revised version, though traces appear in ed. Qu. 8.

[19] Qu. 81 (=127) quoted above.

for before the resurrection of bodies has taken place, and while the bones and fleshy parts of the saints are scattered around, how is it possible for them to be recognized as fully formed men ...?

He feels he must add: "But to prevent some people thinking that I am concocting the sort of legends made up by doctors, pay attention to the scriptural teaching concerning souls.' (Qu. 19 [=89])

How then does Anastasios approach the question of the soul? And if we can be certain of anything it is that he was quite fascinated by this question. Thus he opens his major discussion on the soul with the question:

> Everyone has a positive thirst, as if for a minimum amount of water, to learn and ascertain exactly what is the human soul, what sort of thing it is, and from what it is made up, and when, and how it is active within the body, and where it proceeds to after the separation from the body. (Qu. 19 [=89])

Two comments: first, this whole question and the answer (which is very substantial) was simply omitted in the revised version of the *Questions and Answers* which became the most popular, and was subsequently translated into Slavonic (the *Izbornik* of 1073). It may be significant that these speculative *Questions and Answers* were not to the liking of the more middle-of-the-road, less personal, Reviser who effectively hijacked the work of Anastasios in the ninth century. However the original text continued to be read, and was included in the new amalgam eventually published in the *Patrologia Graeca* as Qu. 89. Secondly, Anastasios returns to the same question of the soul in several of his other works: notably in the definition section of the *Hodegos*, but at much greater length in his *Homilies on the Creation of Man in the Image of God*. The question was an important one for him.

Here I shall restrict myself to some salient points of his teaching. Initially his answer is that there is no answer. We cannot know what the soul is. Just as the eye does not see itself, but only other things,[20] so the soul can know, but cannot be known. In this it is 'in the image and likeness of God', the unknowable in Himself. This is a key principle for Anastasios: the soul is to the body what God is to the world. There is a similar unknowability, but also a similar unity, so that the soul 'blows through'[21] and animates the body as its life principle. The second key point to remember is that if the nature of the soul is unknowable, its activities do appear and can be observed:

> Our soul, which is invisible 'in the image' of God, displays its own activities through the visible body which belongs to it, as if it were a sort of world. The soul has the mind (*nous*) as a steersman (*higemon*) placed in the brain above what is called the 'ouraniskon' [='palate': the Greek word for this (the roof of the mouth) means 'little heaven', and Anastasios uses the image of the mind

---

[20] *Sermo I de creatione*, I.l. 14–17 (ed. Uthemann, *CCSG* 12 [1985], 4).

[21] One of the definitions given in the *Hodegos* II. 5. 60–61 (ed. Uthemann, *CCSG* 8 [1981], 54).

being similar to God, who is placed above the great heaven]...., the mind serves to dispose and control the body, as if it were some earthly cosmos. That is why, should a man happen to receive some violent blow on the head, the mind suffers at once and he can no longer judge properly nor remember as before. On the other hand, the reasoning part is activated by the soul through the heart, the concupiscent part through the liver, the kindly laughing part through the spleen, the breathing through the lung, the generative through the kidneys, the feelings through the blood, the knowing through the eyes, the speaking through the tongue, so that when the latter is cut out, a man can no longer talk. (Qu. 19 [=89])

As you can see, the reasoning is not particularly subtle. This is very much a layman's approach. Similarly his proof that the soul has something to do with the heat or fire element is that if you cut open a dead person, you will find the other three elements present, the cold, the dry, and the wet (bile, humour and phlegm) but not the blood, and it is in the bubbling blood that the soul is giving life.[22] The mysterious soul then needs the body.

Although Anastasios has to be classified as a non-professional theologian, it would be incorrect to suppose that he is completely ignorant of the different theories concerning the soul that were prevalent in earlier times: for example, he explicitly rejects the view attributed to Origen that the soul has pre-existed and is then inserted into an already formed body (Qu. 21 [=91]). Note moreover that for Anastasios, as for Aristotle, the term 'soul' applies also to animals, and even to boiling water (Qu. 22 [=92]). It is clearly the equivalent for him of the term 'life'.

To sum up, Anastasios' teaching on the soul, though mysterious, is lofty and highly respectful. He believes strongly in the free-will, the pre-eminence, the God-like nature of the human soul. So insistent is he on its creative power that he attributes to the human sperm the production of the soul:

> If as the heretics maintain, man were to sow a body without a soul, and if he were not to impart the soul, the irrational beings would be found to be worthy of more respect, for they sow and bring forth a full living being with soul.(Qu. 21[=91]).

This creative power of man is somehow combined with the creative power of God: 'the human soul is a being which really exists, rational, immortal, mindful, which draws its existence not from the elements, but from God....' (Qu. 21 [= 91])

To close, in several of his answers Anastasios tackles the problem of life after death: where are the souls of those who die, and above all what knowledge is possible in the after-life? Briefly his answer is that no knowledge of one another is possible in the after-life, and that to understand

---

[22] Qu. 22 (=92).

the New Testament parable of Lazarus in Abraham's bosom and Dives in Hades one must use allegory and symbol as keys of interpretation. He insists that no mutual recognition is possible:

> How indeed can the souls recognise one another in that other life? They never saw one another in their naked state while in this life. Recognition comes through difference and varied characteristics. But in that state no soul any longer possesses a difference of shape or form.... (Qu. 19 [= 89])

But the problem is even more complicated:

> All of us who have fallen asleep in this world, we shall arise [after the resurrection] in the same form in which Adam came to be – just as the tiny grains that fall from the ear of corn and are buried in the earth do not rise up small, but fill out and become ears of corn as they were before their fall. Resurrection is defined by the holy fathers as an *apokatastasis* [a complete restoration] to the primitive state of the first man. So no one will recognise another for physical reasons.... (Qu. 19[=89])

In other words, all resurrected bodies will look the same, as all will be identical to Adam.[23] Anastasios is forced by the logic of his own premises into the position where if we are to know one another in the future life, it will be by pure miracle, by the mysterious workings of God. For Anastasios it is absolutely obvious that soul and body have to go together: a soul without a body is unrecognizable. We are carnal beings, and yet at the same time, we are made in the image of God. For him this is a source of never-ending wonder. Anastasios certainly does not enter into the category of those who say, 'Deny everything!'

---

[23] The question then arises: does Eve have a place in this theory? There is no clear answer. At several points Anastasios does refer to Eve: e.g. she symbolizes for him the Holy Spirit 'proceeding' from the Father (*Sermo I de creatione*, I.l. 85–7 (ed. Uthemann, CCSG 12 [1985], 11), but her role in the production of a human being seems restricted to that of the passive earth into which the male semen infuses the immortal soul (*Sermo adversus monotheletas*, III.3. 119–26 (ed. Uthemann, CCSG 12 [1985], 70). A study of this particular aspect of Anastasios' teaching would have to take into account the controversial work *In Hexaemeron*.

6. Divine sex: Patriarch Methodios's concept of virginity

Dirk Krausmüller

When, at the end of the eighth century, literary production in Byzantium regained momentum, one looks in vain for writings in which an author develops a coherent anthropology. Instead, there is a plethora of encomia and saints' lives. The work of Patriarch Methodios of Constantinople (after 787–847) is no exception. Methodios is chiefly known as one of the leading figures of the iconodule party under the emperors Michael and Theophilos, and as the restorer of icons and icon worship under the empress-regent Theodora.[1] However, he was also one of the leading intellectuals of his time whose prowess impressed even his enemies, if we are to believe the assertion of his *Vita* that Theophilos had him brought to the Palace to discuss theological questions.[2] Nevertheless, apart from the letters he wrote as patriarch, all that have survived of his writings are narrative texts: three encomia of 'old' saints, Agatha, Nicholas and Dionysios,[3] two lives of contemporary saints, abbot Theophanes the Confessor and Euthymios the metropolitan of Sardes,[4] and a number of canons, including one on Lucy of Syracuse.[5]

---

[1] A short summary of his life can be found in D.Stiernon, 'Méthode', *Dictionnaire de Spiritualité* 10, 2 (Paris, 1979), cols 1107–1109.

[2] *Vita S.Methodii*, chap. 9, *PG* 100, 1252C.

[3] Agatha: E.Mioni, 'L'encomio di S.Agata', *AB* 68 (1950), 58–93 (henceforth EA); Nicholas: G.Anrich, *Der Heilige Nikolaos in der griechischen Kirche*, vol.1: *Die Texte* (Leipzig and Berlin, 1913), 140–50 (henceforth EN); Dionysios: C.Westerbrink, 'Passio S.Dionysii Areopagitae, Rustici et Eleutherii uitgegeven naar het', *Leidse Handschrift Vulcanianus* 52 (Alphen, 1937), 44–63 (henceforth ED).

[4] Theophanes: ed. V.V. Latyshev, 'Life of Theophanes the Confessor', *Zapiski of the Russian Academy of Sciences* 13 (1916–22), no. 4 (henceforth VThC); Euthymios: J.Gouillard, 'La vie d'Euthyme de Sardes (+831), une oeuvre du patriarche Méthode', *Travaux et Memoires* 10 (1987), 1–101 (henceforth VES).

[5] Lucy: A.Kominis, ed., *Analecta hymnica graeca. Canones Decembris* (Rome, 1976), 279–87 (henceforth CL).

In Methodios's case, however, literary genre is a misleading category. While it is true that he gives accounts of the lives of individuals, a closer look at the texts invariably reveals the existence of a dense net of typological relations. These link together the single episodes regardless of their position within the temporal sequence and, in the end, completely subvert the narrative. Methodios was anything but a naïve story-teller to whom the meanings of his stories was self-evident. Quite the contrary: he clearly held the belief that meaning can only be established by transcending the contingencies of the narrative.

In this article, I would like to demonstrate how Methodios uses his encomia as vehicles to develop his own anthropology in which sexuality plays a central role. Since his writings are highly idiosyncratic, however, a few preliminary remarks are necessary. Methodios's main preoccupation is to bring the phenomena of the world into a meaningful order. His system of classification, however, is not based on causal relations but purely on similarity. This concept of similarity is not hazy and undefined; rather, in the hands of Methodios, it becomes a sharp tool. He defines exactly where phenomena overlap and how they are related to each other. In this way, he manages to reduce the wealth of phenomena to a small number of common patterns. Since he writes narratives, he cannot present his concepts in a systematic way and so he develops a series of techniques to 'teach' the reader how to read his texts properly. For example, in the *Life of Theophanes*, Methodios says that the saint did not dare voice his wish to remain celibate when his mother wanted to marry him off: 'He swaddled the more divine thoughts which were still carried in the womb of the mind with the rags of meekness and mother-obeying habit'.[6] Here, Methodios combines two images which do not fit together, for in order to swaddle a baby, one must have given birth to it first. He creates this discrepancy so as to show the reader that it can be transcended once the reader recognizes the basic similarity existing between the membranes around an embryo in the womb and the swaddling clothes round an infant.

Of course, the world does not consist only of parallel phenomena but also of opposites. In these cases, Methodios tries again to domesticate the oppositions by integrating them into more comprehensive patterns. In his encomium of Nicholas, he compares the birth of the saint and that of John the Baptist. He says that in his birth, the saint followed John in an identical and in an opposite way. He explains this by showing that Nicholas's birth was the beginning of a life-long sterility for his mother, whereas John's conception had been the end of Elizabeth's sterility.[7] Wherever possible, Methodios tries to harmonize discrepancies. In his encomium of Dionysios,

---

[6] VThC, chap. 9, 6.27–8.

[7] EN, chap. 6, 143.16.

he manipulates the varying dates for the death of the apostles given in the passio of this saint and in Eusebios's *History of the Church* until he can conclude that 'therefore the apparent discord will rather be a concord.'[8] Nevertheless, he always takes the apparent discrepancy seriously and never feels tempted to gloss over a problem.

Turning to the encomium of the Sicilian martyr Agatha, I will now show how Methodios employs these techniques to develop his concept of virginity. In the introductory part of this text, Methodios presents his heroine to the audience in her roles as 'woman' and 'virgin'.[9] However, when he speaks about her as woman, he adds that she was 'woman by nature, not by choice'.[10]. Thus he creates an opposition between 'woman' and 'nature' on one hand and 'virgin' and 'will' on the other. The reader is led to the conclusion that Agatha has rejected her female nature in order to opt for virginity.

This first statement is then followed by a curious but typically Methodian passage in which he gives the meanings of the terms 'woman' and 'virgin'.[11] Quoting Adam's words from Genesis, he first defines 'woman' as 'because she was taken out of her man'. Then he gives a definition of 'virgin' as 'because she came out of the incorruptible divine Word – the one and undivided Son'.[12] This definition is then given biblical authority through a quotation from the prologue of John's Gospel: 'But to all those who received him, he gave the power to become children of God to those who believed in him, who are born not out of blood, nor out of the will of a man but out of God'.[13] At first, this juxtaposition seems to reinforce the initial opposition between woman and virgin. Nevertheless, there is already a fundamental parallelism here because both woman and virgin 'come out of' somebody else. In the next statement, this parallel is completed. Methodios adapts a passage from II Corinthians and states that Agatha in her role as woman was 'joined well to one man, Christ'.[14] After having come out of him, Agatha is joined to him again, just as in Genesis, Eve was returned to Adam to be married to him. Methodios goes even further: by identifying Christ as Agatha's 'man', he shows that the two statements 'born out of God' and 'taken out of her man/born out of the will of man' can be identical. Being a virgin, then, is just one special case of being a woman – the case where Christ is the husband. This is much more than a play on words. Methodios refuses to see Agatha's womanhood in purely negative

---

[8] ED, chap. 4, 46, 30–48.11.
[9] EA, chap. 3, 77.9.
[10] EA, chap. 3, 77.9–10.
[11] EA, chap. 3, 77.13–24.
[12] EA, chap. 3, 77.18–20.
[13] EA, chap. 3, 77.20–24.
[14] EA, chap. 3, p.77.24–5.

terms. With the expression 'woman virgin' (γυνή παρθένος), he conveys the sense that Agatha is not just virgin as opposed to woman, but woman-virgin, or, rather, that she is a virgin insofar as she is the woman/wife of Christ.[15]

This attempt to give human nature a meaningful role in a virginal life can be found in all other passages where Methodios speaks about the virginity of his heroes. In his canon on Lucy of Syracuse, he presents her as a virgin-martyr who persuaded her mother not to marry her off to her fiancé.[16] When he speaks about her virginity in positive terms, however, he describes it as an 'inner' sexual intercourse with Christ, whom he addresses thus: 'For being twined together in the same spirit, you also preserve the body of the chaste one ever-virginal'.[17] The same idea is expressed in the encomium of Nicholas, where Methodios first states that he 'completely pushed away from himself the yearnings for women' but adds that 'he chastely embraced temperance and twined himself together with her and ate with her'.[18] Since Nicholas is a man, his partner cannot be Christ himself, and so God is represented by the female virtue of temperance who, as bedfellow and companion for meals, fulfils all the roles of an ordinary wife in the life of the saint.

The pattern is clear. The saints refrain from establishing relationships with ordinary husbands and wives, but at the same time imagine such relationships with God or an aspect of the divine. Clearly Methodios is motivated by a wish to justify virginity as an alternative to the social constraints of marriage and procreation, but we must ask why he does so by creating images which exactly reproduce the rejected 'outer' contacts.

Methodios addresses the problem that those who opt for virginity are bound to be haunted by the wish to have sexual intercourse with a partner.[19] In their memories they have stored the respective images which will present themselves and unchain the passion leading to the fulfilment of this wish.

In the system of spiritual ascent which was predominant in late antiquity, the severing of the link between one's body and that of someone else through abstention would have been followed by an inner dissociation from the corresponding passionate feelings and images.[20] Then the soul itself

---

[15] The definition of woman Methodios quotes from Genesis is rather strange for it only applies to Eve and not to other women, who are then – according to this definition – incomplete. It is not unlikely that Methodios tries to insinuate in this way that Agatha, as a virgin, is a super-woman because she is not only married to Christ, she also came out of him.

[16] CL, 283. 89–94, 6th ode

[17] CL, 282. 81–3, 5th ode.

[18] EN, chap. 8, 144.5–7.

[19] EA, chap. 6, 79.14.

[20] John of Carpathus, for example, admonishes his readers to pray to God 'that he may wipe out the images of the passionate mind and make imageless our weaknesses which are full of images', *Capita hortatoria* (Athens, 1957), chap. 78, 290.

would have become imageless and passionless and ready to reach out for the equally imageless and passionless God.

Methodios's solution is radically different. His saints create analogous images of Christ as husband or wife and sustain the relations with Christ in these roles with the same kind of passionate feelings as they would have done in ordinary relationships. Thus the traditional 'vertical' movement from lower types of contact to higher, rarefied ones, which was the backbone of late antique spirituality, has given way to a 'horizontal' movement where one possible role-partner is simply replaced by another. When a nun imagines Christ instead of an ordinary lover, the divine image will not look different from that of any other man. That celibacy is still possible shows that God as a role-partner is considered stronger than any human being and therefore that the images representing him can oust images of ordinary role-partners which might compete with them. Nevertheless, in this competition, God is on the same level as his creatures.

This brings up the question of why Methodios departed from the Late Antique concept of spiritual ascent. I would argue that the reason is a change in the perception of what is real. In Late Antique spirituality, there is a broad consensus that there is a state beyond the images which is where God can be found, a kind of super-reality. This allowed Late Antique authors to have a reserved attitude towards images as a way of conceiving the relationship with God. At best, they could be stepping-stones which might help the untrained soul in the early stages of its ascent, but needed to be left behind by those who wanted to come closer to what God really is.

Methodios's saints, on the other hand, never communicate with an imageless God. They are dependent on God's condescension, since God has manifested himself as man and made all of these relations possible in the first place.[21] If they want to relate to him, they must incarnate him again in their imaginations. Even if Methodios believes in a God beyond the images, it is clear that, for him, such a God is neither accessible to humans nor able to have an effect on them.

Such a view creates severe problems around the Late Antique view of virginity. Defined as not having sexual intercourse and as not procreating, it is a negative concept which mirrors the God of the *via negativa*, equally defined by what he is not.[22] In Methodios' changed world-view, this meant that virginity would both militate against the demands of human nature and not be able to draw the necessary divine power to stave off these demands. It needs to be filled with images and thus empowered. These images are drawn from the ordinary life of men and women. So virginity

---

[21] Therefore Methodios can say about Agatha, as Christ's wife and mother, 'You became everything for him who had become (i.e. incarnated) before your sake', EA, chap. 19, 86.1.

[22] This connection had been stressed by Gregory of Nyssa at the beginning of *De Virginitate*, tr. and ed. M. Aubineau, *Grégoire de Nysse, Traite de la Virginité* (Paris, 1966).

is no longer equated with contemplation in the sense of inactivity, but becomes an inner activity, which leads to a development of male and female nature rather than a neutralization of it.

The conclusion is that while Methodios still aims at liberating the human being from the straightjacket of social relations through virginity, his changed world-view forces him to explore new strategies to make virginity 'liveable'. Escape into abstraction is no longer possible; the mundane takes on a greater weight and cannot be disregarded. As a consequence, Methodios is acutely aware of the conflict of loyalties faced by individuals. The pressure felt by young men and women to perform the actions required by society are not negated, as was the case in Late Antiquity. Rather, they are countered through redirection towards Christ. This inner Christ helps them to become self-sufficient, since they can now do without a real husband, wife or child.

There is a further level to Methodios's concept of virginity, one apparent in his account and interpretation of the martyrdom of Agatha. Following the passio of this saint which relates that her breasts were cut off by her torturer, Methodios first describes this mutilation with the words 'she suffered the cut of the part for Christ the beloved'.[23] He then interrupts the narrative to address it: 'O cut of the part which joins together with God both itself and the rest of the body to a completeness, and which sends it forth to the love of this one as to the mouth of a child...'.[24] With his sense of similar phenomena, Methodios sees the cutting off of the breasts from the body as like the movement of a mother's breast to the child's mouth – in this case, Christ's.

This theme has been carefully prepared throughout the text. When the magistrate, Quintianus, announces the punishment to Agatha, she replies 'that she has another udder inside which is presented to God and which he and his like cannot see or cut at all'.[25] At the very beginning of the encomium, Methodios introduces Agatha as 'a woman by nature, not by choice, whose custom it is to strive to breastfeed even in childish play'.[26] The first two stages show the familiar sequence: Agatha keeps her physical breasts free from physical contact with the mouth of a child and uses her inner breasts to establish an imagined relationship with the infant Christ instead. What is new, however, is that this inner activity is made manifest in Agatha's outer breasts through her martyrdom. In this way, the imagined relationship with God reaches its culmination in a visible manifestation of this imagined contact on Agatha's body.

Methodios tackles an old problem here, one which had always been a main preoccupation of authors of passions. A martyrdom is the ultimate loss of self-control through the destruction of the body by torture. The

---

[23] EA, chap. 18, 85.23–4.
[24] EA, chap. 19, 85.33–5.
[25] EA, chap. 18, 85.21–3.
[26] EA, chap. 3, 77.9–11.

classical solution was to stress that death was freely chosen by the martyr and thus made his or her own: martyrdom was not so much a struggle between the martyr and the torturers but rather the ultimate manifestation of the martyr's love of God. Methodios accepts this basic concept but goes further than that and relates not only the fact of the death of Agatha as a martyr but also the configuration of an individual martyrdom to the person of the martyr. in this way, the cutting off of her breast appears not as something accidental that befalls Agatha but as the fulfilment of her role as the suckling mother of Christ.

To understand the significance of the martyrdom, we must realize that Agatha's reinterpretation of it as breastfeeding is not simply a means of rendering bearable the situation forced on her by others. Rather, it is a necessary step in the development of her relationship with Christ. Methodios makes it clear that right from the start the imagined contacts between saint and Christ are related to their future outward manifestations. This means that the imagined Christ-child can effectively prevent Agatha from succumbing to the temptations of ordinary child feeding because she believes that this relationship with Christ will one day become a real one.

This element of futurity is more obvious in a passage from the *Life* of Theophanes, where Methodios speaks about the renunciation of wealth. Having said that Theophanes' faith had made him give away everything, Methodios then adds: 'Hope strengthened it [faith] greatly, for it persuaded him to consider not-having as having, while future wealth was foreseen in faith'.[27] Methodios can explain Theophanes' poverty only through his imagining the wealth he would acquire later as abbot of a monastery.[28] The alternative explanation that Theophanes could live in complete poverty because material wealth meant nothing to him is clearly alien to Methodios. Renunciation has no value in itself but only as a means to elicit divine wealth. The canon on Lucy reveals a similar attitude. 'We applaud your exchange of virginity, for you remain pure in espousal and virginal in marriage, but you are impregnated regarding martyrdom'.[29] In other words, because Lucy has remained chaste, she will receive in exchange impregnation by Christ. For Methodios, Lucy's renunciation establishes a contract with God, who will then be obliged to manifest himself as the husband she has not had before.[30] This divine obligation must be understood in terms of contemporary social practice: the saints behave like beggars, parading

---

[27] VThC, chap. 25, 17.26–8.
[28] VThC, chap. 28, 19.5.
[29] CL, 282.74–8, 5th ode.
[30] Methodios abounds in passages where God is portrayed as the debtor of man, e.g. EA, chap. 19, 86.22–3.

their poverty, and thus use God's love of honour as a lever to bring about a divine response.[31]

Not every woman opting for a celibate life had the chance to manifest her inner breastfeeding of Christ or her impregnation by him in martyrdom. The question is: in what ways did Methodios's audience benefit from his speculations? The purpose of such isolated cases as those of martyrs is that they function as prefigurations of what is going to happen after the resurrection of the flesh. This is made clear when Methodios presents the healing of Agatha's breast by St Peter in her prison cell as a partial renewal prefiguring the renewal of Agatha's whole body at the Last Judgement.[32] The interpretation of the martyrdom makes it clear that these breasts will not be ornamental then but will perform their proper function. The conclusion is that for Methodios, Agatha's breastfeeding in her martyrdom prefigures the eternal breastfeeding of the Christ-child as one facet of the life of resurrected women.

All of these speculations are based on the belief that what is perceived by the senses has the highest status of reality. In an excursus on the afterlife in his *Vita* of Euthymios, Methodios discusses the significance of visible activities of corpses, such as the flow of unguents, and maintains that these phenomena mirror the state souls are in.[33] He concludes that the invisible souls cannot be alive if they do not act visibly through their bodies.[34] It seems likely that what Methodios says here about corpses also applies to living bodies. This would mean, in turn, that as long as a mental image does not make itself visible on the outside, it has not yet become fully real.

Methodios believes that each part of the human body, including the sexual organs, has a potential for its own specific activity which needs to be developed if the fullness of man is to be realized. A cosmology which values acting-out above everything else, culminating, as it does, in a permanent coitus, leads to an anti-ascetic world-view, one which was held by many of the iconoclasts opposed to monasticism. The description of Agatha's relation with Christ as sexual intercourse shows that an understanding of sexual activity as a consequence of the Fall is alien to Methodios. If sex with Christ is considered pure, then sexuality cannot be bad in itself, but only when directed to the wrong partner.[35]

---

[31] Methodios establishes a link between these two concepts in the encomium of Nicholas, EN, chap. 13, 145.25.

[32] EA, chap. 23, 88.14–15.

[33] VES, chap. 24, 55.485–6.

[34] VES, chap. 26, 59.531–7.

[35] This must be seen in the wider context of a growing belief that one cannot make absolute value judgements about human actions. This relativism shows clearly in John of Damascus who, in the *Contra Manichaeos*, says that to murder someone is not in itself a bad deed, but only insofar as it is a wrongful appropriation of an action that God has reserved for himself. So murder is a good deed if done in the name of God. B.Kotter, ed., *Die Schriften des Johannes von Damaskos*, vol.4 (Berlin and New York, 1981), 360.58–61.

One last look at Agatha's martyrdom will show that Methodios is incapable of justifying the concept of virginity as abstention from sexual intercourse. In his encomium, he presents Agatha's torturer not only as someone who wants to win over Agatha to paganism, but also as someone who wants to entice or force her to be in love with him.[36] He establishes this parallel right from the start when he says that the virgin Agatha was 'untouched by the tortures of Quintianus' and adds that she 'did not give way to the rabies of the sting of passion' by which Quintianus was driven.[37] Her torturer is a danger not only to her faith but also to her virginity. Agatha, of course, bears Christ in her mind, does not yield and is martyred. Her mutilation, however, is not only presented as the manifestation of her inner breast feeding of the Christ-child. Methodios adds '... the offspring of his love – I mean he himself – may sprout in you and become a man in a perfect way'.[38] As a consequence of her martyrdom, Agatha becomes pregnant with Christ, suggesting that the cutting-off of her breasts represents some form of defloration and impregnation by him.[39] Christ does not appear in person to deflower her, but uses the torturer as his instrument. This leads to the paradoxical conclusion that her torturer does, in the end, deflower Agatha.

But she no longer sees him as torturer, for, by the power of her imagination, she has transformed him into Christ her lover. If this were the case, however, the logical conclusion is that once a saint has managed to see God in everything, there is no reason why she should not have actual sexual intercourse with an ordinary man, whom she would experience as a divine incarnation, or why she should not feed an ordinary child. Such a conclusion would have led to the end of virginity and of monasticism as a way of life. In the end, Methodios always shrinks back from this final consequence.

---

[36] EA, chap. 12, 83.11.

[37] EA, chap. 3, 77.29–32.

[38] EA, chap. 19, 85.35–6.

[39] This is preceded by an 'inner' defloration and Methodios speaks once of the 'slaughter by her lover' which Agatha always carries around with her in her mind. EA, chap. 3, 78.8–9.

7. The city a desert:
Theodore of Stoudios on *porneia*

Peter Hatlie

Theodore of Stoudios (c. 759–826) should have had few regrets. After all, he was a prominent monastic leader whose reforms at the monasteries of the Sakkoudion in Bithynia and Stoudios in Constantinople had flourished, a concerned and active churchman who had fought and won a number of high-profile religious crusades, a public figure who was famous and much sought-after in his own day, and a holy man manifestly on his way to sainthood.[1]

So why, during the 820s, the closing years of his life, was the good abbot so visibly distressed? Why did he resort so frequently to the clichés of personal failure and lament the damage that the years had done? Certainly there was good reason to complain about the failure of the emperor Michael II (820–29) to roll back all the iconoclast measures, and everything that that decision implied for Theodore and his followers.[2] But more pointedly, perhaps, was the barrage of reports he received in his last years about sliding standards of Christian morality, both in the world and especially among his own monks. Stories of sexual misconduct (*porneia*), in particular, surrounded him on all sides, from a recurrence of the dreaded 'adultery' (*moicheia*) scandal to frequent reports of moral lapses among his monks. The bitter irony of these developments was that the abbot had invested enormous effort and put himself and his monastic career at risk as a younger man for the very purpose of combating this most pernicious of sins in and around the city of Constantinople, only to watch circumstances eventually overtake him. By the mid-820s there was little more he could do as he sat in his place

---

[1] Good if dated biographies in A. Gardner, *Theodore of Studium, His Life and Times* (London, 1905); A Dobroklonskii, *Prep. Feodor', Ispovednik' i Igumen' Studiskii*, 2 vols (Odessa, 1914). More recently, P. Karlin-Hayter, 'A Byzantine Politician Monk: Saint Theodore Studite', *JÖB* (1994), 217–32.

[2] W. Treadgold, *The Byzantine Revival 780–842* (Stanford, 1988), 244ff.

of exile, sick and ageing, with only his team of letter-carrying messengers at hand to enforce discipline on his flock. Here was an impossible situation that might have looked very much irreversible, indeed a life's failure. Theodore had become a second Chrysostom in more ways than he could have imagined.[3]

Ultimately the City was as immune to the reforming efforts of the abbot as it had been for the great patriarch. Only a fool, as it turns out, could ever hope to end sin in a city completely.[4] To his credit, however, Theodore proved himself an able and resilient opponent of *porneia* until the very end. To monks and nuns he cautioned against exchanging glances and words with members of the opposite sex,[5] being suspiciously alone with someone else in general and with a member of the opposite sex in particular,[6] indulging in 'pornogenerating gluttony' (ἡ πορνοποίον ἀδηάφαγια),[7] and allowing visits from members of the opposite sex to the monastery itself as well as private meetings between two monks in their cells, especially between older male monks and young boys.[8] Meanwhile he warned those in the world against too much laughing, joking and drinking, and extramarital affairs as well as fervently calling for the study of Scripture and honouring one's spouse and children through a chaste marriage.[9] Such counsel, which is found throughout Theodore's works, undoubtedly drew upon the wealth of teachings that had been passed down from early times, notably in ascetical circles. The modern studies of Brown and Rousselle have indicated just how impressive was this body of knowledge on the desires of the body.[10] Yet it would appear that the received written tradition itself did not extend far enough to cover all perceived sexual deviations, nor did it speak with a clear and unanimous voice on all issues. Novel problems presented themselves, and such lacunae as there were in the tradition inevitably sent Theodore to hunt down relevant authorities of his own and reason out appropriate solutions by himself.[11] Let us briefly turn to three

---

[3] For Theodore's conscious identification with John, notably in the Moicheian Affair, see, for example, *Ep.* 33, 92.32–4; *Theodori Studitae Epistulae*, ed. G. Fatouros, CFHB 31 (Berlin, 1991).

[4] Leontios of Neapolis, *Vita of Symeon the Fool*, ed. L. Rydén, *Das Leben des heiligen Narren Symeon* (Uppsala, 1963), 162.17–21.

[5] *Ep.* 250, 382.2–15; *Ep.* 387, 537.16–19; *Ep.* 439, 617.24–6; *Magna Catechesis*, ed. J. Cozza-Luzi, *Novae patrum bibliothecae* 9,2 (Rome, 1888), no. 58, 163.

[6] *Ep.* 10, 33.56–9, 33.63–6; *Parva Catechesis*, ed. E. Auvray (Paris, 1891; repr. Thessalonike, 1984), no. 87, 221–2.

[7] *Catech.parv.*, 480, 702.30.

[8] *Ep.* 10, 33.56–62 and 67–9, and 10, 31–4 passim.

[9] *Ep.* 468, 671–2.5–23; *Ep.* 470, 675.15–23 and 32–4.

[10] A. Rousselle, *Porneia* (Paris, 1983); P. Brown, *The Body and Society. Men, Women, and Sexual Renunciation in Early Christianity* (London and Boston, 1988).

[11] Against the emperor Constantine's second marriage (see more below), the abbot cobbled together canons of Basil, biblical examples, conciliar legislation, early Church precedents, liturgical rites, episodes from Roman history, contemporary rumours about the trickle-down

of the abbot's more troubling bouts with *porneia* and examine both the weapons he amassed and his means of enforcement.

The first struggle is coincident with the impressive growth of his monastic federation and the establishment of the Stoudios monastery in Constantinople after the year 797. The abbot generally welcomed these great changes as a sign of God's favour on his community, notably for its reformed monastic discipline. But this vibrant upswing in Stoudite monasticism, which continued apace from 798 until about 808, also occasioned a number of internal problems. For one thing, the abbot admitted, the queen of cities was a source of great temptation, a place where most of the population was indifferent to true orthodoxy,[12] and where his monks were consequently like sailors tossed and turned by the turbulent sea of urban distractions.[13] New recruits arrived all the same, according to the abbot's reports, with young and old, rich and poor, showing up in great numbers at the monastery gates, indeed 'nearly every day' for a time.[14] Periodic shortages of food, clothing, and space discomfited its monks for awhile.[15] However, more troubling consequences of this rapid growth were the disciplinary problems that appeared in both the large and heterogeneous Stoudios and its smaller satellite houses in the countryside, ranging from a carafe of wine missing from the refectory one day to a group of aristocrats bragging about their origins and refusing to do their share of manual labour the next,[16] and much in between.[17] It may be no accident that Theodore's first written rule, consisting of a short list of disciplinary precepts for one of the Stoudite satellites, dates roughly to this time.[18]

Two admonitions never made it into this or any other Stoudite rule, although the sexual issues prompting them were serious enough to be addressed openly and forcefully in the abbot's contemporary sermons. Both concerned the sin of *parrhesia*, a monk's excessive openness or impudence, about which the ancient ascetic tradition had much to say.[19] In his homilies

---

effect of the emperor's actions, and even, indirectly, Roman law: *Ep.* 21, 55.16–20; *Ep.* 22, 57.16–21, 58.22–45, 59.61–70; *Ep.* 24, 65–6.53–64; *Ep.* 28, 77–8.65–80; *Ep.* 31, 86.57–8, 87, 71–85, 87–8, 92–7; *Ep.* 34, 95.28–43; *Ep.* 50, 145–51 passim; *Ep.* 443, 623–5 passim.

[12] *Catech. magn.* (unpublished ms.), ed. J. Leroy, bk. 1, no. 1.78, 372.62–74.

[13] *Catech. magn.*, Leroy, no. 1.36, 162.4–164.60.

[14] *Catech. magn.*, Leroy, no. 1.55, 258, 86–97; no. 1.70, 338.37–8; no. 1.81, 384.61–71; *Magna Catechesis*, ed. A. Papadopoulos-Kerameus (St Petersburg, 1904; repr. Thessalonike, 1987), no. 75, 516.9–19 (with quote).

[15] *Catech. magn.*, Papadopoulos-Kerameus, no. 30, 211–12; no. 32, 236.6–10; no. 75, 516.19–517.8.

[16] *Catech. magn.*, Cozza-Luzi, no. 33, 92a–93; Leroy, no. 1.80, 379.31–9.

[17] *Catech. magn.*, Papadopoulos-Kerameus, no. 5, 26–7; no. 43, 305–309 passim; no. 44, 315–21 passim; no. 61, 433–4; Cozza-Luzi, no. 10, 28–30.

[18] *Ep.* 10, 31–4.

[19] See, for example, with bibliography, G.J.M. Bartelink, '*Parrhesia* dans les oeuvres de Jean Chrysostome', *Studia Patristica* 162, (1985), 441–8.

Theodore demanded that his monks understand precisely which sins fell under the umbrella of *parrhesia* and how they were to be avoided. The first was the *parrhesia* toward one's brothers:

> May you be ... not unrestrained in your disposition to [your] brothers. For *parrhesia* is a great sin and a death-dealing thing. And the much experienced Devil, if one does not watch out, hurls the sharp arrow of evil into our heart, puncturing and wounding [it]. He presents to us the beautiful faces of young boys. He draws us, with wanton smiles, first to one another and then to an explosion of passion. For when he, after deceiving one person, will persuade that person to love another carnally, he accomplishes that by trying to get the [deceived] person to mount one passion on top of another, and to keep the other person enchanted. Thereupon follow mutual exchanges of glances and fixed stares and spiritual throbbings and burning lusts. And if God does not come to your aid ... then there is complete perdition and a Sodomitic conflagration and Gomorrhic ruin. But let us all flee [these things]. And I, who was before tempted, extend a hand to you who are headed for complete death. And a great security is a policing of the eyes, [as well as] a true confession.[20]

The abbot condemned illicit encounters in other of his homilies as well, warning his monks to resist the crescendo of events beginning with an exchange of glances, moving on to the holding of hands and a stolen kiss, and ending in fatal intercourse.[21]

The second sort of sinful *parrhesia* was that towards oneself:

> Therefore let us not be excessively open toward ourselves either. For there is death in this way, too, and for those who are unaware, it is not necessary [that the thing] be out in the open.... So listen to what I say, you who are guilty of such passions! Don't grasp or handle your member at all, and don't stare deeply at your nudity, lest you bring the curse of Cain upon you. For the great desert monk who fell victim succumbed to no other sin than this one, so says holy Anthony. And it would [still be so] if the wise one did not reveal the way of the spirit. For it is *porneia* even when one does not come close to another's body.[22] So watch out how you walk around. Don't be drawn to death. And when mother nature calls, let yourself down decently, and make water, without looking at what comes out, without manipulating your member with a finger.[23]

---

[20] *Catech. magn.*, Cozza-Luzi, no. 39, 110.

[21] *Catech. magn*, Cozza-Luzi, no. 58, 163.

[22] 'That wise man [Anthony] drew a veil over the nature of the sin, and he knew well that the sin of fornication does not require the availability of another body': John Klimakos, *PG* 88, 885C, in C. Luibheid and N. Russell, trs, *John Climacus, The Ladder of Divine Ascent* (London, 1982), chap. 15, 175, referring apparently to bestiality but followed in subsequent passages with concerns over masturbation or nocturnal emissions. For Anthony's original comments, *PG* 65, 80BC. On associations between masturbation and bestiality in later western medieval sources, J. Boswell, *Christianity, Social Tolerance, and Homosexuality* (Chicago and London, 1980), 323, esp. note 69.

[23] *Catech. magn.*, Cozza-Luzi, no. 39, 110–11.

Such warnings against homosexual activity and genital stimulation were surely not out of place within eastern Christian ascetical traditions.[24] More unusual was the abbot's frank and businesslike treatment of such sensitive topics in public – topics that until his time were probably better left to private discussions between an abbot and his spiritual son. But this was a luxury that Theodore, with hundreds of monks in tow, could simply not afford.

Porneia of a different nature preoccupied Theodore in three separate but closely related 'adultery' cases: the first from 795 to 797 when emperor Constantine VI abandoned his first wife and remarried; the second between 806 and 811 when the priest, Joseph, who had consecrated that second union returned to the Church after a period of disgrace and thus reignited the earlier dispute; and the third, from 823 onwards upon the marriage of the emperor Michael II, a widower, to Euphrosyne, who was none other than Constantine's first child and until then a nun in good standing.[25] These three incidents set the abbot to thinking essentially about two problems, the inherent uniqueness of the marriage bond and the concept of a chaste marriage, issues on which Roman civil law was practically indifferent, Christian traditions incomplete or in transition on some points, and human practice predictably variable.[26]

His views have been treated more fully elsewhere,[27] so a few brief observations will suffice here. First, Theodore flatly rejected the civil criteria, whether it be endangerment of a spouse or treason,[28] which Constantine reportedly invoked for the dissolution of one marriage and entry into another, calling the whole affair an illegal, adulterous, and barbarous act brought about by 'autocratic licentiousness' (αὐτοκρατορικὴ ἀκολασία).[29] He credited the whole incident with provoking governors in Gotthia and Lombardia as well as countless others to do the same,[30] and, following Basil, argued that adultery in general and this act in particular stood on the same level as murder, bestiality, sodomy, witchcraft and idolatry.[31] It was, moreover, fully consistent with the infamous adultery of

---

[24] Brown, *Body and Society*, 224–40.

[25] Treadgold, *Byzantine Revival*, 103–8, 152–7, 246–7.

[26] J. Zhishman, *Das Eherecht der orientalischen Kirche* (Vienna, 1864), 401–34 passim.

[27] Th. Korres, 'The Question of the Second Marriage of Constantine VI. A Symbol for the History of Byzantium Toward the End of the Eighth Century (in Greek)', Ph.D. dissertation (Thessalonike, 1975); D. Gemmitti, *Teodoro Studita e la questione moicheiana* (Naples, 1993); A. Jose Antonio Fuentes, *El divorcio de Constantino VI y la doctrina matrimonial de Teodoro Studita* (Pamplona, 1984); see also Zhishman, *Eherecht*, 412–16.

[28] *Vita Tarasi*, ed. I.A. Heikel, in *Acta Societas Scientiarium Fennicae* 17 (1891), 408–12. On these two conditions for divorce, Zhishman, *Eherecht*, 731–4.

[29] *Oratio Platonis*, in *PG* 99, 829A (with quotation); *Ep.* 24, 65.53ff; *Ep.* 33, 92.18–19 and 31–6; *Ep.* 48, 136.207–22. For civil and canon law on adultery, Zhishman, *Eherecht*, 58–3, 734ff.

[30] *Ep.* 31, 87–8.92–7; *Ep.* 443, 624.39–43.

[31] *Ep.* 22, 57.16–21. Basil, *Saint Basile, Lettres*, ed. Y. Courtonne (Paris, 1961), ii, *Ep.* 188, 126.6–7.

Herod Antipas, reported in Matthew 14:1–12, and therefore merited the same
divine punishment, fitting the crime: whereas Herod had lost his political
power and was held in prison, the young Constantine suffered an
'imprisonment of the eyes'.[32] Second, the abbot objected vehemently to the
ceremonies by which the second marriage was accomplished, especially the
ritual crowning (on the head) of the second union and the ensuing wedding
party. On these points the Christian traditions were less complete,[33] leaving
the abbot to forge a doctrine for himself. The crowning was grossly
inappropriate, he claimed, given that the crown was a sign of victory over
porneia, unique to first marriages, which alone were untouched by carnal
passion (ἀνάλωτος πορνικῷ πάθει). Second marriages never met that
standard of purity, in his view, neither under conditions of widowhood
accompanied by penance, nor in the event of a penitent digamist marrying
a virgin, and least of all in second marriages compromised by adultery. Even
if a priest were to try to put a crown on the shoulders or legs of those seeking
remarriage, Theodore says wryly, it would still be illegal.[34]

It will be observed that the abbot was on fairly unsure ground here,
forced to rely analogies and comparisons in the absence of canons that fully
addressed the complexities of second marriages.[35] In the end, his message
seems to have been as follows: that between the extremes of the chaste first
marriage and utterly unchaste adultery lies the rather ambiguous institution
of second marriage, which, although permitted by the Church, is in fact a
carnal defeat of sorts. In other words, a second marriage does not merit
crowning because it is not entirely free of *porneia* – even if it were to follow
upon a chaste first marriage and were itself chaste. An equally dubious
circumstance was that of someone who had quit the monastery for a secular
marriage, as had the nun-princess Euphrosyne. Theodore was considerably
less generous with his judgements in this instance, hesitating to comment
on it at all, though finally characterizing it more in terms of adultery than
second marriage and condemning those who looked the other way.[36]

For a third and final illustration of Theodore's concern with *porneia*, it is
necessary to return to the Stoudite monastic world about the year 818, some
ten years after it had reached its peak. The iconoclast persecutions were

---

[32] *Ep.* 22, 58–9.46–60; *Ep.* 28, 77–8.65-80; *Ep.*, 443, 624.21–32 (with quote).

[33] K. Ritzer, *Formen, Riten und religiöses Brauchtum der Eheschleissung in den christlichen
Kirchen des ersten Jahrtausends* (Münster, 1962), 52–7.

[34] *Ep.* 21, 55.13–20; *Ep.* 22, 60.83–95; *Ep.* 28, 76.24–44; *Ep.* 50, 145–50, esp. 147.39–40 (with
quotation) and 149–50.87–101. On Theodore's views, Ritzer, *Formen*, 77–9, 102–3.

[35] His use of the canons prohibiting a priest's dining with digamists as applying to a
priest's crowning of legitimate second marriages. See esp. *Ep.* 50, 146.33–148.62.

[36] *Catech. parv.*, no. 74, 192-3; *Ep.* 514, 766.20–8. Cf. Theophanes Continuator, *Chronographia*,
ed. I. Bekker, CSHB 33, 2 vols (Bonn, 1838), 2.24.78–79.4–12.

already three years old and only sporadically violent.[37] Pockets of Stoudite monks were hiding here and there, and would continue to do so until long after their abbot's death in 826. The year 818 marked a decisive turning point because it was then that Theodore and a great many of his hundreds of monks began to realize that the persecutions would endure for many years. More to the point, they also began to orient themselves toward this new future, and not necessarily in complementary ways.[38]

Most monks remained remarkably faithful to their monastic vows and iconodule confession. Others slipped in a myriad ways, from living a chaste but unseemly life with a family or group of virgins, to the more outrageous dirty weekend, or indeed dirty decade.[39] From 818 onward news of these irregularities reached Theodore, first in a trickle, then in a stream. Rumours travelled outside Stoudite circles, too, and soon the abbot had to face accusations that he and his monks were resisting a compromise with iconoclasts because they preferred their life of carnal sin. After some time and study, the abbot came up with a rather compelling answer to his critics, which doubled as a warning and exhortation to his monks:

> I beg you, brothers, in the name of Our Lord Jesus Christ, to comport yourself nobly in the monastic vocation, the confession which we confess, and the persecution under which we are persecuted.... For there are some who consider that your confession of Christ is flawed, is a pretext for *porneia*. I shiver to say it. Yet they say, and they will be rightly judged for saying, that 'it is better to commune with the heresy than let the persecution for Christ capture you'[40] which is like the advice of Balaam when he put a scandal before the children of Israel.[41]... Now there are two kinds of *porneia*: one in respect to belief, the other in respect to the body. Someone who is captured by heretical communion is indeed committing fornication against God, and is liable to commit fornication also with the body. Those who say such things [about us] are deceived and crazy, therefore, laying traps for unsteady souls. So let us establish our lives more securely, brothers, for our own sake and for others who struggle for the truth.[42]

---

[37] A. Tougard, 'La persecution iconoclaste d'après la correspondance de Saint Théodore Studite', *Revue des questions historiques* 50 (1891), 80–118; Dobroklonskii, i.377–89, 647–51, 752–60, 863–4; P. Alexander, 'Religious Persecution and Resistance in the Byzantine Empire of the Eighth and Ninth Centuries: Methods and Justifications', *Speculum* 52,2 (1977), 242–6.

[38] P. Hatlie, 'The Politics of Salvation: Theodore of Stoudios on Martyrdom and Parrhesia', *DOP* 50 (1996), 277–80.

[39] *Catech. parv.*, no. 35, 101; *Ep.* 450, 636–7.7–36; *Ep.* 503, 744–5 passim.

[40] Discussion in John Klimakos, *PG* 88,889BC, in Luibheid and Russell, *John Climacus*, 177 (with explanatory note 68), when asked the question why heretics are sooner readmitted to the church than those caught in *porneia*. Klimakos claims not to know.

[41] A reference to Rev 2:14–15, the Redeemer, through John, saying: 'You have in Pergamum some that hold to the teaching of Balaam, who taught Balak to put temptation in the way of the Israelites. He encouraged them to eat food sacrificed to idols and to commit fornication, and in the same way you also have some who hold the doctrine of the Nicolaitans.'

[42] *Catech. parv.*, no. 3, 16.

The abbot's message here is clear enough: hold strong to both iconodule confession and sexual continence, since the one discipline reinforces the other just as the absence of the one facilitates the absence of the other. But there was more to it than that. In another passage he turns the logic around, saying that, 'The same result obtains when someone does not turn his back on a harlot as when he does not give proskynesis to the icon.'[43] Thus although Theodore acknowledged that *porneia* was not a heresy, his fundamental point was that iconoclasm and *porneia* were equally serious sins insofar as they both negated Christ, 'for in both there is adultery'.[44] Both constituted a surrender of the senses to the forces of Satan and heathenism, and both sought nothing more from life than mere carnality. Whether this was a new revelation to Theodore or simply the political device he needed at the moment is not clear. Yet at all events the abbot now insisted that his movement was rigorously opposed to both sorts of *porneia*.[45]

By way of conclusion, it may be useful to recall that this novel attack on porneia – combining the best of both icon theology and the ascetic tradition – dates to the very last years of the abbot's life. It demonstrates clearly that although he was distressed about the revival of *porneia* within his world, he was not yet ready to announce defeat. Armed with an array of ancient authorities, which he had learned to handle skilfully over the years, he was determined instead to develop new weapons against a sin that he now put forth – in a very late catechism – as one of two primary evils in the world, from which all other sins originated and because of which countless catastrophes had visited the earth.[46] Many of his contemporaries considered this too alarmist, too fussy. But for Theodore, looking back upon the Christian tradition and the events of his own lifetime, the choice was clear between the good fortunes of a continent people and the utter disasters associated with those ruled by the 'temptations of the eyes'.[47]

---

[43] *Ep.* 303, 446.22–4.

[44] *Ep.* 303, 446.28. See Boswell, *Homosexuality*, 103, 336–7 for a discussion of the broader meanings of *moicheia* beyond mere adultery.

[45] *Ep.* 303, 446. 19–29. *Ep.* 164, 285–6.12–31; *Ep.* 503, 744–5.17–47.

[46] *Catech. parv.*, no. 40, 114–15.

[47] *Catech. parv.*, no. 40, 114.

Section III

Problems with Bodies

8. Desires denied: marriage, adultery and divorce in early Byzantine law

Bernard Stolte

Marriage law is one of those fields in which we may expect to see a clear reflection of prevailing moral and social values. Perhaps it would be more accurate to say that we may expect to find a development in the law of marriage which corresponds with, but in time follows after, a change of moral and social values. Sometimes the law will even be used by the legislator as an instrument in order to effect a change in behaviour. Examples abound in our own time: to name but one, in many European countries the gradual social acceptance of concubinage has led to a legal equalization of that phenomenon with the institution of marriage, thus transforming it itself into a legal institution with important legal effects.

From this point of view there is every reason to consider the law of marriage as one of the precursors of a truly Byzantine, as opposed to Roman, law. Christianity took a clear view of marriage as an institution about which definite moral precepts had been given in the Bible.

It could be argued that with Constantine we see the first attempt at Christianization of the law, just as it could be argued that precisely the Christianization of Roman law transformed Roman law into Byzantine law. As it is my brief to present the way desire and denial have been dealt with by the law, and, furthermore, as desire and denial lead us to questions of morality and ethics, obviously the vexed problem of Christian influence on the law cannot be avoided.[1] It seems therefore practical to start with the

---

[1] J. Gaudemet, 'Roman Law, Christian Influence on', *New Catholic Encyclopedia* 12 (New York, 1967), 583–4, gives a concise summary of his views on the relations between Roman law and Christianity, which he has studied in several books and articles. See also the classic treatment by B. Biondi, *Il diritto romano cristiano*, 3 vols (Milan, 1952–54), and, recently, the general remarks by P.E. Pieler, 'Das Alte Testament im Rechtsdenken der Byzantiner', in Sp. Troianos, ed., *Analecta Atheniensia ad ius Byzantinum spectantia* I (Athens and Komotini, 1997), 81–113, esp. 81–91.

fourth century and not to be dogmatic about the distinction between Roman and Byzantine law.

There is no shortage of literature on our subject. An excellent recent treatment of a wider area, which takes in our subject as well, is by Joëlle Beaucamp, to whose bibliography I refer,[2] the more so as she deals with the early Byzantine period, to which I wish to restrict myself here.

Desire and denial then. Certain desires have been curbed by law from the earliest times. The Ten Commandments, preserved in two slightly different versions (Exod 20:1–17; Deut 5:6–21 and also Exod 34:11–28), spring to the mind, for example, 'Thou shalt not commit adultery. Thou shalt not steal. Thou shalt not kill.... Thou shalt not covet thy neighbour's wife, thou shalt not covet thy neighbour's house, nor his field, nor his servant, nor his maid, nor his ox, nor his ass, nor any of his cattle, nor whatever belongs to thy neighbour' (Exod 20:13–17). Why these precepts and not others, has to be explained from the circumstances of the time, whether one attributes them to a historical Moses or to the time of the prophets of the eighth to seventh centuries. A modern lawyer would probably class them under the law of nature, which only means that he is unable, or unwilling, to imagine a society that would not abhor adultery, murder and theft, although the precise definitions of them might still diverge according to place and time. The crimes so described generally offend morality.

I have selected marriage as the topic central to this paper, because it well illustrates the uneasy relationship between morality and law. 'Thou shalt not commit adultery. Thou shalt not covet thy neighbour's wife'. Not only do we preserve morality in this way, we also preserve order in society, and at that point we enter the province of the law. The two spheres need not coincide entirely, and sometimes they do not do so at all. In an ideal world law is superfluous as morality suffices; law only comes in where morality alone provides insufficiently strong deterrents or incentives. Great activity of the legislator usually indicates a moral crisis. The question in those cases is, whether a changing moral attitude is giving rise to a change of the law, or whether the law is being harnessed in order to bring about a change of moral attitude. When two groups are competing in a society, each with its own desires, it may become difficult to disentangle cause and effect in the development of that society's law.

Marriage may be seen both as a curb on, and therefore a denial of, a desire for unlimited sexual freedom, and as an expression by the parties concerned of the desire for mutual support and protection, an expression that entitles them to recognition of their relationship and even the awarding of certain advantages by society. Adultery threatens marriage, and divorce, in

---

[2] J. Beaucamp, *Le statut de la femme à Byzance (4–7 siècle), I: Le droit impérial, II: Les pratiques sociales* (Paris, 1992).

addition to death, dissolves it. Just as Byzantine law did, we start from Roman law.

Marriage is the formalization of a relationship between a man and a woman, meant to be permanent. It is a contract, usually accompanied by certain formalities. It would be foolish to expect the view of marriage to have remained constant during more than a thousand years of Roman history before Constantine, but a glance at the first three centuries of the Roman Empire is sufficient for our purpose. The well-known definition of *(nuptiae sunt) coniunctio maris et feminae et consortium omnis vitae, divini et humani iuris communicatio*, 'marriage is the union of a man and a woman, a partnership for life involving divine as well as human law' (tr. Watson *et al.*) stems from the jurist Modestinus of c. 240 AD. Whether or not Modestinus has really described marriage in this way is of little moment, as it is the form in which the definition occurs in Justinian's *Digest* (D. 23,2,1) and has lived on in East and West until modern times. As for Byzantium, it has been included in the *Basilica* in a literal Greek translation (*B*. 28,4,1), and it is perhaps significant that the commentary in the scholia on the *Basilica* does not mention religion apart from the fact that both parties have to be of the same faith (*BS* 1815, 10 ff.). As famous as Modestinus's definition is the legal maxim of *consensus facit nuptias*, a phrase coined from Ulpian's slightly fuller statement that *nuptias non concubitus, sed consensus facit* (D. 50,17,30=35,1,15; cf. *B*. 2,3,30; 44,19,15), 'for it is consent, not sleeping together, which makes a marriage' (tr. Watson *et al.*). The aim of the marriage was held to be the procreation of legitimate children (*liberorum quaerendorum causa*).

Despite Modestinus's 'partnership for life', both the conclusion and the dissolution of a marriage were simple matters and there was no impediment to conclude a subsequent marriage once the previous one had been dissolved. It was not so much the marriage itself that was considered important; rather it was the place of the family in society and the continuation of that place that counted. This view goes a long way to explain certain peculiarities of the Roman law of marriage. Moral or religious considerations hardly mattered. That is not to say that marriage itself did not matter; it was a monogamous relationship accompanied by certain rights and duties, and sanctions in certain cases of disregard, but not to be explained by moral or religious considerations. Considerations that did play a role were, for example, the preservation of a certain class-structure in society, and therefore the birth-rate within that class. A case in point is the legislation of Emperor Augustus, whose laws were to be designated later collectively as the *lex Iulia et Papia*. The point to remember is that Augustus's marriage legislation was hardly, if at all, inspired by moral considerations. Even if it had been otherwise, the Roman satirists Martial and Juvenal are witness to its utter failure, and from Seneca stems the image that certain upper-class women counted the years not by the consuls, but by their husbands (*De benef.* III,16,2).

With Christianity moral and religious considerations were brought into play and could not fail to impinge on the traditional view of marriage. As we have seen, despite Modestinus's *consortium omnis vitae*, the idea of indissolubility of marriage was foreign to the Roman mind. The New Testament taught otherwise. In the Christian communities the rights and duties of man and wife towards each other and towards their marriage were being defined in a new manner, and the new definition brought with it disciplinary measures if the flesh had been weak. Questions of discipline were dealt with by the local synods – the ecumenical councils rather tended to occupy themselves with doctrinal matters – and especially by the Fathers, whose writings provide an interesting mirror of late antique and early Byzantine society in this respect. Pronouncements by councils and certain Fathers came to be regarded as 'canons' and together these constituted the canon law of the early Church.

The emancipation of Christianity, and even more so its elevation in 381 to the position of the official religion of the Roman Empire, inevitably brought up the problem of the relationship between secular and canon law wherever the two spheres came into contact. Marriage was one of these points of contact. Legislation of the fourth to sixth centuries shows the meandering course of the secular legislator in his attempts to come to terms with the teachings of Christian doctrine, from the over-zealous efforts of Constantine to the more balanced laws of Justinian. At the end of the day, however, we must conclude that a complete fusion of secular and canon law on this subject never was reached. Jerome's much-quoted dictum that *aliae sunt leges Caesarum, aliae Christi, aliud Papinianus, aliud Paulus noster praecepit* (Jerome, *Ep.* 77, ad Oceanum), in short, that the apostle Paul and the jurist Paul – and they really were different persons! – would never fully agree, held good in Jerome's time and for several centuries to come.

This is not the place to deal with the details of the development of the law of marriage, civil and canon, in the first few centuries of the Byzantine empire. Instead I should like to examine a few aspects of the matter that seem interesting to me in a wider context.

We must remember that the development of legislation concerning marriage was gradual, fragmented and therefore not always consistent, or perhaps I should say, often inconsistent and haphazard. Justinian, whom we cannot charge with an aversion to grand projects, to a certain extent recodified the law concerning marriage in Novel 22 of 536, only two years after his great codification. Its Latin rubric reads *De nuptiis*, the Greek one Περὶ δευτερογαμούντων. The latter is misleading in the sense that it dealt with more than second marriages only, but at the same time it is correct to say that marriage was not dealt with in all its aspects. Moreover, already in 542 some changes were regarded necessary in Novel 117.

The Church never managed to formulate its rules in an official, comprehensive statement. It reacted to what it perceived as abuses, but there can be no doubt that the lead in reforming the law was in the hands of the emperor, not of the Church. That the emperor allowed himself to be counselled by prominent churchmen is another matter. What we do emphatically not see is a retreat from this field by the secular legislator, as in the West, where we may observe the Church taking over jurisdiction and law-making from the secular authorities. No wonder that the views of the Church, which were by and large the same in East and West, asserted themselves more clearly in the West. Eventually, moreover, the canon law of marriage of the Roman Catholic and the Orthodox Churches was to show quite important differences.

The way in which the Byzantine law of marriage developed is often presented as the result of a conflict between Roman and 'Christian' law, Roman law representing the forces of traditionalism and conservatism. Let me illustrate this from a concrete example.

As Joëlle Beaucamp and many others have noticed, Byzantine legislation on sexual relations does not treat men and women in the same way. The balance is often tilted in favour of men, who are allowed more freedom than women in a similar position. A good example is the crime of adultery, which has always been seen as a fault of the woman rather than of the man or indeed of both parties. Briefly, in Byzantine law we may only speak of adultery, μοιχεία, if a married woman has sexual intercourse outside marriage. If a married man sleeps with an unmarried woman, that does not constitute adultery, but fornication, πορνεία, which does not carry the same penalties, but lighter ones. In other words, the crime of adultery is not conceived of as an offence against marriage, irrespective of the gender of the offender, but as a fault of the woman against her marriage.

Although it would be incorrect to say that Byzantine law has always treated adultery in exactly the same way, this 'asymmetrical' notion of adultery has never been replaced by what would be in our modern, western view a fairer one; a notion, we may add, which would be more acceptable to the Church, and not only to the Church of today but also to that of early Byzantine times.

The 'asymmetrical' view has often been attributed to the effect of Roman law, where the same attitude may be observed. The ancient Roman attitude is held to have persisted until the end and thus to have prevented the victory of a more modern, Christian view. If certain changes toward a more equal treatment of man and wife take place, these are the signs of Christian influence and therefore deserving to be termed Byzantine as opposed to Roman.

This, however, is not much of an explanation. In the first place it supposes law to have been the cause of a certain moral attitude, rather than a prevailing moral attitude to have been expressed in certain legal rules. In other words, it attributes to law a much more important role in society than law can ever play by itself. That is not to say that law cannot be used as a means to effect changes in behaviour which seem desirable to those in power. But it is not so much existing law that opposes changes in the law, but patterns of behaviour, social attitudes. In order to be successful, reform by law is dependent on more than just the power of the legislator. Secondly, it is not helpful to distinguish between Roman and Byzantine law unless as a rough indication of time. It does no harm to call law in the time of Augustus Roman, and law in the time of the Komneni Byzantine, but is does not explain anything. The remarkable continuity of the formal law during what we call the Roman and Byzantine periods, that is, the time during which the Byzantines preferred to call themselves Rhomaioi, should make us wary of the distinction. If we must have one at all cost, let us by all means have the watershed of Justinian's codification. Even then, it is not superfluous to remember that Justinian used a great deal of non-Christian, pagan material,[3] and that this material, translated into Greek, was incorporated into the *Basilica* as well. The material collected in the *Digest* and the *Code* is of course a selection from the writings of the ancient Roman, non-Byzantine jurists, made from a sixth-century point of view, but our other sources do not give us reason to believe that the selection distorts the historical picture: despite a number of changes that occurred, the legal view of adultery was remarkably consistent during the first six centuries of our era and survived the change from pagan and Roman to Christian and Byzantine. In other words, the law reflects a remarkable continuity in society's view of adultery.

That is to say, as long as we are dealing with secular law. If we move to canon law, matters are different. But precisely because they are different, they confirm at the same time our conclusion about the civil law.

We have already observed that the attitude to adultery of the secular law was not what the Church would preach. On the contrary, in the formative

---

[3] At the earliest moment that we may speak of Byzantine law, in the time of Constantine, adultery had been described and its consequences regulated in Roman law and in that form had been commented upon by Roman lawyers. The oldest articulated legal treatment of adultery is 'Roman'. The relevant sources have mainly reached us via Justinian's *Digest*, in which they have been arranged under the title 'Ad legem Iuliam de adulteriis coercendis' (D. 48,5). Similarly, in Justinian's *Code* a title treats 'Ad legem Iuliam de adulteriis et de stupro' (C. 9,9). Both titles refer back to the time of Augustus, of course, and thus once more emphasize their 'Roman' character, but that did not prevent Justinian from allowing one of his laws to be included under that heading, together with seven constitutions of his predecessors from Constantine onwards; more significant even, these eight constitutions of Byzantine emperors follow after 27 laws issued by Roman, non-Byzantine emperors, the first dating from 197 AD.

period of canon law, in the fourth and fifth centuries, that is, in early Byzantine times, we see the Councils as well as the Fathers take a different position and explicitly state that their position was different from that of the secular authorities. When the Council in Trullo in 691–2 confirmed in its second canon the catalogue of authorities recognized as sources of canon law, it preserved a number of statements about adultery which were still as divergent from the civil law as ever. Especially interesting on this theme is St Basil, whose three letters of 374–5 had been recognized as canonical. Like other Fathers, Basil deplored the lack of symmetry in the rights and duties of men and women in marriage and advocated a more even-handed approach, but without success. His relevant canons are 9 (letter 188) and 21 (letter 199), which both are worth quoting. In canon 9 he states (tr. Deferrari [Loeb]): 'And the decision of the Lord that it is not lawful to withdraw from wedlock save on the ground of fornication, according to its logical sense applies alike to both men and women. Yet custom does not so obtain. Furthermore, in canon 21 (same tr.): 'In the case of a man married to a woman, whenever not being satisfied with his marriage he falls into fornication, we judge such a person to be a fornicator, ... but we have no canon which subjects him to the charge of adultery, if the sin be committed against some unmarried woman. ... Therefore the wife will receive her husband when he returns from fornication, but the husband will dismiss the polluted woman from his house. But the reasoning in these matters also is not easy, but the custom has so obtained.'

Two points need to be made. First, Basil admits that not even the Church felt able to treat men and women the same way in this respect, even though the New Testament seemed to prescribe it. The right to end the marriage by *repudium* on the ground of the partner having sexual relations outside marriage was denied to the woman: 'We do not have this observance in the custom of the Church', as canon 9 has it. But the opposite was sanctioned on the authority of the Old Testament (Jer 3:1 and Prov 18:22). Second, Basil does not attribute this lack of symmetry to outside influences, such as Roman law. His study of the New Testament had convinced him that Christ had meant the rights and duties of both parties to be the same, but this doctrine had not even prevailed in canon law. The terminology of adultery and fornication is not always consistent (see Basil's canons 58–9 and 77 [letter 217]), but the underlying differences in the positions of husband and wife are maintained.

At first sight, Gregory of Nyssa takes a different attitude. According to his canon 4, if one wishes to make a distinction, fornication is 'the satisfaction of desire without causing injustice to someone else' and adultery is committed where there is 'deliberate injustice towards someone else', the latter also including sexual offences 'against nature'. The canon does not distinguish between men and women. But we must note that Gregory does not speak of the possibility of divorce, but only of the ecclesiastical penalties (ἐπιτιμία). Although the number of years in each stage of penance is different from what we read in St Basil, there is no reason to believe that Gregory would fundamentally disagree from Basil as to the possibility of divorce on grounds of adultery.

Within its own province the Church was in a position to legislate fairly and treat men and women equally: adultery committed by either of them would entail the same ecclesiastical penalties. A disruption of the marriage, however, was a different matter. The doctrine of Christ could not set aside the inveterate, deeply rooted custom, as noticed by Basil.

A point of conflict between Roman and canon law was the termination of marriage by divorce. The Church firmly defended the indissolubility of marriage except for certain specific circumstances, whereas Roman law recognized the possibility of *dissensus*; just as it stressed consensus as a requisite for marriage, it assumed that marriage lasted as long as this *consensus*.[4] Divorce by mutual consent was the logical expression of the end of the consensus. The Church thought otherwise: it, too, required consensus, but once the parties had given mutual consent, it was irrevocable. Secular legislation from Constantine onwards shows the influence of Christian doctrine. For unilateral divorce, originally possible without restriction, specific grounds were being introduced; if these were not present, the marriage was brought to an end but the divorcing party was subject to penalties as to his property and restrictions as to remarriage. Divorce by mutual consent underwent restrictions, too, was forbidden altogether by Justinian in 556 (Novel 134,11 pr.), but allowed again by Justin II in 566 (Novel 140). The latter measure seems to have been ignored in later legal compilations. Second marriages were frowned upon, and so on, and so forth. In short, through a series of measures, the law was organized so as to favour a marriage lasting a life-time, even if the consensus of the parties was lacking. The impetus came from Christianity.

So far, we have only spoken about marriage in the strict sense of the word. At least as important are its consequences for the worldly goods of the spouses, the law of matrimonial property. That was one of the major considerations for the secular legislator to pay attention to the institution of marriage. There is no time to go into the various complications. Suffice it to say that under imperial Roman law the property of both parties remained separate. There would be a *dos*, a dowry, and its counter-part, the *donatio propter nuptias*, a donation on the occasion of marriage. On dissolution of the marriage each would return to the party which had provided it. Through alterations in the law of matrimonial property the legislator

---

[4] See for the Roman law of divorce O. Robleda, 'Il divorzio in Roma prima di Constantino', *Aufstieg und Niedergang der römischen Welt* II 14 (1982), 347–90, with bibliography, 388–90.

gradually made it increasingly unattractive for the spouses to divorce without good grounds. The beginnings may be observed with the early emperors, and Christianity reinforced the tendency, but for different reasons. The Christianization of the law of marriage has not resulted in a fundamental change in the law relating to matrimonial property. Byzantine law may have incorporated a Christian marriage, albeit reluctantly, but on matrimonial property it never did entirely shed its Roman vestment. Here it is worth taking note of a series of investigations instigated by Dieter Simon.[5]

I conclude with an observation about the way the law on divorce has developed since the Justinianic legislation. In the early seventh century the so-called *Nomocanon of the Fourteen Titles* summed up some of the relevant provisions in the fourth chapter of its thirteenth title 'On those who are divorced'. It lists some canons, among them several by St Basil, and has a longish section with the civil law on the subject, consisting of references to Justinian and to Novel 140 by Justin II, mentioned before. Only one canon was added later, namely the 87th of the Council in Trullo. In other words, the author of the revision of 882/3 did not have to add much to the status quo of the early seventh century. The corresponding title of the *Basilica* (28,7), stemming from the same time as the revision of the *Nomocanon*, is unusual in that it starts with the Justinianic Novels (117 and 22) and only then does it give the sections that represent the *Digest* and the *Code*. And in fact the two Novels had largely superseded the latter two collections on this point and were therefore more important. In a scholion on *Basilica* 28,7,8, at which point the section from the *Digest* begins, we read: 'Note that the exposition of the chapters on *repudium* [i.e. unilateral divorce] is entirely obsolete', meaning briefly that what follows has fallen into abeyance. I am unable to tell from when the scholion dates, nor can I tell whether the scholiast meant the form or the substance of unilateral divorce as described there; I rather suspect the latter. The next title of the same 28th book of the *Basilica* deals with 'The way in which the dowry is claimed on the dissolution of marriage'. Now that got the lawyers going. Here we meet with nothing but *Digest* and *Code* and very full commentaries.

To sum up: I do not believe in a distinction between Roman and Byzantine law as far as marriage is concerned. Rather I see a slow development from early imperial Roman law onwards, in which Christianity has played an important role.

The innovations brought about by Christianity were the idea of the indissolubility of marriage and the introduction of moral and religious considerations into the law of marriage. Both were in principle foreign to Roman law, but a preferential treatment of marriage accompanied by a

---

[5] D. Simon, ed., *Eherecht und Familiengut in Antike und Mittelalter* (Munich, 1992).

reduction of adultery and divorce were perceived as favourable to the preservation of the fabric of society already by Augustus. Certain changes in the law of matrimonial property and succession were the result. Many of them did not have the desired effect, as we know. Christianity supplied, or at least reinforced, the moral justification of a tendency that had already become official policy. If we must believe our sources, the combined efforts of State and Church were often woefully inadequate to effect a change in inveterate patterns of behaviour.

Zhishman wrote in his book about Byzantine marriage law[6] that the Christian idea of marriage emerged in the end triumphant, thanks to the combined efforts of Church and emperor. It cannot be denied that precisely in this field the influence of Christianity made itself felt much more clearly than in other parts of the law. It is also true that the law of marriage of the present day in many European countries shows its origin from canon law. Recent legal reforms in England of the law of divorce prove that the days of what I should like to call a secularized canon law of marriage are by no means over. Other countries are not much different. The secularization of the State has not brought with it an automatic return to a non-Christian marriage. It may have dispensed with the religious ceremony as a requisite for a valid marriage, a requisite that was slow to develop in any case, but in several respects the idea of a *consortium omnis vitae* as championed by Christianity is still present, though now resting on a different foundation. The motives of the legislator for resisting too far-reaching reforms are no longer exclusively Christian-inspired; a modern politician seldom campaigns along the lines of St Basil and St Augustine. Nevertheless that is how we have received our modern law of marriage, in East and in West. Just as the Byzantines held tenaciously fast to elements of the Roman law of marriage, which was based on non-Christian ideas, modern Europeans are slow to abandon their marriage law. Do they really know its origin?

---

[6] J. Zhishman, *Das Eherecht der orientalischen Kirche* (Vienna, 1864), 11.

9. Body vs. column:
the cults of St Symeon Stylites

Antony Eastmond

'Mind you,' [Colonel Porter] replied, 'I've seen a good deal of Mohammedan architecture one way and another ... and I've given a good deal of thought to the matter. I can tell you the key to the problem if you like.' 'Really. What is it?' 'The whole thing's *phallic*,' he uttered in a ghoulish whisper. I was surprised at first to note the influence of Freud on the North-West Frontier, but soon discovered that for Colonel Porter the universe itself was phallic.[1]

St Symeon Stylites is the most famous of all the early Syrian ascetic saints: as a model of denial he attracted the attention of thousands during his lifetime,[2] and many thousands more as pilgrims after his death. He effectively created a new industry, and 123 more stylites have been recorded, the most recent in 1848.[3] However, the extremism of his actions led him into trouble: his fellow monks were suspicious of him and forced him out of one monastery, and modern theological scholars have anguished at the form of his asceticism. As the Franciscan Ignace Peña has pondered: 'We can wonder whether it is really necessary to follow Christ by standing almost immobile at the top of a pillar for many long years and in view of all. Was this way of life not a little exhibitionist?'[4]

Symeon's life was one of paradoxes: he sought to escape the world, but the further he removed himself from it, the more the world sought him out. He sought to deny his body, but the more he denied it, the greater its allure became to those who wished to venerate him. The role of the holy man as

---

[1] R. Byron, *The Road to Oxiana* (London, 1937), 281–2.

[2] Theodoret of Cyrrhus, *Historia Religiosa*, P. Canivet and A. Leroy-Molinghen, eds and trs, *Théodoret de Cyr: Histoire des moines de Syrie*, Sources Chrétiennes 234, 257 (Paris, 1977–9), XXVI.11; R.M. Price, Eng. tr., *Theodoret of Cyrrhus: A History of the Monks of Syria*, Cistercian Studies Series 88 (Kalamazoo, 1985), 4.

[3] A list is given in I. Peña, P. Castellana and R. Fernandez, *Les Stylites Syriens* (Milan, 1975), 79–84.

[4] Peña, Castellana and Fernandez, *Les Stylites Syriens*, 5.

From *Desire and Denial in Byzantium*, ed. Liz James. Copyright © 1999 by the Society for the Promotion of Byzantine Studies. Published by Ashgate Publishing Ltd, Gower House, Croft Road, Aldershot, Hampshire, GU11 3HR, Great Britain.

an important social intermediary for the people of Syria is well known. Peter Brown has demonstrated the ways in which these exceptional figures could act as a prime arbiter of social justice,[5] and Symeon is recorded as deciding disputes ranging from the price of cucumbers to more serious matters involving the government of Antioch and imperial policy towards the Jews.[6] However, the most important paradox came on Symeon's death: the nature of the rival cults that grew up around his memory. It is these paradoxes that this paper addresses.

Three texts describe the life of St Symeon.[7] Two were written posthumously and are dedicated entirely to the first stylite: the Syriac *Life* and that by the monk Antonios. The third was written during Symeon's lifetime: Theodoret of Cyrrhus's *History of the Monks of Syria* (*Historia Religiosa*). It was composed in 444 by which time Symeon had already been standing on his column for some thirty-two years, and it fits Symeon into the context of ascetic Christianity in Syria in the fifth century.[8] The stylite appears as just one of thirty-five holy men and women living in the Syrian desert, and the column is all that marks him out as being more exceptional than his contemporaries. The Prologue to Theodoret's *History* is very explicit in its desire to establish all their memories in relation to the pagan society at the edges of which they lived. In particular, the asceticism of the monks and nuns is held up as a model against which to contrast the pagans around them. The audience Theodoret addresses is one conversant with the pagan society of the late antique city and its culture. Thus, in the most famous parallel drawn by Theodoret and other authors, the monks of Syria are the new athletes of God, and are contrasted against the athletes training for the Olympic Games in Antioch.[9] It is an image of strength and vigour depending on two very different training regimes. The Syriac *Life* of Symeon uses the athlete comparison, but includes other materialistic metaphors, describing Symeon's spiritual victory in commercial terms: 'The skilful sailor and watchful pilot [Symeon] whose ship arrived at a safe harbour ... all with help from his Lord, and made its sailor happy by its huge profits'.[10]

Theodoret's *History* also contrasts his holy men and women with a second group: those men whose memories are venerated in painted panels,

[5] P. Brown, 'The Rise and Function of the Holy Man in Late Antiquity', *JRS* 61 (1971), 80–101.

[6] Evagrios, *Ecclesiastical History*, in J. Bildez and L. Parmentier, eds, *The Ecclesiastical History of Evagrius with the Scholia* (London, 1898; repr. Amsterdam, 1964), I.13; A.M. Festugière, tr., 'Évagre: Histoire ecclésiastique', *B* 45 (1975), 219; also the *Syriac Life of St Symeon*, in R. Doran, ed. and tr., *The Lives of Simeon Stylites*, Cistercian Studies Series 112 (Kalamazoo, 1992), 189–91.

[7] The three texts are brought together in Doran, *Simeon Stylites*.

[8] Introduction to Theodoret, *HR*, 21–2.

[9] On the survival of the Olympic games in Antioch see G. Downey, *A History of Antioch in Syria from Seleucus to the Arab Conquest* (Princeton, 1961), 439–46.

[10] *Syriac Life*, in Doran, *Simeon Stylites*, 191.

but who are 'womanish and effeminate, so that it is ambiguous whether they are men or women [... and whose] memory causes not profit but injury to the soul'.[11] Theodoret's subjects, in opposition, are new 'living images and statues'. There is a fine distinction here between the pagan idolatry aimed at the inanimate panels of those who worship the flesh, and the true power contained in the living images of holiness produced by the immobile holy people. This comparison also serves, implicitly, to sexualize Theodoret's monks and nuns, although their virility, of course, lies in the renunciation of their sexuality.

Theodoret concentrates on particular aspects of his subjects, especially their renunciation of the flesh. It is an area that has been well studied in recent scholarship.[12] Indeed, the body is central to Theodoret's conception of the holy man. Susan Ashbrook Harvey has pointed out how much of the power of the holy man in society derived from his body. It was the fact that the stylite had voluntarily put his body through the same privations suffered involuntarily by those who sought his advice that gave him his authority.[13] But it was also the body that gave the saint power after death. This is why the cult of St Symeon is so interesting, since the cult of his body seems to have been particularly fragile.

The importance of the body of the saint is well known in all early Christian cults throughout the Christian world, but in Syria it seems to have been of especial significance. Theodoret stresses the power of the body continually, both before and after death. When the emperor Jovian surrendered Nisibis to the Persians in 363 the displaced inhabitants of the city took the body of their local martyr James with them.[14] Rival tombs awaited the hermit Marcianos on his death, forcing the monk to ask to be buried in secret so that there could be no squabbling over his remains (and no attempts to claim forged relics as his own).[15] And when the ascetic Maron died there was a 'bitter war' between rival villages for his body, which ended when one village seized the corpse. The spiritual (and no doubt also commercial) value of the body is clear as Theodoret notes that 'they reap benefit therefrom even to this day'.[16] The two most extreme cases he gives are those of the holy men Salamanes and James of Cyrrestica. The former, who blocked himself up in a cell as a form of living corpse, was subsequently treated as one by his local villagers. He was stolen while still alive and

---

[11] Theodoret, *HR*, Prologue, 3.

[12] For example, P. Brown, *The Body and Society. Men, Women and Sexual Renunciation in Early Christianity* (London and Boston, 1988).

[13] S. Ashbrook Harvey, *Foreword* to Doran, *Simeon Stylites*, 11–12.

[14] Theodoret, *HR*, I.14.

[15] Theodoret, *HR*, III.18. It was only after 50 years that it was deemed safe to reveal his body and give it a special burial. Theodoret, *History*, 118.

[16] Theodoret, *HR*, XVI.4.

carried to a new village where he was incarcerated in a new cell. When this theft was discovered the first village came and stole him back again – all, we are told, without Salamanes ever speaking or resisting.[17] In a similarly ghoulish manner no one could wait for James of Cyrrestica to die. Rivals from a local town and village gathered to seize his body while he was still alive. But when James recovered from his illness, all the locals were forced to leave empty-handed (and no doubt disappointed), only to gather like vultures when the monk fell ill again. This time the townsfolk came well prepared and used their greater military might to ensure that they would gain possession of the body. The relic-taking began even before the saint's death: 'he was not even conscious of his hair being plucked out by the peasants'.[18]

Against this background the treatment of Symeon's body after his death comes as no surprise. Indeed, it fits in neatly to the *topos* of the miracle-working, valuable corpse. When Symeon died many groups gathered in the hope of taking possession and advantage of his body. Antonios's *Life* describes the crowds, including groups from local villages and armed Arabs, that gathered in the hope of seizing the body in order to carry it off for their own benefit and protection. Ardabourios, the *magister militum per Orientem*, required a force of 600 men to guarantee his own possession of the body, in order to deliver it to the patriarch and people of Antioch. The city could already boast the relics of a number of important holy men, including the martyr saint Babylas, reburied in 383,[19] and Ignatios, an early bishop of Antioch.[20] However, Symeon was far and away the most important and influential saint to have lived near Antioch, and his body took on extra value accordingly. The corpse was transferred to the city in a long and impressive procession which took five days, and on arrival it was displayed in the church of Cassianus for thirty days. After that it was moved to the city's cathedral, the great octagonal church built by Constantine the Great – the Domus Aurea. Symeon, we are told, was the first man to be laid to rest in this church. John Malalas claims that a special martyrium and shrine were then built for the body.[21] Antonios's *Life* is adamant in proclaiming the centrality of Symeon's body to his cult. He writes that when the Emperor Leo I requested that a relic of the saint be sent to Constantinople he was refused. The people of Antioch claimed that the body was central to the defence of the city. When the walls of the city had collapsed in the terrible earthquake of 459 the people of the city had

---

[17] Theodoret, *HR*, XIX.3.

[18] Theodoret, *HR*, XXI.9.

[19] Downey, *Antioch*, 415–6.

[20] Downey, *Antioch*, 455.

[21] John Malalas, *Chronographia*, ed. L. Dindorf (Bonn, 1831), 369; E. Jeffreys, M. Jeffreys and R. Scott, eds and trs, *The Chronicle of John Malalas*, Byzantina Australiensia 4 (Melbourne, 1986), 203.

travelled to Symeon's hermitage at Telanissos (called the *mandra*) where they stayed for 59 days for aid and protection, and now they envisaged St Symeon as the principal defence of the city: 'the very holy body was a fort and a rampart for the city'.[22] Symeon's body was the guarantee of Antioch's security, even after death.

Other attempts were made to gain relics from Symeon's body at this early stage, but all were unsuccessful. The bishop of Antioch saw his hand wither as he tried to cut hair from Symeon's beard,[23] and all bribes were refused by the clergy in the city.[24] All these stories testify to the importance of the body. It is clear that the wholeness of the body and its physical presence were the two requirements of his cult. It was these that gave him his power. His asceticism and denial of his body before his death gave his body power and virility after it.

I have outlined the importance of the body to Theodoret and have described the history of Symeon's body in some detail, because at this point in its power the cult of St Symeon diverges from the norm: the power of the body begins to wane, and its subsequent history is more confused and ambiguous. The first clue to this comes in the *Life of St Daniel the Stylite*. This records that the Emperor Leo I, on the prompting of Symeon's main disciple, the Constantinopolitan stylite Daniel, did finally manage to persuade the people of Antioch to give up a relic of the saint for the imperial capital, sometime in the 460s; at just the time that Antonios was proclaiming the importance of Symeon's bodily inviolability. The emperor then built a church in Constantinople to house it to the north of Daniel's own column by the Bosphoros, and when Daniel died he was buried next to the body of his inspirer.[25] This seems to undermine the emphasis placed on the body in Antioch. Evagrios, writing in the 590s, over 140 years after Symeon's death, records witnessing with a number of priests the relics of the saint in the Octagon church in Antioch, and he states that in his day the 'vast majority' of the body was preserved in Antioch. He gives a detailed description of Symeon's head, noting his hair, skin and missing teeth, which he claims to have seen when the head was sent by Gregory, Patriarch

[22] Evagrios, *Ecclesiastical History*, I.13; Festugière, 'Évagre', 220; also in the *Syriac Life*, Doran, *Simeon Stylites*, 194.

[23] Antonios, *Life of the Blessed Symeon the Stylite*, eds H. Lietzmann and H. Hilgenfeld, *Das Leben des heiligen Symeon Stylites*, Texte und Untersuchungen zur Geschichte der altchristlichen Literatur 32/4 (Leipzig, 1908), 70; Doran, *Simeon Stylites*, 98.

[24] Antonios, *Life*, 76; Doran, *Simeon Stylites*, 100.

[25] *Life of St Daniel the Stylite*, ed. H. Delehaye, *Les saints stylites* (Brussels and Paris, 1923), 55–6, E. Dawes and N. Baynes, trs, *Three Byzantine Saints* (New York, 1977), 40–41. The only reference to the monastery (from the *Life of St Daniel the Stylite*) is discussed in R. Janin, *La géographie ecclésiastique de l'empire byzantin. Le siège de Constantinople et le patriarcat oecuménique. III: Les églises et les monastères*, 2nd edn (Paris, 1969), 86 and 479.

of Antioch, to the general Phillipikos and the eastern armies in around 582.[26] The records seem to be contradictory: did Leo I succeed in gaining the body or did the people of Antioch retain it for their own protection? Most modern commentators have regarded this as somewhat a non-issue, arguing that the body could have been divided, with relics being kept in both Antioch and Constantinople.[27] This is an obvious solution, but it is marred by the implications in the *Life of St Daniel* and in Evagrios's *History* that the whole body had either been transferred to Constantinople or witnessed in Antioch, [28] and, more seriously, by the stress in the *Life* of Antonios laid on the inviolability of the body, which had previously driven the people of Antioch to refuse an imperial command, and had caused the hand of the bishop to wither.[29] The sources seem confused, and if the solution proposed by modern scholars is accepted, then it provides evidence of a definite shift in the status of the body as talisman of Antioch and as inviolably whole within ten years of Symeon's death. Why should Symeon's body lose its power so quickly?

The fate and status of St Symeon's body in the longer term is even harder to determine. After the period of the Persian occupation of Antioch (609/10–28) and its subsequent fall to the Arabs in 636/7 the body disappears from history. The recapture of the city by John Tsimiskes in 969 brought the city back into Byzantine hands, and saw the revival of many of its churches;[30] but there are no references to the cult or body of St Symeon. If the body had remained in Antioch in the fifth century, then its loss would be understandable: the devastation of the Persian and Arab invasions or, more probably, the earthquakes of the sixth century could easily account for its disappearance. But the disappearance of Symeon's body from its other possible home, Constantinople, is less comprehensible. Yet there is no record of it in Constantinople after the translation of the relics recorded in the *Life of St Daniel*: when Antony of Novgorod went to venerate the relics at the monastery of St Daniel the Stylite in Constantinople in c.1200 he prayed before the relics of Sts Daniel, Akakios and Xene, but he makes no reference to what would surely have been the monastery's prime possession,

---

[26] Evagrios, *Ecclesiastical History*, I.13; Festugière, 'Évagre', 220–21. P. Allen, *Evagrius Scholasticus the Church Historian* (Louvain, 1981), 3–4, states that Evagrios saw the head en route from Qalat Siman to Phillipikos via Antioch, but I can find no evidence to support the idea that the head had ever been returned to Qalat Siman.

[27] This, for example, is what is argued by Delehaye, *Les saints stylites*, lvi; and Allen, *Evagrius*, 85.

[28] The *Life of St Daniel*, 56–7, trs Dawes and Baynes, *Three Byzantine Saints*, 41 implies that the whole body was translated to Constantinople.

[29] Antonios, *Life*, 70; Doran, *Simeon Stylites*, 98.

[30] On the later history of Antioch see H. Kennedy, 'Antioch: from Byzantium to Islam and back again', in J. Rich, ed., *The City in Late Antiquity* (London and New York, 1992), 181–98.

the body of the first stylite.[31] An argument based on silences in the sources is perhaps not very strong, but it is certainly striking: Symeon was, after all, the first saint in the liturgical calendar and so must have had a symbolic importance in the Byzantine world (and also a commercial value to the monastery that possessed his relics).[32] Symeon's body had simply disappeared; it was forgotten.

In contrast to this tale of loss and neglect, the history of the site of Symeon's column at Telanissos (now Qalat Siman) is very striking. Here the memory of the saint was preserved well into the twelfth century at the site of the enormous monastery built around the saint's column. Qalat Siman was first described by Evagrios, who visited it in the second half of the sixth century and recorded the continuance of miracles being performed there and the large number of pilgrims and peasants who processed around the column with their beasts of burden.[33] However, its history can be traced back to the years immediately after Symeon's death.

The monastery stands only some forty kilometres from Antioch, the supposed site of Symeon's principal cult, yet here was built the largest and grandest church of the age, part of a large complex of buildings. The local village of Deir Siman was also expanded to house the very large numbers of pilgrims that attended the church.[34] The church seems to have been built between 476 and 490, very soon after Symeon's death. Its enormous size and the quality of its decoration all testify to the wealth of the site and it has long been assumed to have owed much to imperial patronage under the emperor Zeno.[35] The fate of the monastery after the Arab invasions is unknown, but it was certainly active after the reconquest of Antioch. There is evidence of restoration work in 979, and of attacks on the monks in 985 and 1017 from Aleppo and Egypt.[36] After that there is no more evidence of activity at the site, although the patriarch Michael of Syria knew of it at the end of the twelfth century.[37]

The church was designed in the shape of the cross, with four basilicas making up the four arms, and an open octagon containing Symeon's

---

[31] Janin, La géographie écclesiastique, 86. No other later pilgrims to Constantinople mention the body of St Symeon: G.P. Majeska, Russian Travelers to Constantinople in the Fourteenth and Fifteenth Centuries, Dumbarton Oaks Studies 19 (Washington DC, 1984).

[32] See, for example, the opening image of the imperial menologion of Basil II, Il Menologio di Basilio II (Cod. Vaticano Greco 1613), Codices e Vaticanis Selecti 8 (Turin, 1907), 2.

[33] Evagrios, I.14; Festugière, 'Évagre', 221–3.

[34] See G. Tchalenko, Villages antiques de la Syrie du Nord (Paris, 1953), 1. 205–22 and plates LXVII–LXX; I. Peña, The Christian Art of Byzantine Syria (London, 1997), 151.

[35] Tchalenko, Villages antiques 1. 231–3.

[36] See Tchalenko, Villages antiques 1. 242–3 for references.

[37] J.-B. Chabot, ed. and tr., Chronique de Michel le Syrien, patriarche jacobite d'Antioche (1166–1199), vol. 2, (Paris, 1905), 422.

column at their centre.[38] The north, south and west basilicas had the
column as their focus, and the eastern basilica was more traditionally
oriented around the liturgical core of the apse at the east end of the church.
This architectural form fits in closely to the standard design of martyria in
this period, although on an unprecedented scale. Gregory of Nyssa, writing
in 380 of a martyrium in his home town, describes a building which was
octagonal with four exedrae,[39] and in Antioch the martyrium which had
been built for St Babylas in 383 took an identical (although smaller scale)
form to venerate the relics.[40] What is extraordinary about Qalat Siman is
both its scale (it has been estimated that the church could hold a congregation
of up to 10,000) and its focus: whereas other martyria had saints' bodies at
their centre, Qalat Siman was focused on the column of the saint; the body
lay elsewhere. This is the core of the problem. Why did a cult emerge
around the column at a time when we know that the body cult was still
prospering? And why did the column cult outlast that of the body, when
all other contemporary cults were still centred on the power of the body?
It is remarkable that no source should comment on this change. The shift
away from the body, which provided physical proof of Symeon's asceticism,
and which gave his holiness meaning and importance to the impoverished
villagers and emperors of the fifth century, to its physical symbol, the
forty cubit-high column, seems to have been regarded as entirely natural
and unnoteworthy.

The evident primacy of the column cult stands markedly at odds both
with the evidence outlined already about the importance of the body in early
Christian society, and more importantly with the aims of Symeon's
promoters during his lifetime. This is the most apparent in Theodoret of
Cyrrhus's account of Symeon's life. Theodoret is careful to stress the
importance of Symeon's ascetic body as the site of his holiness, and to
minimize the role of the column. In the *History* the nature of Symeon's fame,
holiness and popularity are very clearly described: it was to see the man
that the vast crowds came to the mandra, and it was portraits of the man
that adorned houses in Rome and elsewhere.[41] The column appears only
as a means to an end, not an end in itself. Indeed, Theodoret is desperate

---

[38] Tchalenko, *Villages antiques* 1. 223–76.

[39] Gregory of Nyssa, *PG* 46, 1093; J.B. Ward-Perkins, 'Memoria, Martyr's Tomb and Martyr's Chapel', *JTS* 17 (1966), 34; A. Grabar, *Martyrium. Recherches sur le culte des reliques et l'art chrétien antique* (Paris, 1946), 152–75.

[40] E. Baccache and G. Tchalenko, *Églises de village de la Syrie du nord: Planches, Documents d'archéologie: la Syrie à l'époque de l'empire romain d'orient* (Paris, 1979), 348–51; J. Lassus, 'L'église cruciforme (Antioche-Kaoussié 12-F)', and G. Downey, 'The Shrines of St. Babylas at Antioch and Daphne', both in R. Stillwell, ed., *Antioch-on-the-Orontes* 2: *The Excavations, 1933–1936* (Princeton 1938), 5–44 and 45–8.

[41] Theodoret, *HR*, XXVI.11.

to explain it away; its seems to be an embarrassment. He excuses the column as merely a means to escape from the crowds;[42] as just a gimmick to attract barbarians for conversion.[43] Theodoret seems to be replying to contemporary criticism about Symeon's actions and cites a series of Old Testament precedents for the saint's unorthodox practices. He concludes his defence of the column by saying that: '[God]... arranged this extraordinary novelty to draw everyone by its strangeness to the spectacle and make [Symeon's] proffered counsel persuasive to those who came.'[44] Theodoret prefers to locate Symeon's sanctity in the more acceptable Syriac tradition of *stasis*: the motionless and standing saints.[45] Viewed in this way, Symeon is one of an army of Christian ascetics working for God.

Bernard Flusin, who was concerned with the authority of the different *Lives* of the saint, has provided a partial answer to the problem of the possible rivalry between the cults of the body and the column.[46] He has argued that the *Life* of Antonios and the Syriac *Life* were written for different purposes: the former to promote the cult of the body, the latter to legitimize and popularize the site of Symeon's column at Telanissos. This goes some way to explaining Antonios's stress on the inviolability of Symeon's body. It is aimed at a similar urban constituency to Theodoret, who is equally uncomfortable with the theatricality of Symeon's asceticism. The Syriac *Life*, composed by 473, was aimed at promoting Telanissos, in which aim it seems to have been remarkably successful: the great church around the column at Qalat Siman was begun less than three years later.

However, we cannot ascribe the success of Qalat Siman just to the power of the Syriac *Life*, nor can the new church there be regarded simply as imperial compensation for the removal of the body: in both cases the scale of the church and surrounding village indicates an already thriving cult. To divert attention away from the body, Qalat Siman must have had other attractions. So what was the attraction of the column? With the benefit of hindsight it might seem obvious that the column should act as a major relic of the saint, but the contemporary accounts of the cult, as we have seen, all concentrate on the body, and *loca sancta* were normally only associated with

---

[42] Theodoret, *HR*, XXVI.12.

[43] Theodoret, *HR*, XXVI.13.

[44] Theodoret, *HR*, XXVI.12.

[45] On this see Delehaye, *Les saints stylites*, clxxxi–clxxxiii. Theodoret, *HR*, XXVII.1. On the importance of Theodoret's primarily Greek audience: S. Ashbrook Harvey, 'The Sense of a Stylite: Perspectives on Simeon the Elder', *Vigiliae Christianae* 24 (1988), 378–9.

[46] B. Flusin, 'Syméon et les philologues, ou la mort du stylite', in C. Jolivet-Lévy, M. Kaplan and J.-P. Sodini, eds, *Les saints et leur sanctuaire à Byzance: textes, images et monuments* (Paris, 1993), 1–23. However, D.T.M. Frankfurter, 'Stylites and *Phallobates*: Pillar Religions in Late Antique Syria', *Vigiliae Christianae* 44 (1990), 192 note 8, argues that the Syriac *Life* 'had the added purpose of defending Antioch's claim to the body'.

the stories of the Old and New Testaments – usually events for which there no other physical relics.

In trying to explain the phenomenon, many authors have looked for local precedents to column worship, and have also searched for deeper human motivations for its attraction. At the centre of this has been the lure of the phallus. As is well known, the basis for this argument lies in Lucian's *De Dea Syria*, which describes the *phallobates* at the cult site of the goddess Atargatis at Hierapolis in the second century.[47] In the late 1960s G.R.H. Wright explored these links and stressed the fertility symbolism of both.[48] But in the same way that Robert Byron was surprised at Freud on the North-West Frontier, so most other scholars have been unable to accept this link. Most recently, David Frankfurter has tried to reinterpret this association.[49] He has endeavoured to explain away the 'phallic' aspect of Lucian's description and has suggested instead there was a 'general tradition of pillar symbolism and ritual in Greco-Roman Syria', and that Symeon fitted in to a well-established need for this form of worship. He notes Evagrios's account of witnessing men dancing round the column in the moonlight as a clear example of local ritual survival. To that can be added one more piece of evidence from the twelfth-century chronicle of the Jacobite patriarch of Antioch, Michael (1126–99). This describes the arrival of the Persians in Syria in 618. Michael claims that the invaders arrived at Qalat Siman on Symeon's feast day and found the site jammed full of men, women and children who 'in place of fasting, vigils, and psalmody ... had abandoned themselves to intemperance, to drunkenness, to dancing and other forms of lust and debauchery ... and had irritated God'.[50] Michael was certainly just trying to explain the Persians' victory by highlighting the moral decline of the Christians in Syria, but it seems significant that it is Qalat Siman that is used as the one example to demonstrate it (rather than Antioch itself, for example).

However, to interpret all this evidence in terms of local cults and the survival of pagan Syrian forms of worship restricts its relevance to Syria, and does not explain the popularity of the cult throughout the Roman world.[51] While it is possible that the origins of the pillar cult may lie in local

---

[47] Lucian, *De Dea Syria*, eds and trs H.W. Attridge and R.A. Oden, *The Syrian Goddess (De Dea Syria) Attributed to Lucian*, Society of Biblical Literature, Texts and Translations 9 (Missoula MT, 1976), 38–40 (chaps 28–9).

[48] G.R.H. Wright, 'Simeon's Ancestors (or the Skeleton on the Column)', *Australian Journal of Biblical Archaeology* 1,1 (1968), 41–9; G.R.H. Wright, 'The Heritage of the Stylites', *Australian Journal of Biblical Archaeology* 1,3, (1970), 82–107.

[49] Frankfurter, 'Stylites and *Phallobates*', 168–98.

[50] Chabot, ed. and tr., *Chronique de Michel le Syrien*, 2. 422.

[51] Theodoret, *HR*, XXVI.11: 'Not only do the inhabitants of our part of the world flock together, but also Ishmaelites, Persians, Armenians subject to them, Iberians, Homerites,

precedents, although this cannot be proven, these cannot explain Symeon's international popularity, nor the long-lasting nature of the cult. None, after all, of the other holy men and women in Theodoret's *History* were to enjoy such popularity.

It is therefore necessary to look for broader contemporary parallels for Symeon's appearance on a column, which might explain the cult's international popularity.[52] The most obvious potential parallel for Symeon, of enormous international significance, is that of imperial columns.[53] When Symeon first ascended his column in 412 Constantinople was at the peak of its column-building programme. The most famous two, the monumental historiated columns of Arkadios (erected in 402), and of Theodosios I (erected in 386) were merely the tallest in a long line stretching back to Constantine I's original porphyry column set up at the foundation of the city in 324, and beyond that back to the second-century columns of Rome.[54] In the course of the fifth century Eudoxia, Theodosios II (in Hebdomon), Leo I and Marcian all erected columns, and the tradition continued through the reign of Justinian to that of Phokas in 609.[55] Antioch also had its own range of imperial statues set up in the decades before and during Symeon's life, including two statues of the empress Eudokia (set up in 438), and images of Theodosius II and Valentinian III (erected 439), as well as the earlier statues of Theodosius I, Aelia Flaccilla and Arkadios which had been destroyed in the riot of the statues in 387.[56]

---

and men even more distant than these; and there came many inhabitants from the extreme west: Spaniards, Britons, and the Gauls who live between them. Of Italy it is superfluous to speak. It is said that the man became so celebrated in the great city of Rome that at the entrance of every workshop men have set up small representations of him to provide thereby some protection and safety for themselves.'

[52] One such attempt has been made by H.J.W. Drijvers, 'Spätantike Parallelen zur altchristlichen Heiligenverehrung unter besonderer Berücksichtigung des syrischen Stylitenkultes', in G. Wießner, ed., *Göttinger Orientforschungen I. Reihe: Syriaca* 17, vol 2: *Erkenntnisse und Meinungen* (Wiesbaden, 1978), 78–113, who has attempted to explain the popularity of the column cult in terms of *imitatio Christi*. But as Frankfurter, 'Stylites and Phallobates', 175, 186 has pointed out, the majority of Symeon iconography does not emphasize or imitate Christ on the Cross.

[53] R. Janin, *Constantinople Byzantine* (Paris, 1950), 77–84.

[54] For descriptions of the historiated columns, see G. Becatti, *La colonna coclide istoriata* (Rome, 1960); J.-P. Sodini, 'Images sculptées et propagande impériale du IVe au VIe siècle: recherches récentes sur les colonnes honorifiques et les reliefs politiques à Byzance', in J. Durand, ed., *Byzance et les images, Louvre conférences et colloques* (Paris, 1994), 41–94; for an impression of the range of other imperial statues set up in Constantinople by the eighth century see A.M. Cameron and J. Herrin, eds, *Constantinople in the Early Eighth Century: The Parastaseis Syntomoi Chronikai* (Leiden, 1984), 48–51.

[55] C. Mango, 'The Columns of Justinian and his Successors', in G. Dagron and C. Mango, eds, *Studies on Constantinople* (Aldershot, 1993), Study X, 1–20.

[56] For references to these statues see Downey, *Antioch*, 426–9, 451, 454.

The visual similarity between the great monumental columns, each surmounted by a statue of the emperor, and that of St Symeon standing atop his own column in the Syrian desert is undeniable, but the comparison can be taken much further. The two types of column also shared similarities in the way they functioned. In the same way that the statue of an emperor on a pedestal or column acted as an object worthy of veneration, so too did people come to pray to Symeon. Throughout the fourth century a series of theologians and ecclesiastical writers from Eusebios to Chrysostom to Athanasios and Gregory of Nyssa had commented on the power and importance of the imperial image and the need to perform proskynesis before it.[57] Whereas on the imperial column the statue stood in for the prototype, at Qalat Siman, Symeon became the image. And in the same way that the imperial image was a powerful symbol of authority, so too could people turn to Symeon to look for justice and guidance: the column of Eudoxia in Constantinople of 403 was adorned with an inscription which established it as a place for the dispensation of justice,[58] just as Symeon's column acted to attract those seeking resolution to their disputes.[59] In both cases the column seems to have acted as as important an aspect of the monument as the statue or stylite surmounting it, but what is remarkable is that the stylite's column retained these functions after Symeon's death.

In the long-term, the veneration of the two types of column, imperial and stylite, became ever more closely intertwined, although it is impossible to say how early this began. Just as pilgrims processed round the column at Qalat Siman, so too the great columns in Constantinople became centres of veneration on processions through the city.[60] At the great porphyry column of Constantine the Great the centrality of the column to the imperial cult is most clear. A chapel was built at its base, possibly in the eighth century, in order, according to Mango, 'to enhance and sanctify the symbolic significance of the column.'[61] The column took on an increasingly autonomous importance, appearing in the *Life of St Andrew the Fool* as the only monument to survive the ultimate destruction of the city.[62] More significantly, in the same way that the column of St Symeon became the focus of veneration after the body of the saint was removed, so too did the

---

[57] For a summary of this see K. Setton, *Christian Attitude Towards the Emperor in the Fourth Century Especially As Shown in Addresses to the Emperor* (New York, 1941), 196–211.

[58] The inscription is given in Janin, *Constantinople Byzantine*, 80–81.

[59] For example the story of the man who vandalized a cucumber field in the *Syriac Life*, Doran, *Simeon Stylites*, 124–5.

[60] M. McCormick, *Eternal Victory. Triumphal Rulership in Late Antiquity, Byzantium, and the Early Medieval West* (Cambridge, 1986), 217, provides one possible interpretation of their function.

[61] C. Mango, 'Constantine's Porphyry Column and the Chapel of St Constantine', Deltion les Christianikes Archaiologikes Hetaireias 10 (1981), 110 (reprinted in *Studies on Constantinople* [Aldershot, 1993], Study IV).

[62] L. Rydén, 'The Andreas Salos Apocalypse. Greek text, Translation, and Commentary', *DOP* 28 (1974), 197–261 at 211 (868B).

imperial columns retain their importance, even after they had lost the imperial statues that once crowned them. The columns, in particular the Xerolophos, came to be seen as sites of prophecy,[63] and this had become well embedded by the beginning of the thirteenth century. Robert de Clari recorded that the people of Constantinople on the eve of the fall of the city in 1204, looked to the column of Arkadios for an explanation of their fate, even if, as Robert maliciously notes, they could only interpret the imagery contained in the reliefs on the column with the benefit of hindsight.[64] It is possible that this way of viewing the imperial columns was itself influenced by the continued veneration of the [empty] stylites' columns. In the fifth century, the veneration accorded to Symeon's column seems to have been based on that given to imperial columns, but later the miraculous powers of the stylites' columns rubbed off on the now incompletely understood imperial columns. Perhaps the ultimate elision of the two phenomena came in the twelfth century when the imperial columns in Constantinople themselves became homes to stylites.[65] At this point the various aspects of the column – its aura of piety and of authority and its symbolism of ascent to God became one.

The imperial parallel for the cult of the stylite on his column appears compelling, and certainly relies on a broad stream of evidence from throughout the empire, rather than just on postulated local links with regional pagan cults. Its weakness, however, lies in the silence of the sources. No Byzantine commentator ever noted such a parallel, striking as it now appears. The closest to such a mention comes in the Prologue to Theodoret's *History*, noted earlier in this paper.[66] Theodoret there calls his holy men and women 'living images and statues'. However, his aim there was to contrast the hermits and ascetics with the lifeless images of athletes which were so revered by pagans; he does not seem to imply any comparison with imperial imagery, and he makes no other similar comparison. There are several possible reasons for this: the imperial image, as all church writers made clear, was a special case and so the imperial cult might not have seemed a suitable comparison (whether for an ascetic to assume the symbolism of imperial power, or for an emperor to appear as an ascetic); also at this stage the imperial column itself might not yet have assumed the cult status it was later to attain. Moreover, imperial art might still have been too closely associated with pagan idolatry for Theodoret's

---

[63] Cameron and Herrin, eds, *Parastaseis*, 82–4 (chap. 20); G. Dagron, *Constantinople imaginaire. Etudes sur le receuil des «Patria»*, Bibliothèque byzantine. Etudes 8 (Paris, 1984), 74–6, 149; G. Dagron and J. Paramelle, 'Un texte patriographique: Le «récit beau et profitable sur la colonne de Xèrolophos» (Vindob. suppl. gr. 172, fol. 43v-63v)', *TM* 7 (1979), 491–523.

[64] Robert de Clari, *The Conquest of Constantinople*, tr. E.H. McNeal, (Columbia, 1936), 110–11.

[65] Robert de Clari, *Conquest*, 111.

[66] Theodoret, *HR*, Prologue, 3.

purposes. Despite the weight of Church Fathers who supported veneration of imperial images, others were more suspicious of them. Theodosios II issued a law in 425 condemning the *adoratio* of imperial images,[67] and Theophanes's *Chronographia* records that the statues set up by Eudoxia in Constantinople attracted Manichaean supporters of paganism who danced round the column, apparently in the same way as those condemned by Michael of Antioch, who danced round Symeon's column at Qalat Siman.[68] The revolt of the statues in Antioch in 387, might also have had the effect of making all those in and around Antioch more sensitive about referring to imperial art.

The absence of any direct references to imperial columns and their possible relationship to that of the stylite mean that it is now only possible to provide circumstantial evidence of any connections between them. However, enough clues survive to suggest that the two functioned in very similar ways. I hope that it shows that the column had a greater lure than just as a distant echo of earlier Syriac column religions, and that its influence had greater repercussions throughout the empire. In the short term the column was able to act as an early rival to the cult of Symeon's body, which itself had proved to be very powerful in the immediate aftermath of his death. In the long term, the stylite's column, with its miraculous powers, was able to act in a similar way to that of the great imperial columns; indeed, it seems as if the two each influenced the way in which the other was regarded as a source of power and authority.

---

[67] T. Mommsen, ed., *Theodosiani libri XVI cum Constitutionibus Sirmondianis* (Berlin, 1905), XV.4.1; C. Pharr, tr., *The Theodosian Code and Novels and the Sirmondian Constitutions* (Princeton, 1952), 432.

[68] Theophanes Confessor, *Chronographia*, ed. C. de Boor, (Leipzig, 1883), 79; C. Mango and R. Scott, trs, *The Chronicle of Theophanes Confessor. Byzantine and Near Eastern History AD 284–813* (Oxford, 1997), 121.

10. Christian bodies: the senses and early Byzantine Christianity

Béatrice Caseau

In looking at studies on the body in Late Antiquity, it is clear that one theme dominates: the recurrent topic of the virginal life in patristic literature. Many studies dealing with the body in Late Antiquity have insisted on sexual attitudes. Their focus has been mostly on the meaning and consequences of the refusal of sex and sexual desires.[1] A distrust of the other sex and different means to reduce one's sexual drives, such as deprivation of food,[2] of sleep, of physical comfort and the control of the senses seem to dominate the *Sayings* of the Desert Fathers, the *Lives* of many of the monastic saints and the discourse of patristic writers such as Jerome and John Chrysostom.[3] Yet to study the body through these texts makes one dependent on a specific trend in Late Antique Christianity, one well represented among church writers inclined towards monasticism, but not necessarily adopted by all Christians. The risk is 'to assume without analysis that discourse has general social effect',[4] to believe without discussion that the norms of the ascetic lifestyle were adopted by large numbers when, in fact, the question of the impact of monasticism on Late Roman society remains open.

---

[1] H. Chadwick, 'The Ascetic Ideal in the History of the Church', in W.J.Sheils, ed., *Monks, Hermits and the Ascetical Tradition* (Oxford, 1985), 1–24; E.A. Clark, 'Ascetic Renunciation and Feminine Advancement: A Paradox of Late Ancient Christianity', *Anglican Theological Review* 6 (1981), 240–57; P. Brown, *The Body and Society. Men, Women and Sexual Renunciation in Early Christianity* (London and Boston, 1988).

[2] Fasting to curb the desires of the body is a recurrent theme in ascetic literature. See, for example, Evagrios Pontikos, *Praktikos*, A. and C. Guillaumont, eds and trs, *Evagre le Pontique, Traité pratique ou le moine* (Paris, 1971); H. Musurillo, 'The Problem of Ascetical Fasting in the Greek Patristic Writers', *Traditio* 12 (1956), 1–64; C.W. Bynum, *Holy Feast and Holy Fast: The Religious Significance of Food for Medieval Women* (Berkeley, 1987); V. Grimm, *From Feasting to Fasting: The Evolution of a Sin. Attitudes to Food in Late Antiquity* (London and New York, 1996).

[3] A de Vogüé, *Histoire littéraire du mouvement monastique dans l'antiquité* (Paris, 1991–96).

[4] B. Turner, *The Body and Society* (Oxford, 1984), 175, criticizing books written under the influence of Michel Foucault.

Because so many of the sources originate from religious communities, we risk over-emphasizing the influence of monastic ascetic practices and values on the majority of Christians. Virginity and extreme asceticism were exceptional statements of a life devoted to God. They were not an option open to everyone. Antony and Symeon Stylites the Younger shared one characteristic: they were both orphans at an early age and could therefore avoid following in their fathers' footsteps in society. Monastic lifestyles touched only a minority of Christians and even when, through preaching, monastic values reached the ears of the crowds, it is not clear whether they felt concerned.[5]

We also have to be careful to remember that most of the prominent figures among the saints, such as the stylites, were not offered as an example to follow but as one to admire. The way they treated their bodies, working to make them transparent to the presence of God, visible signs of the ability to overcome the natural limits of one's physical nature through God's grace, was not the only way to create a lifelong relationship with God. It was not the only path to holiness.[6] Henry Maguire has shown that the Byzantines were aware of the differences between the bodies of different sorts of saint.[7] Different degrees of corporeality or immateriality displayed on images of saints corresponded to their different lifestyles. Soldier saints were represented with more bodily presence and movement than monks.[8] These later iconographic divergences direct us to pay attention to the diversity of Christian lifestyles. To study common attitudes through the lens of monastic texts alone leaves open the question of what were the expected bodily attitudes in the sight of God among those Christians who lived and reproduced in the world.

There are other ways of exploring the subject. Aline Rousselle has used Greek and Roman medical literature to reconstruct ideas about the moulding of the body and the sensory education of élite young Romans.[9] She has also paid attention to the voice-training of the educated layman.[10] Maud Gleason has taken this one step further and asked what constituted an appropriate

---

[5] J. Beaucamp's *Le statut de la femme à Byzance (4e–7e siècle)* (Paris, 1990–92) draws attention to the fact that monastic life was not the concern of the majority by the few pages devoted to monastic women.

[6] M. Van Uyfthanghe, 'L'origine, l'essor et les fonctions du culte des saints. Quelques repères pour un débat rouvert', *Cassiodorus* 2 (1996), 143–96, and in the same volume, Peter Brown's revision of his views on the holy man, 'Arbiters of Ambiguity: A Role of the Late Antique Holy Man', 123–42.

[7] H. Maguire, *The Icons of their Bodies. Saints and their Images in Byzantium* (Princeton, 1996).

[8] Maguire, *Icons of their Bodies*, 49–50.

[9] A. Rousselle, *Porneia: de la maîtrise du corps à la privation sensorielle* (Paris, 1983); Eng. tr. F. Pheasant, *Porneia* (Oxford, 1988).

[10] A.Rousselle, 'Parole et inspiration: le travail de la voix dans le monde romain', *History and Philosophy of the Life Sciences* 5 (1983), 129–57, and also *La contamination spirituelle, science, droit et religion dans l'Antiquité* (Paris, 1998), 87–114.

deportment for men of the high Roman Empire and the training imposed on them in order to achieve it.[11] Works such as these invite us to read religious sources of Late Antiquity in a different light and to reconsider what might have been the non-monastically rooted attitudes towards the body and its desires. If we stop focusing on ideas about virginity and ask the sources about gestures, bodily attitudes, and the use of the senses in a religious environment, quite a different picture of the body emerges from that offered by scholars of the virginal life. In what manner did the Church invite Christians, including the *kosmikoi*, married men and women and soon-to-be-married children, to use their bodies in sacred spaces?

One avenue of approach is to balance the normative discourse of Christian pastors on the senses with the religious experiences involving the senses revealed by liturgical sources, sermons and saints' lives. My research on the use of incense and perfume in churches reveals a striking contrast between the insistence on the necessity of a strict control over the senses in the world and the richness of sensory experiences offered to the faithful in church.[12] The chronology of this is particularly interesting: the tightening of the discourse on sensory control appears at the exact time that the field of sensory experiences expands in churches. Moreover, the senses were considered a tool by which to know God and teach the faithful about the unseen realities of the other world.[13] The sweetness of the perfumes of Paradise was rendered by the fragrance of incense and the perfumes burning in the oil of the numerous lamps in churches; the music of the angels was echoed by the singing choirs and the warmth of human voices praising God. In richly decorated churches, the contrast between the cold, smooth marbles and the warm softness of coloured textiles hanging around doors, windows and sometimes between columns was striking.[14] The lights flowing from windows and lamps, the colours of the mosaics, the geometry and the volumes of the different spaces inside Christian sanctuaries fostered a sensory approach to God and his court of angels and saints.

Specific rituals were also created for the faithful to express their instant recognition of the sacrality of religious spaces through their own bodies. Touch, in particular, was the sense used to show love and respect for the divine persons, the saints and the sacred space itself. Kisses on doors,

---

[11] M.W.Gleason, *Making Men. Sophists and Self-preservation in Ancient Rome* (Princeton, 1995).

[12] B. Caseau, *Euodia: The Use and Meaning of Fragrances in the Ancient World and their Christianization (100–900)* (Ann Arbor, 1994).

[13] On the role of the body as an instrument for knowing God, see A. Guillaumont, *Les "kephalaia gnostica" d'Evagre le Pontique et l'histoire de l'origénisme chez les Grecs et chez les Syriens* (Paris, 1962), 110–13; S. Ashbrook-Harvey, 'St Ephrem and the Scent of Salvation', *JTS* 49 (1998), 109–28.

[14] M. Flury Lemberg, *Textile Conservation and Research* (Bern, 1988).

columns and icons, gestures involving the whole body such as bowing, kneeling, prostrating, all presented diverse responses to the sacred in church. Unlike rituals organized for them by the clergy, these gestures allowed a personal input for the faithful who could communicate their religious feelings to the divine as well as to members of their own community present in church at the same time. This personal touch had to respect a grammar of acceptable gestures, that came to be defined regionally, but inside this grammar there was a relative freedom of expression for each individual.[15] The historical study of the senses is still in its infancy and it is not the purpose of this chapter to present a full investigation of the religious use of the senses.[16] However, I wish here to draw attention to the particular and complex role of perfume and the sense of smell in early Byzantine Christianity.[17]

Let us take two examples of normative discourse on the Christian use and control of the senses. If we compare Clement of Alexandria (c.150–c.215) with John Chrysostom (c.354–407), who both wrote on sense education for young Christians, it is easy to see a tightening of the discourse. The two writers follow similar lines on the appreciation of the body and assert that God's creation should be treated with respect, but they diverge on what constitutes a reasonable use of the senses. Chrysostom advises that the young should be kept in an environment as deprived of sensory experiences as possible; Clement calls for caution but does not suggest keeping the Christian completely out of touch with the common practices of Alexandrian society.

In the *Paedagogus*, on the subject of the senses, Clement has a balanced position.[18] He promotes control of the senses and avoidance of sensuality, but he refuses to contemplate complete asceticism. On perfumes, for example, he acknowledges the link between the pleasure created by sweet-smelling perfumes and an inclination towards other bodily pleasures.

---

[15] For the Western medieval church, J.C. Schmitt offers a synthesis on religious gestures, *La raison des gestes dans l'Occident médiéval* (Paris, 1990). See also F. Garnier, *Le language de l'image au Moyen Age. Signification et symbolique* (Paris, 1982). For Byzantium, see C. Walter, *Art and Ritual of the Byzantine Church* (London, 1982).

[16] D.Howes, review article, 'Scent and Sensibility', *Culture, Medicine and Psychiatry* 13 (1989), 91–7.

[17] It is now possible to refer to a general, diachronic approach to smell: C. Classen, D. Howes, A. Synott, *Aroma: The Cultural History of Smell* (New York, 1994). See also A. Le Guérer, *Les pouvoirs de l'odeur* (Paris, 1998); J.P.Albert, *Odeurs de sainteté: la mythologie chrétienne des aromates* (Paris, 1990).

[18] I use and refer here to the Greek text and French translation, *Clément d'Alexandrie. Le Pédagogue*, intro. H.I. Marrou (Paris, 1960), vol. 1, tr. M. Harl (1960); vol. 2, tr. M. Mondésert (1991); vol. 3, trs C. Mondésert and C. Matray (1970); Eng. tr. S.P. Wood, *The Instructor* (New York, 1953).

Clement, aware of the association between perfumes and eroticism, notes that there can be danger in smelling some perfumes at night-time and in letting the open door of the senses experience too much pleasure. To warn Christian males against perfumes, Clement raises the traditional bogeys of effeminate charm and unmanly softness: perfumes have a relaxing power, they make the body soft and limp. Although he tries to find a Christian meaning for perfumes – he recalls that Christ himself was anointed with perfumes by a woman, and was pleased about it – he sticks to the familiar invectives of gender deviance to condemn the passion for perfumes of some of his contemporaries. By asserting that perfumes belong to the world of women and should be avoided by men, he shows his allegiance to the Roman thought-world so well-described by Gleason. He mocks women who wish to have everything around them perfumed, but thereby admits that perfumes are part of a woman's world and points in the direction of a moderate use of perfumes for Christian women. The reproach of crossing the gender boundaries for well-bred males is, however, soon replaced by a Christian analysis of the body as God's creation. Clement teaches that Christians must be respectful of the body, by which he means, above all, that they should keep it as God created it. To women, he gives the advice not to use make-up or anything artificial, for it covers God's beautiful creation. To men, in a similar manner, he recommends keeping the body as God has intended it to be, warm and hairy. Men should not use depilatory creams or colour their hair. Perfumes belong to the world of unnecessary substances added to an already perfect creation.

However, Clement refuses to reject all perfumes completely. Some fragrances are useful for one's health. They have a good impact on the brain, they help the stomach work better and they warm up the nervous system in a beneficial way. Clement shares with his society an understanding of the positive impact of what we now call aromatherapy. In ancient medicine, as well as in common lore, some odours were deemed to be relaxing, others to bring actual cures. Recipes of various medicines included fragrant gums and resins, whose power to cure lay in their smell.[19] Clement, for example, recommends placing perfumes on the nose to cure the common cold. So, although he chooses to ask for caution when using perfumes, he does not opt for a perfumeless environment for the young. Perfumes have a role to play in Christian households. They can have an allegorical meaning for Christians, who are invited to see in them the image of virtue and the fragrance of Christ's divine nature. However, no mention of any Christian religious use of perfumes appears in Clement's text. In his time, incense was

---

[19] B.Caseau, 'Les usages médicaux de l'encens et des parfums. Un aspect de la médecine populaire antique et de sa christianisation', *Air, miasmes et contagion* (forthcoming).

used in pagan sacrifices and avoided by the faithful. The oil of baptism seems simply to have been olive oil with no addition of perfumes.[20]

Turning now to John Chrysostom, two centuries later, the discourse on the senses, in particular the sense of smell, and on perfumes, has changed. In his treatise *On vainglory and the education of children*, Chrysostom offers his advice to Christian parents about how to raise young boys.[21] Superficially, it looks very similar to Clement's. Chrysostom compares the soul of a child to a city. The senses are the gates of this city. Parents should control what comes in, because the senses are also the gates of desires and pleasures. Smell is the first sense that Chrysostom denounces as dangerous. Like Clement, he warns of the relaxing powers of perfumes, and like Clement, he notes medical lore on the effect of perfume on the mind. The difference between them lies in the fact that Chrysostom emphasizes only the dangers of smelling perfumes and getting aroused by them. Unlike Clement, he has no space for safe, useful perfumes that can be employed in different therapies for various ailments as well as for general well-being. Instead, he denounces all perfumes as irrevocably dangerous: they act on the brain and soften the body, lighting up desires. As a consequence, no Christian child should ever be given the opportunity to smell a perfume.

A similar rigid attitude is found in his approach to the other senses. A strict control over what is seen and heard should be enforced. No lascivious poses or stories should pollute the soul. A tight surveillance over what the child touches should also be maintained. The child should have nothing soft, clothes or blankets. No physical contacts should be allowed between the child and other people. Sensory deprivation is therefore strongly recommended to Christian parents who wish to raise Christian children. The control of the passions and in particular of sexual desires is at stake here. The goal is moral purity during childhood, the teenage years and married adulthood. The recommendations of Chrysostom are particularly interesting, for they concern young Christians destined to be married, not future monks, although he admits he wishes a monastic vocation to all.

If we were to stop the investigation of the senses with these normative discourses, we would conclude that early Byzantine writers wanted, at all costs, to close all gates to pleasurable experiences and that they denied any kind of sensory experience to Christians in search of holiness. The relationship between individual and body was one of strict control over the

---

[20] The oldest liturgical sources of Armenian and Syriac origin never refer to the oil as myron, but use a word meaning olive oil. G.Winkler, 'The Original Meaning of Prebaptismal Anointing and its Implications', *Worship* 52 (1978), 24–5.

[21] A.M. Malingrey, ed., *Jean Chrysostome, Sur la vaine gloire et l'éducation des enfants* (Paris, 1972); Eng. tr. M.L.W. Laistner, *Christianity and Pagan Culture in the Later Roman Empire* (Ithaca, 1951).

senses, keeping them closed to any external influences which could entice the believer to sin through the sights, sounds, smells and touches of the world. Church Fathers could not condemn any part of the body, since this would amount to criticizing God's creation, but they could warn against the fallen nature of human desires. The senses were the main gate through which sinful desires took form; through them, all worldly pleasures reached the soul and polluted it. In this discourse, there was only a thin line between laymen and monks.

However, a different view is apparent in saints' lives and liturgical sources. Inside churches, around the persons of saints and their relics, the senses were deeply involved and participated in a complex process of communication with the divine world. It is interesting to note that the first certain reference to incense burning in churches is contemporary with Chrysostom's treatise on vainglory. This was written in the 380s, at the same time that the pilgrim Egeria was both impressed and charmed by the sweet-smelling incense floating in the church of the Anastasis in Jerusalem at Easter.[22] The use of incense was one of many ways to involve the senses in the process of approaching and knowing God. The appeal of these rich sensory experiences is apparent from texts, such as John Chrysostom's complaint that the faithful paid more attention to lamps being lit than to the words of Scripture being read to them.

The testimonies on the sensory experiences offered to Christians inside churches expands considerably between the late fourth and the seventh centuries. Smell was particularly important in signifying the place of the church in the other world. It was of great significance that the inner space of consecrated buildings smelt good. The fragrance floating in the air was meant to remind worshippers of Paradise, of holiness, and of God's approval for one's orthodoxy and form of worship. A multi-layered symbolism mixed images of the divine with a sense of material and physical security.

One of the most common ways to spread fragrances in the air of Christian churches was to pour perfumes into lamps. Nard oil and balsamic oils were poured into the lamps of Roman basilicas, according to the text of the *Liber Pontificalis*, creating a fragrant source of light.[23] Censers were a further source of fragrance. In major churches, it appears that censers were originally fixed around the sanctuary. Here again, Constantine's donation described in the *Liber Pontificalis* mentions censers of finest gold to perfume the new Roman churches. By the second half of the fifth century, even a

---

[22] *Itinerarium Egeriae*, 24.10., ed. P. Maraval (Paris, 1982), 242; Eng. tr. G.E. Gingras, *Egeria: Diary of a Pilgrimage* (New York, 1970).

[23] *Liber Pontificalis*, ed. L. Duchesne, *Le liber pontificalis* (Paris, 1955); Eng. tr. R. Davis, *The Book of Pontiffs* (Liverpool, 1989).

country church, such as the Italian church which received a donation from
Fl. Valila in 471, could count a censer among the precious vessels kept in
its treasury. From this, one can assume that incense was freely available.

Incense and perfumed air not only welcomed the faithful. They also
belonged to the list of gifts appropriate to offer at the shrines of saints.
Fragrant offerings on the tomb and fragrant emanations from the holy place
mingled, creating a source of healing and miracles, a place of the epiphany
of the divine, testified to by the odour of sanctity. Paulinus of Nola invited
the faithful to decorate the shrine of St. Felix for his *natalis* in 397. He
describes the white curtains adorning the threshold, the countless fragrant
lamps ablaze night and day, the blossoms strewn on the floor and the
garlands on the martyr's tomb.[24] Such practices continued in Byzantine
times. The sixth century *Acts of the Egyptian Martyrs* record that before their
martyrdom, saints Apater and Irai had a vision of Christ accompanied by
this promise: 'Even in the case of serious sinners, if, on the day of your
festival on earth, they care to offer to your holy place either bread or wine
or incense or sacred vessels or oil, I shall wash away their sins and I shall
give their persons to you.'[25]

In the martyria where incubation was practised, censers were often kept
at the disposal of the faithful, who began their prayers by offering incense
to the saint. It was a reminder that the saint was perfumed in Paradise, and
was also a conciliatory offering before asking a favour. The mother of
Symeon Stylites the Younger went to the sanctuary of John the Baptist
outside the walls of Antioch to ask for a child. She took a censer and threw
a large quantity of incense into it, so that the whole church was redolent
of its strong perfume.[26] This practice of placing incense before saints'
tombs is also recorded in the West, by Gregory of Tours among others. It
may be that the habit of starting prayers with incense had spread to
churches from martyria. This would explain two texts from the *Liber
Pontificalis* that have puzzled commentators.[27] One claims that Pope Soter
(162–70) forbade monks to offer incense in the holy church. The other
asserts that Pope Bonifacius (418–22) forbade women and nuns to offer
incense in church. This offering should only be carried out by a priest. It
is clear that in the time of Soter, incense was not offered in churches by
clergy because of the links with pagan religious practice. By the time of
Bonifacius, the problem was not pagan religion but women, suggesting a
wider spread of the practice. Both texts, however, reveal a rising prevalence

[24] Paulinus of Nola, *Poem* 14, ed. G. de Hartel (Vienna, 1894); Eng. tr. P.G. Walsh, *The Poems of St Paulinus of Nola* (New York, 1975).
[25] *Actes des martyrs de l'Egypte*, ed. and tr. H. Hyvernat (Hildesheim and New York, 1977), 92–93 (reprint of 1886 edn).
[26] *La vie ancienne de S.Syméon Stylite le Jeune*, ed. P. Van den Ven (Brussels, 1962).
[27] *Liber Pontificalis*, ed. Duchesne, 135.

of private incense offerings in churches, a practice which bothered the Roman clergy of the late sixth century when the text was composed. It might even be that these passages reflect a sixth-century disquiet with this particular practice, if the historical background of this period is also taken into account.

What this brief investigation of the fragrant world of early Byzantine churches reveals is that the senses were clearly used as instruments of communication with the divine. In that context, pleasurable sensory experiences were allowed and even encouraged. This is far from the image of a disincarnated or disembodied Christianity. On the contrary, private and public devotions involved the body and offered spiritual experiences which were not abstract or intellectual, but which were very physical and called for the full use of the senses. It is possible to conclude that in Byzantium, neither desire nor pleasure were cancelled or denied; rather, they were transferred to different objects.

11. Writing on the body:
memory, desire, and the holy in iconoclasm

Charles Barber

In July of 836, two brothers, the Palestinian monks Theodore and Theophanes, suffered an unusual punishment. In the course of debating the question of the legitimacy of religious icons with the Emperor Theophilos, the two saints, at the emperor's command, are reported to have had verses inscribed upon their foreheads. These read as follows:

> When all men long to speed towards the town,
> Wherein the Word of God's all-holy feet
> Once stood to succour and preserve the world,
> These men were seen within the sacred place,
> Foul vessels of perverted heresy.
> There the villains did many shameful deeds,
> Through lack of faith and impiousness of mind,
> Until they were driven forth as apostates.
> But fleeing to our city, seat of power,
> They did not lay down their lawless foolishness.
> So, inscribed like criminals on the brow
> They are condemned and chased off once more.[1]

The poem proclaims that the brothers were branded and exiled as criminals because of their heretical views, their heresy being the support of icons

---

[1] The poem is found in *The Life of Michael the Synkellos*, ed. and tr. M.B. Cunningham (Belfast, 1991), 86. The translation is Anna Wilson's, Cunningham, *Life*, 87 note 145. The *Life* provides a full account of the events surrounding the torture of the brothers. While a number of sources offer reports on these events (see Cunningham, 7–8), the fullest comparable text is that of Theophanes of Caeasarea, J.-M. Featherstone, 'The Praise of Theodore Graptos by Theophanes of Caesarea', *AB* 98 (1980), 93–150. Only the *Theodore Psalter* (London, British Library, Additional 19.352, fol. 120v) and the *Barberini Psalter* (Rome, Vatican Library, Barberinianus gr. 372 fol. 155r) show the act of inscription. Other representations of the saints: *Menologion of Basil II* (cod. Vaticano greco 1613) and Mount Athos, Lavra D 51, fol. 156r are without narrative content. A visual narrative of the tortures of the monks is available in the Madrid *Skylitzes* (Madrid, Biblioteca Nacional, MS Vitr. 26–2, fol. 51v).

111

during a period of official iconoclasm.[2] This specific form of punishment, this act of bodily inscription, was an appropriate gesture at this point in the unfurling history of Byzantine iconoclasm as it placed the body at the centre of the values ascribed to representation. The following consideration of the relationship between memory and the holy, as outlined during the period of iconoclasm, will indicate a role for the saint's body in this debate. This should not surprise, as the body was an essential element in the definitions of Christ's representation that were debated at this time.[3] But in extending the argument so that it incorporated the saints an additional ethical theme was introduced into Byzantine theories of representation. It is this development that will be mapped in this chapter.

One of the earliest, and longest-running defences of Christian religious imagery is that painting can serve as an aide-memoire. In terms of Byzantine Christian writing the implications of this defence were richly explored in the mid-seventh century works of Leontios of Neapolis and those who came after him. For Leontios the image was a sign of the physical reality that is at the origin of memory, a point that within his text privileges the incarnate Christian God.[4] John of Damascus, for one, developed this thesis in his defences of the icons. In his first *Oration on the Icons*, perhaps dateable to c.730, he argued that: 'The saints during their earthly lives were filled with the holy spirit and when they fulfil their course, the grace of the holy spirit does not depart from their souls or their bodies in the tombs, or from their likenesses and holy images; not by the nature of these things, but by grace and power.'[5] The saints are thus worthy of remembrance, not only because of their deeds during their lifetimes, but also because they maintain within their bodies and their images the grace of the holy spirit that made them holy. Thus, for Leontios of Neapolis and John of Damascus, memory

---

[2] For an overview of the history of iconoclasm see J. Martin, *A History of the Iconoclastic Controversy* (London, 1930). For a recent history of this second phase of iconoclasm (815–43) see W.J.T. Treadgold, *The Byzantine Revival 780–842* (Stanford, 1988).

[3] These well-known arguments are discussed in C. Barber, 'The Body within the Frame: A Use of Word and Image in Iconoclasm', *Word and Image* 9 (1993), 140–53.

[4] The most recent edition of Leontios's text is found at V.Déroche, 'L'*Apologie contre les juifs* de Léontios de Néapolis', *TM* 12 (1994), 61–85. For the relationship between memory and the incarnation see Déroche, 'L'*Apologie*', 67 lines 30–42. For discussion of this text see now C. Barber, 'The Truth in Painting: Iconoclasm and Identity in Early-Medieval Art', *Speculum* 72 (1997), 1024–33.

[5] This passage is from John of Damascus's *First Oration on the Images*. For the Greek text see B. Kotter, ed., *Die Schriften Johannes von Damaskos*, 5 vols (Berlin, 1969–88), 3.95. Note the reservations that Kotter has regarding this text. Comparable statements on the presence of holiness can be found at 3:137–8. The English translation is from Saint John of Damascus, *On the Divine Images: Three Apologies Against Those Who Attack the Divine Images*, tr. D. Anderson (Crestwood NY, 1980), 27. From his quotations of Leontios and his redeployment of a number of Leontios's texts, it is apparent that John of Damascus draws heavily upon Leontios's text.

operates as a mark of a continuing state of being, rather than as the recall of something that is absent. As such, in their writings, both the bodies and icons of Christ and the saints remain locations of their holiness and objects suitable for worship. In effect the icon is now embraced by the notion of the relic, that has already been granted to the bodies of the saints.[6]

In response to this claim for a continuing presence of the holy within the material traces of the saints, the iconoclasts questioned the terms of this relationship between memory and its object by enquiring into the exact nature of that which is remembered. They asked: what is it that is remembered when the holy is called to memory? One of the *Enquiries* attributed to the Emperor Constantine V can represent this question. The Emperor wrote: 'Since that which concerns Christ is dispersed and dissolved, it follows also that that which concerns the saints disappears at the same time, and that that which remains is not worth remembering.'[7] In this statement Constantine's concern is the 'holy', by which his broader writings imply the transformation of the human into the divine.[8] In this regard his thinking is close to that of John of Damascus.[9] But, following on from his Christological precepts, Constantine argued that Christ's post-Resurrection body, now wholly divine, has ascended to the heavens and is thus dispersed and dissolved. In its material form the holy has now absented itself.[10] In the same passage Constantine then applies this model to the saints, and in so doing introduces a key value judgement on the status of the saint's body. He argues that there is that which concerns the saints (their holiness) and then that which remains (their bodies). Unlike John of Damascus, Constantine distinguishes between the holy, the body, and the icon. To each of these he assigns a different value.

This reading of the *Enquiries* text is guided by a clarification found in the *Horos* of the iconoclastic council of 754: 'Let, therefore, every mouth that speaks iniquities and blasphemies against our opinion and our vote, which have been approved by God, be silent. For the saints who have pleased God

---

[6] This line of argument obviously draws no distinction between a relic and an icon. This reading reflects a common correlation in the pre-iconoclastic era. See the examples in E. Kitzinger, 'The Cult of Images in the Age before Iconoclasm', *DOP* 8 (1954), 112–18 and G. Vikan, *Byzantine Pilgrimage Art* (Washington, DC, 1982).

[7] The *Peuseis* were composed by Constantine V as a preparation for the iconoclastic council held at the Hieria in 754, see G. Ostrogorsky, *Studien zur Geschichte des byzantinischen Bilderstreites* (Breslau, 1929), 7–45. Note the additions to this suggested in Nikephoros, *Discours contre les iconoclastes*, tr. M.-J. Mondzain-Baudinet (Paris, 1989), 301–2 and in *Textus byzantinos ad iconomachiam pertinentes. In usum academicum*, ed. H. Hennephof (Leiden, 1969). The text referred to here is found at *PG* 100, 469A.

[8] *PG* 100, 337CD.

[9] See my comments in C. Barber, 'From Image into Art: Art after Byzantine Iconoclasm', *Gesta* 34 (1995), 6–7.

[10] *PG* 100, 469A.

and been honoured by him with the dignity of sainthood live with God
forever, even though they have departed from here. Thus he who thinks
to reinstate them on the poles by means of a dead and accursed art which
has never been alive but rather has been invented in vanity by the adversary
pagans, proves himself blasphemous.'[11] Clearly, the saints are considered
by this text to have departed from the earth at their deaths. Even though
their bodies and other relics may remain, these have little value as the saints
are with God.[12]

The strategy in both of these iconoclastic texts is to define the location
of holiness as other than the body. As is well known, for Constantine, and
for his fellow iconoclasts of the eighth and the ninth centuries, holiness is
primarily conceived in terms of the category of the spiritual, as opposed
to that of the material.[13] Hence, the body is not worth remembering, as
holiness resides elsewhere, within the spirit. Within these terms the saints
have indeed departed. For that which made them saints, their holiness, is
with God rather than with their bodies. In the absence of this holiness, the
saints cannot be revived by means of painting, as this pertains to dead
matter, rather than the living spirit.[14]

Thus we find that for both the iconophiles and the iconoclasts the saint's
body is central to the enquiry over the legitimate object of memory and
therefore of representation. On the one hand the iconoclasts deny any
value to the body. Holiness is understood as a temporary resident of the
body, whose departure at the moment of death introduces a spiritual

[11] Mansi 13, 276D. The translation is from D.J. Sahas, *Icon and Logos: Sources in Eighth-Century Iconoclasm* (Toronto, 1986), 103.

[12] S. Gero, *Byzantine Iconoclasm during the Reign of Constantine V* (Louvain, 1977), 152–65 provides a reading of this iconoclastic material that argues for leipsanoclasm on the part of the iconoclasts.

[13] On the spiritual aspect of iconoclasm note the discussions of G.Florovsky, 'Origen, Eusebius, and the iconoclastic controversy', *Church History* 19 (1950), 77–96, Gero, *Byzantine Iconoclasm*, and especially the discussion of the iconoclastic council of 815, P.J. Alexander, 'The Iconoclastic Council of St Sophia (815) and Its Definition (*Horos*)', *DOP* 7 (1953), 35–57, M.Anastos, 'The Argument for Iconoclasm as Presented by the Iconoclastic Council of 754', *Late Classical and Mediaeval Studies in Honour of Albert Mathias Friend, Jr.*, ed. K.Weitzmann (Princeton, 1955), 177–88, and M. Anastos, 'The Ethical Theory of Images Formulated by the Iconoclasts in 754 and 815', *DOP* 8 (1954), 153–60.

[14] This question of the departure of the spirit raises an important question regarding the fate of relics during iconoclasm. If the spirit has departed from the body, then is there any value in the relics of the saints? Occasional attacks on relics appear to have taken place during the course of iconoclasm, but official iconoclast policy does not appear to have condemned the cult of relics. Indeed one might read defense of such a cult into the legislation forbidding the destruction of reliquaries found in the Horos of the council of 754. Since the cult appears to have been protected it is important to consider how this is possible, given the play of matter and spirit in the texts noted here. For a full discussion of the issues involved in the cult of relics during iconoclasm see J. Wortley, 'Iconoclasm and Leipsanoclasm: Leo III, Constantine V and the Relics,' *ByzF* 8 (1982), 253–79.

economy of memory and emulation. On the other hand, the iconophiles argued that holiness is founded upon the experience of the body as a site of the holy spirit. Thanks to this transformational experience the body remains central to the act of remembering and remains empowered by its continuing relationship to grace.

From the texts already introduced it is apparent that the centrality of the body to the discourse on the holy also impinges upon the notions of representation at play in this culture. In particular, the respective definitions of the location of holiness have an effect upon the media chosen by both sides to represent the holy. For the iconoclasts, the visual, with all of its implications of boundaries and limitations, is too close to the material aspects of religion that they are critiquing.[15] Consequently they propose verbal and symbolic forms as the legitimate media of representation.[16] For the iconophiles, the visual must be privileged because their conception of Christianity is bound to the body as the vehicle of the incarnation and as the medium of martyrdom.[17]

In the second phase of iconoclasm, the defining theoretical issue remained the possibility or the impossibility of the representation of an incarnate God. Such continuity is reflected in the council called by the Emperor Leo V in 815, where the arguments in favour of iconoclasm drew on many earlier iconoclastic theses.[18] These included the central claim that the eucharist was the only true image of Christ, and that the icon was therefore a false image. The grounds for this assertion lay in the assumption that an icon cannot represent both the divine and the human natures in Christ for fear of transgressing the Second Commandment. In contrast, Christ was wholly present in the God-given eucharist, hence this was to be identified as a true image.

Where the council of 815 was novel was in its emphasis upon an extended analysis of the nature of the falsehood identified in the icon. For the iconoclasts, the attribution of falsehood to the icon depended in part upon assigning different values to verbal and visual representation. In particular, they argued that the visual medium was an inadequate means of representing the holy, and hence it was false.[19] In place of the false or

---

[15] The relationship between the visual, the material, and boundaries is specifically addressed in the *Peuseis* at *PG* 100, 236C, 248D–249A, 253A, and 296C. In the *Horos* of 754, see Mansi 13, 252AB, 256AB, 256E–257B, 257E–260B.

[16] *PG* 100, 425D and see the discussion below.

[17] This case is clearly set forth in K. Parry, 'Theodore Studites and the Patriarch Nicephoros on Image-making as Christian Imperative', *B* 49 (1989), 164–83.

[18] The key texts on this are noted in footnote 15 above. To these should be added Nikephoros's *Refutatio et Eversio*, published as *Nicephori patriarchae constantinopolitani refutatio et eversio definitionis synodalis anni 815*, ed. J.-M. Featherstone (Turnhout and Leuven, 1997).

[19] Alexander, 'Iconoclastic Council', 59–60. This notion of the spurious icons is already found in the Horos of the Hiereia council of 754, Mansi 13, 268C.

inadequate icon the iconoclasts proposed a further interpretation of what constituted a true image. This was the imitation and embodiment of the virtues found in Christ and the saints and narrated in verbal texts. The body of the listening believer was thus to become the site for imaging holiness.[20]

The chief architect of this revived and developed thesis was John the Grammarian. A taste of his argument can be gleaned from this fragment preserved in a later refutation. For John the verbal is the superior means of representing an individual:

> It is hopeless to characterise a man, unless one has been led to this by words. When it happens that the particular features of a man are seen to be of a similar form and like those of another, it is not possible effectively to grasp them and render them by visual means. For if his people or his father are not described, nor the fact that he is blessed in his deeds, his companions and the customs of his land, all of which are made known by verbal means, and through which one might judge his worth, it follows that the visual arts are a waste of time. Hence it is impossible truthfully to discern the man by means of depictions.[21]

Here John argues that the visual is an inadequate means of representation. First, it cannot clearly differentiate between those that look alike. Second, it cannot give a complete idea of them, being limited to appearance alone and lacking the fuller descriptive habits of rhetorical representation.

The florilegium attached to the *Horos* of the iconoclastic council of 815 broadens the scope of John the Grammarian's verbal bias by using the model of encomia (as he does) to define an appropriate, adequate and verbal means of representing the saints:

> The saints do not beg for our written encomia, as they are already inscribed in the book of the living, being the righteous guarded by God. But we desire, through the darkness of writing, to make public that which has been impressed upon our minds in commemoration of them, and to know of them through hearing, so that having been uplifted by this sound we can be transported.... We do not anxiously desire that the flesh of their faces be presented to us by colours on boards, rather to imitate their truth and to repeat their good deeds and to figure the love of God and to be imitators of their good deeds; these post-mortem memories of them are inscribed in those listening so that they might know of their presence in the world.[22]

---

[20] The florilegium attached to the Horos of 815 exemplifies this attitude, particularly in the texts of Theodotos of Ankyra, Basil of Seleukia, Amphilochios of Ikonion, and John Chrysostom (Alexander, 'Iconoclastic Council', 61–2). The texts by Theodotos of Ankyra, Amphilochios of Ikonion, and John Chrysostom had already been used in the council of 754, Mansi 13, 309E, 301D, and 300A.

[21] J.Gouillard, 'Fragments Inédits d'un Antirrhétique de Jean le Grammairien', *REB* 24 (1966), 173–4.

[22] Alexander, 'Iconoclastic Council', 61, Amphilochios of Ikonion, from his *Encomion on Basil*.

and:

> ... for if a soulless icon can manifest a child or friend or relation, making present the image of the one who has gone away and bringing them to mind through this soulless image, it is even more beneficial to have the souls of the saints present in what is written, rather than having their bodies in icons: for it is their sayings that are the images of their souls.[23]

From the use of these texts it is clear that the iconoclasts privilege the verbal over the visual in correlation with a privileging of the spiritual over the material. The saints, it is claimed, are made known to us more clearly and more completely by means of words. The audience is asked to take these words into themselves, to inscribe the virtues attributed to the saints into their own living bodies.

Given this position, it is perhaps understandable that the iconoclasts chose to write on the faces of Theodore and Theophanes. The mark of the words inscribe upon their bodies the iconoclast party's assessment of their character, their criminality. In choosing this medium to present their case they make a further claim. As I have suggested, the text on their faces re-presents their bodies as those of criminals. This act of literal inscription is, in this context, also a claim on the possession of the body by verbal discourse, and so returns us to the wider context of the debate over the relative values of the verbal and the visual as modes of representation.

For the iconophiles, the body possesses holiness as a consequence of experience. This is evident in the writings of Nikephoros, who responds to the question asked by Constantine V above with a lengthy and powerful discussion of the suffering of the saints in the flesh.[24] When Nikephoros turns to the representation of this suffering he privileges the visual as a medium through which to remember that the saints embody the virtues that gave them their status as holy.[25] For the iconoclasts on the other hand, holiness belongs to a living spiritual domain that is distinct from the material world, and that can only be represented in the living body of the Christian. This relationship only has value while the body lives. With death, and the departure of the spirit, words alone remain as the medium that is adequate to the representation of the absent spirit. What the iconoclasts have tried to do is to replace the body of the departed saint with the body of the audience for the saint's life.[26]

---

[23] Alexander, 'Iconoclastic Council', 62, John Chrysostom, from his *On the Gaoler*.

[24] *PG* 100, 468D–476B.

[25] *PG* 100, 477B.

[26] I do not want to imply that the iconophiles did not also value the reading of saints' lives. Their value is made clear in the *Little Catecheses* of Theodore the Stoudite, where reference to the verbal models of holiness is repeatedly made. For example see E. Auvray, *Parva Catechesis* (Paris, 1891), 139f.

To a great extent Nikephoros has appeared to continue the use of the body to legitimate the icon that was found in John of Damascus. There is however an important difference. In the period that separates John of Damascus from Nikephoros the iconophile camp has introduced a distinct set of relational terms into their analyses of the icon.[27] The icon is now to be considered absolutely distinct from the body represented therein.

As we have seen, the iconoclasts denied the validity of visual representation on the grounds that the true subject of that representation, the holiness of the saint, was absent from the material rendering of the body. The body on its own was an unworthy object of representation, and the material icon was unfit to revive the holiness of the ones depicted therein. In response, the iconophiles needed to demonstrate that the icons of their bodies were both an adequate and a valid medium for the presentation of the saints.

The terms that made this possible can be found first in the rather complex text known as the *Adversus Constantinum Caballinum*. This iconophile tract exists in two versions, one longer and one shorter, both of which sustain a strong polemic against the iconoclastic policies of Leo III and Constantine V. The longer version of the text, that found in the *Patrologiae graeca*, probably marks the third revision of an original work composed c.730. My quote comes from the section of this text that was probably composed around 785–7.[28] The passage discusses the icons of the saints:

> I honour and embrace their holy and honourable icons; not as gods, but as a concise inscription and exegesis of their sufferings. For the icons of the saints are not only of the forms of the flesh and of discourses, but also of the suffering of the flesh. For it is through their sufferings, which Christ our God brings to an end, that they are blessed and honoured and worshipped. For if these were not brought to an end by Christ we would not inscribe their honourable icons, either in books or in churches.
>
> For many have inscribed icons of people in their homes, sometimes parents of their children, sometimes the children of their parents, through which [they manifest] their desire for (πόθον) and relation to (σχέσιν) those others, and thus they do not lose them to forgetfulness, having their inscribed icons in their houses. Whence they also embrace them, not as gods, but as was said previously, because of desire and the relationship to them.
>
> One may also follow this reasoning in regard to the icons of the saints. The martyrs have been inscribed in the churches and in books in order to indicate their beauty; [this is] for the sake of our remembrance and our love and our

---

[27] The term is used to define the expectations brought to bear on saints' images in the long version of the *Adversus Constantinum Caballinum* of ca. 785–787, *PG* 95, 313AB and in the Horos of the seventh oecumenical council of 787, Mansi 13, 377D.

[28] For discussion of the *Adversus Constantinum Caballinum* text see, M.-F. Auzépy, 'L'Adversus Constantinum Caballinum et Jean de Jérusalem', *BS* 56 (1995), 323–38, and A. Alexakis, *Codex Parisinus Graecus 1115 and Its Archetype, Dumbarton Oaks Studies* 34 (Washington, DC, 1996), 110–16.

conduct, just as it was for those nations who came to and believed in Jesus Christ. For what the Divine Scripture makes known, these [icons] also make known, and lead us quickly towards the love of God. And if indeed those afore-mentioned artful images of carnal love lead us wholly towards remembrance, then how much more bound are we to paint icons of the saints with their sufferings, of those who spilled their blood for the love of Christ.[29]

Through the repetition of the idea of suffering this text seeks to legitimate both the bodies of the saints and their representations by introducing suffering as a specific attribute of the body. It is this suffering in the body that defines the holiness of the saints. This should not surprise. John of Damascus used martyrdom as a means of introducing his notion of the transforming indwelling of the holy spirit.[30] But in the *Adversus* text this martyrdom in the flesh is the point of departure for an altogether different defence of representation.

For John of Damascus, the icon and the saint's body marked a continuing and present space for the holy. The *Adversus* text, on the other hand, sought to differentiate more clearly the locations of the holy and the icon. First, the text introduces an alternative model for the expectations of representation: 'For many have inscribed icons of people in their homes, sometimes parents of their children, sometimes the children of their parents, through which [they manifest] their desire for and relation to those others; and thus they do not lose them to forgetfulness, having their inscribed icons in their houses. Whence they also embrace them, not as gods, but, as was said previously, because of desire and the relationship to them.'

Derived from notions of family portraiture, this model deploys some important terms in its definition of the expectations of the portrait. First the text underlines the manufactured quality of the images by referring to them as inscribed icons. Second, the presence of the portrait is understood to assist memory. Third, the icon is not to be embraced as if it were divine. Fourth, the text introduces and repeats two key concepts when desire and relation are used to define the relationship between the viewer and the viewed. The portrait mediates relationships within the family group. It both marks the absence of the one portrayed and maintains the family relationship, through the promise of the likeness that the portrait presents. The second term, that of 'relation' will be developed much further in the writings of the ninth century iconophiles.[31] The first term, that of 'desire' was put to immediate use in the *Horos* of the Seventh Ecumenical Council,

---

[29] *PG* 95, 312C–313A.

[30] Kotter, *Schriften*, 3:137–8.

[31] In particular, see the discussion by M.-J. Baudinet, 'La Relation iconique à Byzance au IXe siècle d'après Nicéphore le Patriarche: un destin de l'aristotélisme', *Les Etudes philosophiques* 1 (1978), esp. 95ff.

where there is this famous definition of the proper function of the icon: 'For the more these (saints) are kept in view through their iconographic representation, the more those who look at them are lifted up to remember and to desire the prototypes.'[32] In both the *Adversus* and the *Horos* texts desire and memory are used to establish a relation to the necessarily absent figure portrayed in the icon.

The *Adversus* text then declares that this relational model is applicable to the icons of the saints when it states: 'One may follow this reasoning in regard to the icons of the saints. The martyrs have been inscribed in the churches and in books in order to indicate their beauty.' What is given to vision in these icons is the beauty of the saint; not simply their good looks, but the virtue that is inscribed in their bodies. It is this ethical theory of representation that is explored in the discussion of saints' icons in the course of the ninth century.

The problem of the portrayal of the saint's body was defined by the implications of their holiness. For both John of Damascus and Constantine V the debate over the possibility of religious representation was predicated upon the presence or absence of holiness in the body. For John of Damascus the holiness of the body remained with it for ever. This holiness extended to and was present within icons of that body. For Constantine, the close relationship between holiness and the material world that John's discussion highlighted had to be denied. Instead he proposed a strong delimitation of the boundaries separating the material and the spiritual. For him, the holy was absent from both body and icon as both were mere dead matter. The *Adversus* text offered a response to Constantine's writing by bringing a wholly different discourse to bear upon the question of holiness and its representation. The *Adversus* text praised the saint's body as a site of his holiness, a continuing witness to his suffering. But this text, in contrast to that of John of Damascus, refused to extend this notion of holiness to the icon itself. Indeed, the icon was denied as a site of present holiness and was considered in terms analogous to those of domestic portraiture. The icon was now embraced within a discourse of inscription, desire, and relation. So that through the operation of desire the relation between portrait and portrayed was cemented, such that the one portrayed, necessarily absent from his or her depiction, may never be forgotten. What the *Adversus* text discloses is a search for an economy that can contain and exploit both desire and denial in defence of the representation of the saint's body in the icon and so police and validate the icon's operation as a medium of representation.

---

[32] Mansi 13, 37

Section IV

Fine Manly Bodies

12. Passing the test of sanctity:
denial of sexuality and involuntary castration

Kathryn M. Ringrose

This paper is part of a larger project that seeks to explore the development of eunuchs as a gender category in the Byzantine empire. Eunuchs probably represent the ultimate socially constructed gender category, but we should not assume that the social expectations and roles assigned to this category of individual remained consistent over an extended period of time. In fact, if we trace changes in the way this category was constructed we can gain valuable insights into changing social structures and cultural norms within the Byzantine world.

The specific piece of the puzzle that I plan to explore in this paper involves the relationship between castrated eunuchs and the spiritual life. In the fourth century, St Basil of Caesarea wrote that the eunuch was 'damned by the knife.'[1] Yet in the tenth century, Symeon Metaphrastes reconfigured the life of the Old Testament prophet Daniel, offhandedly identifying him as a eunuch and discussing his castration.[2] Even more striking perhaps is the image of Symeon the Sanctified, a court eunuch who was allowed to live as a monk on Mount Athos. What intellectual and cultural transformations accompanied such a distinctive shift in status for eunuchs? What kinds of stereotypical language and imagery came into play as the gender-defining attributes of eunuchs changed over time and what can that change tell us about the social context of middle-period Byzantium?

The first part of this paper examines the link between voluntary celibacy and sanctity and suggests that the essentially negative images of the eunuch that pervade the sources of Late Antiquity precluded the possibility of eunuchs achieving sanctity. The second part shows that by the ninth to the twelfth centuries, attitudes and assumptions about eunuchs had changed

---

[1] Basil of Caesarea, *Letters* (Cambridge MA, 1961), 229.

[2] Symeon Metaphrastes, 'Vita S. Prophetae Daniels', *PG* 115, 371–403.

From *Desire and Denial in Byzantium*, ed. Liz James. Copyright © 1999 by the Society for the Promotion of Byzantine Studies. Published by Ashgate Publishing Ltd, Gower House, Croft Road, Aldershot, Hampshire, GU11 3HR, Great Britain.

significantly. Moreover, these changes interacted with an expansion of the ways in which the spiritual individual could achieve sanctity. Eunuchs still could not achieve sanctity through the narrowly defined process of denial of the flesh that is associated with sanctity in earlier centuries, but they could achieve sanctity through other forms of denial and selflessness. This shift was one of the various ways in which the gender construct of eunuchs was 'normalised' in the Byzantine world.

The language and imagery involved has to be approached with considerable caution. The Classical world contributed a collection of stereotypes about eunuchs to later Byzantine authors, and such stereotypes were for centuries enshrined in literary tradition and the language of vindictive discourse. In reading later diatribes against eunuchs, it is worth remembering that most of these diatribes consist of topoi drawn directly from earlier sources and were used for rhetorical effect, traditions which can be found, for example, in the writings of Claudian and Lucian.[3]

In that hostile Classical tradition, eunuchs were men who had been turned into women. Since they had lost their testicles, they had lost their 'loom weights', an old Aristotelian notion which is repeated in Galen. Their bodies' regulatory apparatus, like a loom without weights, was 'sprung', and even a well-woven physical or moral fabric could not be created on the structure that was their physical bodies. Thus, like women, they lacked balance, moral fibre and self-control. This analogy to the loom and to the assumed weaknesses of women reinforced the assumption that eunuchs could not control their desires for sexual pleasures, food or wealth. It implied that their emotions lacked the control and balance so important to the Eastern Mediterranean and Roman concept of perfect masculinity. These notions were further enshrined in Galen's theory of humours. Eunuchs, like women, were cool and moist.[4] As a result their physiology was assumed to resemble that of women not men and observers and commentators characterized them by using the negative stereotypes that classical culture applied to women. These assumptions about the physiology of eunuchs were repeated by physicians throughout the Byzantine period.

The eunuchs of the late classical period were further burdened by the fact that they were usually foreign-born and easily became a cultural 'other'. Moreover, they were almost always slaves. As a result, they were perceived to have a 'slave mentality', one which was morally deficient and untrustworthy.

---

[3] See, for example, Lucian, 'The Eunuch' in Lucian, *Works* (London and Cambridge MA, 1936), 341 and Claudian, *Works* (London and Cambridge MA, 1946), 151.

[4] Aristotle, *Generation of Animals*, 4.1.766a, 20–35, and Galen, *Opera omnia*, ed. C.G. Kuhn (Leipzig, 1821–33), 8,1. 40–1. Also M. Gleason, *Making Men: Sophists and Self-Presentation in Ancient Rome* (Princeton, 1995).

Furthermore, since eunuchs were almost always slaves and dependants, young eunuchs were exploited as passive partners in same-sex relationships with adult men. Indeed, it is likely that this issue of passivity was more important culturally than the biological sex of partners in a sexual encounter. In this context, eunuchs were thought capable of sexual pleasure. At the same time, it was assumed that they desired women and could give them pleasure, but they themselves experienced sexual frustration because they could not consummate the sexual act. In other words, in a Roman and late classical world that measured masculinity in terms of reproductive capacity and sexual dominance, eunuchs functioned as passive objects or givers of sexual pleasure.

While eunuchs were thus considered capable of sexual activity, the late Roman world also assumed that they were incapable of natural affection. In modern society, where sexual pleasure is associated with affection, this seems incongruous. In the classical world, however, affection tended to be associated with one's children and family, not one's sexual partners.

The existence of eunuchs, often in powerful positions in government, confronted the early Christian Fathers with a serious dilemma. In a world that valued celibacy, eunuchs were unquestionably celibate, at least in the sense that they could not procreate. If the real value of celibacy was to avoid emotional ties and obligations to one's extended family, then eunuchs were perfectly celibate. Yet the perception persisted that at least some eunuchs were sexually active and perhaps even experienced sexual pleasure.

Although the real goal of the celibate life was probably to avoid the complications of earthly ties, literary topoi increasingly emphasized the role of the devil, who used sexual desire to entrap men who were pursuing the celibate life. If eunuchs were sexually active, and, when young, offered sexual temptation to men attempting to achieve celibacy, and if eunuchs thus assisted the devil in his evil work, how could they possibly achieve holiness? What kind of a role could a eunuch play in the emerging structure of Christian sanctity?

Two leitmotifs emerged that affected the status and general perceptions of eunuchs. One focused on the man who achieved holiness through the renunciation of the world and family duties, the most important of which was procreation. The devil, using the beauty of women and boys as bait, and preying upon the ungovernable nature of men's genitalia, attempted to bind mankind to the world. When a holy man had overcome all sexual desires, he had defeated the devil's snares and won another battle for the heavenly kingdom. The signs of victory for the holy man were the inactivity of his sexual organs and the absence of wet dreams. The eunuch was perceived to be unable to participate in this drama. He could not be tempted by the devil, nor could he display the outward signs of victory over the devil.

The other motif focused on the moral duties of the Christian holy man and teacher working within the world. A holy man who wished to serve women and children in the church had to be above all sexual reproach. Whether the holy man was guilty or not, the devil would whisper accusations of sexual sin against him in order to entrap him and frustrate his efforts. The only effective defence against this was perfect, easily demonstrable, celibacy. Stories of religious figures who had themselves castrated for this reason appear in Late Antique sources – Origen is certainly the best known, but there are others. This is not a particularly surprising topos since the medical techniques needed to accomplish a kind of vasectomy or the excision of one or both the testicles were a part of the surgical literature of the period.

This castration motif spawned a hagiographical topos in Late Antique and Byzantine sources, in which a woman who is posing as a man is accused of fathering a child and is ultimately revealed as a woman and incapable of the deed.[5] The companion to this is the tale told about the Patriarch Methodios, a man who at the instigation of the devil is accused of fathering a child. He publicly displays his mutilated genitalia and proves that he is a eunuch and thus incapable of the deed.[6]

While castration might have appeared to be a practical solution to these questions of propriety, it flew in the face of long-standing norms regarding the integrity of the body, and especially the priestly body. It also defied Roman legislation that forbade the mutilation of the genitalia of any male Roman citizen.[7]

Faced with these two emerging motifs – achieving sanctity through victory over one's sexuality and castration for the sake of holy service – and their implications, the Church Fathers of Late Antiquity wrestled with two serious theological problems regarding eunuchs. First, could a castrated man achieve true holiness, since the measure of holiness was determined by each man's ability to control his sexual desires? In other words, did eunuchs 'cheat' because they were not born to 'struggle' to achieve the celibacy that is central to sanctity? Second, is the act of castration an 'unnatural' act, an act that violates the physical integrity of the body? Can religious duty justify this act or is it, like murder, socially unacceptable? This second question leads to a thicket of discussion regarding changing cultural definitions of 'nature' and the cultural relativism of the 'natural' versus the 'unnatural'. This paper will concentrate on the first question: did eunuchs 'cheat', or could denial somehow play a part in their lives?

---

[5] See, for example, the life of St Mary/Marinos, in the excellent translation of Nicholas Constas in *Holy Women of Byzantium*, ed. A.-M. Talbot (Washington, 1996), 9.

[6] The tale of Methodios' sterility appears in almost all the historians who discuss his patriarchate, Theophanes Continuatus, ed. I. Bekker (Bonn, 1838), 4.158; John Skylitzes, *Synopsis Historiarum*, ed. A. Thurn (New York, 1973), 1.52, 86.

[7] *Corpus Iuris Civilis, Codex Justinianus*, vol.2, ed. P. Krueger (Dublin, 1954), chap. 42.

The Church Fathers, faced with this question, of course looked to the Old and New Testaments for guidance. They looked at Isaiah 56, 'Let not the foreigner who has joined himself to the Lord say "The Lord will surely separate me from his people" and let not the eunuch say "Behold, I am a dry tree." For thus says the Lord: "To the eunuchs who keep my sabbaths, who choose the things that please me and hold fast my covenant, I will give in my house and within my walls a monument and a name better than sons and daughters; I will give them an everlasting name which shall not be cut off."' This 'eunuch as dry tree or twig' metaphor continues and was subjected to interesting modifications in twelfth-century Byzantium. The Church Fathers also asked why the eunuch of Queen Candaces (Acts 8: 26–40) could achieve such honour, given that he was a eunuch. They wrote endless glosses on Matthew 19:12, 'For there are eunuchs who have been so from birth, and there are eunuchs who have been made eunuchs by men, and there are eunuchs who have made themselves eunuchs for the sake of the kingdom of heaven.' This passage led them to ask questions about what a eunuch was, what was the relationship between castrated men and those who forced themselves to be celibate, and who among the above could enter the kingdom of heaven and achieve true sanctity.

These Late Antique commentaries on Biblical texts regarding eunuchs all illustrate the fact that 'eunuch' is a very general term that applies to a great variety of non-reproductive individuals. By the fourth century, as an omnibus term, 'eunuch' was applied to men who were born with seriously deformed sexual organs or undescended testicles. It was also applied to men who had no natural sexual desires, and in fact such men were considered especially blessed by God. It was the usual designation for castrated men, and reflected their non-reproductive condition, not the nature of their mutilation. Finally, it was becoming the designation of celibate holy men and women. Specific labels for different kinds of eunuchs did not appear in Byzantium until the tenth century.

Most Late Antique and Byzantine commentators assumed that Matthew 19:12 should be interpreted literally. In their interpretation, the passage was assumed to apply to three categories of men, those who were born without sexual desire, a particularly blessed state, those who had been castrated by others, and those who chose to remain celibate. Epiphanios in the *Panarion* sets up his categories in a slightly different way. He says that the passage refers to three groups of people, those castrated involuntarily by others, those who have castrated themselves, something he sees as a wicked act contrary to the power of Christ, and celibate men who 'imitate the angels'.[8] In the same vein, Clement of Alexandria offers an elaborate classification scheme

---

[8] Epiphanios, *Panarion*, in K. Holl, *Die Griechischen Christlichen Schriftsteller der Ersten Drei Jahrhunderte* 2 (Leipzig, 1915), 361.

for eunuchs. Using the term in its broad definition, he distinguishes between 1) those men born without desire for women; 2) those born without fully functioning sexual organs or those who are made eunuchs 'of necessity' by others; and 3) those who conquer their own bodies through the practice of celibacy.[9] Eusebios comments that Origen took Matthew 19:12 too literally when he castrated himself as a way of achieving celibacy.[10]

Athanasios glosses the passage by dividing eunuchs into two groups, one of which includes people castrated by other men 'for the sake of the kingdom of women, to guard them and be conspicuous over others', a worldly goal of which Athanasios disapproves. Where this group is concerned, Athanasios is almost certainly thinking of servants of aristocratic households or the court. He is reiterating two standard charges against castrated eunuchs, that they live in the soft and effeminate world of women, not in the open, public world of men, and that they attempt to overcome their sexual deficiencies by behaving arrogantly.

Athanasios' second group is made up of those who castrated themselves.[11] In this context, when he talks about men castrating themselves, he is using the phrase in its metaphorical sense and saying that these individuals are electing to ignore their sexual natures and live the celibate life for the sake of the kingdom of heaven. For Athanasios, this is the highest goal to which a man can aspire. Epiphanios echoes Athanasios' negative opinion about castrated eunuchs by saying that 'These [eunuchs castrated by men] cannot be foremost in faith'. He goes on by saying that those who 'castrate themselves for the sake of the kingdom of heaven' are men who, though remaining whole in body, practice celibacy as the apostles did. These will enter the kingdom of heaven.[12]

Similarly, John Chrysostom divides eunuchs into two groups, those castrated by other men and those who castrate themselves, again metaphorically, and live the celibate life.[13] Those in the former group, he says, deserve no reward for their virtue, since their enforced celibacy comes from having their nature imposed upon them, not from their own efforts. The latter group will be crowned in heaven because its members have practised celibacy through their own efforts, for the sake of the kingdom of heaven. Chrysostom goes on to suggest that castration is the devil's work, since it injures God's creation and allows men to fall into sin.

---

[9] Clement of Alexandria, *Stromata*, Book I–IV, eds O. Stahlin and L. Fruchtel (Berlin, 1985), 3.1.

[10] Eusebius, *Ecclesiastical History* 6, 29.

[11] Athanasios, *Homily on the Song of Songs*, PG 27, 1332.

[12] Epiphanios, *Panarion*, ed. Holl, vols 1–3; *Ancoratus und Panarion*, in *Die Griechischen Christlichen*, nos 25, 31, 37 (Leipzig, 1915, 1922, 1933), II, 360.8.

[13] John Chrysostom, *Homily XXXV on Ch. XIV of Genesis*, PG 58, 599.

Epiphanios agrees with Chrysostom when he says rather explicitly: 'It doesn't matter whether castration is done by oneself or by another. It still doesn't count towards sanctity. It still isn't done "for the sake of the kingdom of heaven". He (the castrated eunuch) has failed to win the prize or win the game, since he has not achieved grace by shedding his own power, but rather has destroyed his sexual desire through the removal of those parts that lie under his penis. He who mutilates his own limb is like one who cuts down another's vineyard, for he does not do this in accordance with law, but in accordance with a plan which is counter to the holy power of Christ.'[14]

Gregory of Nazianzos puts another hostile twist on his gloss of this passage. For him, the first group consists of men born as eunuchs, the second of men who have been taught celibacy by others, the third of men who have the spiritual power to teach themselves celibacy. Castrated eunuchs have no place at all in Gregory's gloss.[15]

So, by the end of the fourth century, as celibacy is becoming an increasingly important measure of sanctity, the castrated eunuch is being denied participation in the holy life. This is because the eunuch was perceived to be an individual who did not have to confront the sort of personal spiritual effort required of a whole man striving for true celibacy. Furthermore, since eunuchs were perceived to belong to a class of individual that was associated with sexual sin and worldliness, their mutilation was perceived to be 'against nature', contrary to God's plan, and perhaps even a part of a trap set by the devil himself.

The evils of eunuchs are summed up in Basil of Caesarea's vituperative letter to Simplicia. The tone of the letter is so angry and negative that some scholars have even suggested that a churchman like Basil could not have written it. I think that he could have. The angry rhetoric about eunuchs used by Basil is standard for Late Antiquity, and is aimed at a group he has clearly dismissed as less than human. Basil says that the eunuch is damned by the knife, and although he is chaste, his chastity will go unrewarded. He claims that eunuchs cannot make moral judgements because 'their feet are twisted'.[16] Backward feet are a sign of being in league with the forces of evil, particularly the devil. Finally, he claims that eunuchs experience sexual passion, they rave with passion, yet this passion cannot achieve fruition.

Basil articulates most of the important negative charges levelled against eunuchs in late antiquity. Because they are castrated they can never achieve salvation. This is the case because they need not fight against their sexual

---

[14] Epiphanios, *Panarion*, 2. 362, 1.7.
[15] Gregory of Nazianzos, *Discours* 32–7, ed. C. Moreschini (Paris, 1985), 305.
[16] Basil, *Letters*, 229.

passions in pursuit of true celibacy. In other words, they 'cheat'. They are part of the devil's scheme to undermine God's plan for man's salvation and as such, their moral judgement cannot be trusted. Moreover, though castrated, they are subject to sexual passion. Basil's writings were widely read, especially by later churchmen and this letter was cited as the definitive word on eunuchs.[17] It was a key part of the repertoire of negative stereotypes available to any later author disposed to be critical of eunuchs.

As we pursue the issues of sanctity and the moral attributes of eunuchs into the Byzantine period, we find that while there is rich source material for the fifth and sixth centuries, these sources rarely talk about eunuchs who are also church men or holy men. The seventh century is thin indeed. By the ninth and tenth centuries, however, we have a variety of hagiographical sources that illuminate parts of the problem, but the issues we are addressing here are not raised in a comprehensive way until the early twelfth century. At that moment we have some remarkable writings of the theologian and essayist Theophylact of Ochrid, particularly his discussion of Matthew 19:12 and his essay the *Defence of Eunuchs*. The latter, presented as a full-blown dialogue, is a piece written for his brother, who was both a eunuch and a cleric on the staff of Hagia Sophia.[18]

By Theophylact's day, 'eunuch' had been accepted as a general omnibus term for non-reproductive men and women of all sorts. Within this large group, castrated men were identified using specific terminology such as 'crushed' or 'cut', terms that describe their mutilation. Thus, when Theophylact writes his gloss on Matthew 19:12, he does so in terms which are very similar to those of Gregory of Nazianzus. Eunuchs 'born as eunuchs' are those who are born lacking sexual desire or functioning genitalia. Those who are made eunuchs by men are those who have learned celibacy from others. Those who are 'eunuchs for the kingdom of heaven' are those who have been able to teach themselves celibacy. In this gloss, Theophylact does not mention castrated men at all. I believe that this represents an important shift in the rhetorical approach to eunuchs in general and to castrated men in particular. For Theophylact, the biblical passage refers to men, castrated or not. It is part of his overall strategy, apparent in the *Defence of Eunuchs*, of presenting eunuchs as individuals whose souls are untouched by the physical nature of their bodies. For Theophylact, there are good and bad eunuchs just as there are good and bad men; the physical fact of castration has no effect on the quality of an individual's soul.

In the *Defence of Eunuchs*, he reminds his readers that the term 'eunuch' covers a wide variety of individuals. Some are castrated, some are not. Some

[17] See, for example, John of Damascus's collection of texts relevant to eunuchs, including Basil's letter to Simplicia, *PG* 95, 1564.

[18] *Theophylacte d'Achride, Discours, traites, poésies et lettres*, ed. P. Gautier (Thessalonike, 1980–86), 291–331 [hereafter *Defence of Eunuchs*].

are honourable, celibate men, some are not. He applauds the virtues of
castrated saints, bishops and patriarchs, while acknowledging the faults of
eunuchs of the palace and theatre. His central message encourages others
to examine eunuchs on a case by case basis. While admitting that eunuchs
are aided in their chastity by their castration, he argues that celibacy is still
for them a matter of personal choice between good and evil.

His position regarding the act of castration is startling in view of both
modern and Late Antique attitudes to the topic. He maintains that there are
two sorts of castration with very different motivations. The first is castration
that is done to an adult of his own volition. This, he says, is wrong, a sin
equal to murder and against nature. I suspect that Theophylact's real
objection to this kind of castration is that it represents a voluntary change
in a man's gender assignment after he passes puberty. For Theophylact, this
was culturally unacceptable.

The second kind of castration is, however, laudable. This is castration that
is arranged for a young child by a concerned parent acting to enable a child
to fulfil God's plan for him. This kind of castration is not an unnatural act
that violates nature because these eunuchs live beyond nature. God has a
plan for each man and His plan for the celibate man is that he be made
fruitful outside the world of sexuality and fertility. To assure this fruitfulness
beyond nature, a young child, like a growing vine tended by a careful
farmer, must be pruned. Here we have a very different, positive interpretation of the traditional 'dry twig or tree' imagery so often used about
eunuchs.

I suspect that Theophylact can place this second type of castration in a
separate mental category because he perceive prepubescent children as
unformed, malleable beings, destined to be moulded by forces outside
their own control. The idea that society moulds a male child into a model
of perfect masculinity is very old in Greek society.[19] It is only a short step
to the suggestion I believe Theophylact is making here, that concerned
parents and teachers can 'mould' a prepubescent male child, through
castration and special training, into a perfect servant either of God or of
powerful men; a servant who has not only been freed from the distractions
and taints of active sexuality, but is angelic in appearance.

Theophylact goes on to remind us that he considers he lives in difficult
times and that the devil's many temptations make it difficult to remain
chaste. Early castration is helpful if a child's chastity is to be ensured.
Finally, he outlines the positive contributions that eunuchs make to society.
They are excellent and devoted servants of society, the church and God. They
guard and provide for women and orphans, and engage in philanthropy.
As far as achieving holiness though chastity and celibacy is concerned

---

[19] Discussed in P.Brown, *The Body and Society* (New York, 1988), 10.

Theophylact considers that eunuchs are like other men. Some are celibate
and some are not, though castration does aid in their struggle for chastity.
  What are we to make of these ideas? Is Theophylact an anomaly? Is it
possible that eunuchism had achieved this level of acceptance within the
religious community? Despite the negative rhetoric still found in many
sources from the tenth to twelfth centuries, I believe that it had. Theophylact
stands at that interesting intersection between the period of political power
of the eunuchs of the Byzantine court in the tenth and eleventh centuries
and the later political marginalization of the eunuchs in the second half of
the twelfth century under the Komneni. Theophylact is looking back over
a period in which the status of eunuchs, both at court and in the church,
had developed in significant ways, and his *Defence of Eunuchs* reflects
these changes. The historical sources of the ninth to eleventh centuries are
generally hostile or neutral regarding eunuchs, in part because they tend
to replay the rhetoric and attitudes of late antiquity. The rich hagiographical sources of this period however, while they also contain some standard
negative tropes about eunuchs, clearly anticipate Theophylact's more
positive views.
  In some cases, the *vitae* assume that eunuchs could be sexually active,
implying that eunuchs could sometimes serve as tools of the devil. This is
apparent in the vivid description of the eunuch who befriends St Andrew
Salos's friend Epiphanios.[20] The saint calls him a sodomite and suggests that
he is in league with the devil, saying 'Alas for your youth which Satan sent
headlong with the most violent and vehement force into the lowest regions,
cut wretchedly by wounds'. Even Epiphanios' argument that the eunuch
was a slave and for that reason was forced to engage in sexual acts did not
change the saint's mind about him. In the *Life* of Anna Euphemiana[21]who
is living in a monastery and pretending to be a eunuch, we find the story
of a man who tries to seduce her, assuming that since she was a eunuch,
she would be receptive to his sexual advances. When she rejects him, he
suggests that perhaps she is a woman pretending to be a eunuch since she
does not seem to be interested in sex.
  During this period, however, it is also easy to find hagiographical
vignettes that reflect positive assumptions about the sanctity accessible to
eunuchs. This is illustrated in the *Lives* of St Niphon of Konstantiniane and
of St Basil the Younger.[22] In the first, the saint comes across a situation in
which the angels and demons are fighting for possession of a eunuch.

[20] *Vit.Andrew Salus, Acta Sanctorum*, May v.6 (1688), 30.
[21] *Vit.Anna Euphemiana, AASS*, Nov. Propylaeum Synax.Actes Const. (1902), 170–78.
[22] For Niphon, see *Vit.Niphon of Konstantinane*, A.V. Rystenko and P.O. Patapow, ed., *Materialien
zur Geschichte der byzantisch-slavischen Literatur und Sprache* (Odessa, 1928). For Basil, see *Vit.Basil
the Younger* (BHG 263), ed. A.N. Veselovskij, *Sbornik Otdelanija russkago jazika ... imp.akad.nauk.*
46 (1889–90), suppl. 3–89, and 53 (1891–2), suppl.3–174, and S.G.Vilinskij, *Zitie sv.Vasilija Novago
v russkoj literature II*, Zapiski imp. Novsiossijskago Universiteta 7 (Odessa, 1911).

Their debate evolves into an interesting discussion about whether a eunuch can achieve salvation. The demons claim that because he is a eunuch he cannot be saved. To make matters worse, they claim that he had engaged, as a passive partner, in sexual activity with a man. The angels argue that the fact of being a eunuch should not automatically condemn him and that, since he is remorseful, his sexual activity can be forgiven. He proceeds, 'limping', into heaven. Another eunuch in the same *vita* is damned for his greed and no forgiveness is possible. This suggests that there are standards of holiness that can be applied to eunuchs other than the standard of perfect celibacy. In this *vita*, a eunuch's failure to achieve celibacy can be forgiven but another eunuch's lack of charity cannot. A similar contrast appears in the life of St Basil the Younger. There we find a detailed portrait of the eunuch Samonas, an historical figure of the ninth century who was the *praepositus sacri cubiculi* under Leo VI. He is accused of all the traditional eunuch faults. He is arrogant, his temper is undisciplined and he is a sodomite. Yet in the same *vita*, the hagiographer celebrates the eunuch Epiphanios, a very holy and ascetic monk, and the Gonzaales brothers, both retired court eunuchs who were generous supporters of their rural community.

While the term eunuch has an omnibus meaning in some contexts and is occasionally used to refer to a celibate man, several of the *vitae* of the period centre on figures who have clearly been castrated. This is also true of the life of the Patrician Niketas who entered the household of the empress Eirene. After a career as a civil servant and military commander, he became a monk and specialized in healing men who were tormented by sexual desires. This same pattern appears in the life of St Nikephoros, Bishop of Milesius, who began his career as a court eunuch,[23] and in the life of St Kosmos who was *koitoniles* to the Emperor Alexander in the early tenth century.[24] Indirectly we find this same attribution of sanctity in the life of Metrios, the father of Constantine, a court eunuch in the reign of Leo VI and subsequently the favourite of the empress Zoe.[25] Moreover, we have the lives of two of the great eunuch Patriarchs, Germanos and Ignatios,[26] and the probability that the patriarch Methodios was also a eunuch.[27] Some scholars have suggested, based on his career path, that St Symeon the New Theologian might also have been a eunuch.[28] Finally, there is Symeon

---

[23] *Vit.Nicephoros, Bishop of Milesius* (BHG 1338), *AB* 14 (1895), 129–66.

[24] C.Angelide, 'Vision du moine Cosmas', *AB* 101 (1983), 73–99.

[25] *Vit.Metrios AASS*, Nov. Propylaeum Synax. Eccl. Const. (1902), 721–4.

[26] I have been unable to locate a copy of A.Papadopoulos-Kerameus's edition of the life of Germanos (BHG 697). *Vit. Patriarch Ignatios* (BHG 817), *PG* 105, 487–574.

[27] Above, note 6.

[28] See the changing position of Rosemary Morris between 'The Political Saint of the Eleventh Century', in S. Hackel, ed., *The Byzantine Saint* (London, 1981) and her *Monks and Laymen in*

Metaphrastes' rewriting of the life of the Biblical prophet Daniel: Symeon
has no hesitation in attributing sanctity to Daniel while he matter-of-factly
describes Daniel's castration and training as a court eunuch.[29]

Furthermore, Theophylact's logic about whether it was appropriate for
parents to castrate their sons is anticipated in several *vitae*. The lives of the
patrician Niketas and of Nikephoros, Bishop of Milesius, tell us that they
were castrated by their loving parents. Both hagiographers say that they
find this hard to talk about, but indicate that it was done to preserve the
boys' chastity. There is ample evidence from a variety of sources that by
the twelfth century, the castration of sons had become an acceptable action
for free, moderately affluent families, and one that opened career options
for bright young men.

A few sources even suggest that castration under those circumstances was
condoned by God. An angel rewarded St Metrios's good deeds with a son,
to be called Constantine. Metrios is explicitly told that he could 'do as he
wished' with the boy. In the context of this *vita*, God is clearly authorizing
Metrios to castrate his son as his neighbours have done, and to send him
to the city to make a fortune for the family.[30] In the often repeated story
about the false accusation brought against the patriarch Methodios, the saint
was so troubled by sexual desires that, while travelling in Rome, he prayed
to St Peter for relief. His prayers were granted: his genitalia shrivelled and
ceased functioning. In this case, God Himself seems to have undertaken the
crucial act.[31]

In a more general way, by the tenth century eunuchs make appearances
in popular stories and are being described using language and imagery
previously reserved for celestial beings. Eunuchs and angels are increasingly
being confused with one another, perhaps because they are portrayed as
doing similar tasks.

By the twelfth century, some eunuchs had moved from careers as
courtiers to the monastic life. While monasteries had long served as places
of luxurious retirement or enforced exile for eunuchs, we now encounter
eunuchs who become monks and ascetics and are celebrated for their
holiness. One of the best historical examples is Symeon the Sanctified.
Symeon, a court eunuch, served the emperor as *droungarios*, an office that,
in this period, was probably president of the imperial tribunal.[32] There is

---

Byzantium 843–1118 (Cambridge, 1995). I suspect the question can only be settled by a detailed
examination of Symeon's writings, see A.J. van der Aalst, 'The Palace and the Monastery in
Byzantine Spiritual Life', in A. Davids, ed., *The Empress Theophano* (Cambridge, 1995), 326–7,
for a preliminary attempt.

[29] I have discussed this in some detail in a forthcoming paper, 'Reconfiguring the Prophet
Daniel: Gender, Sanctity and Castration in Byzantium'.

[30] See K.M. Ringrose, 'Eunuchs as Cultural Mediators', *ByzF* 23 (1996), 75–93.

[31] See note 6.

[32] N. Oikonomides, *Les listes de présence byzantines des IXe et Xe siècles* (Paris, 1972), 331.

considerable evidence that Symeon also served as a close confidant, ambassador and perhaps also spiritual father to Alexios Komnenos. At some time just before 1078, Symeon retired from court life, took over the restoration of the monastery of Xenophon on Mount Athos and became a monk. The 1089 *Acts* of Paul, *protos* of the Athonite monasteries, says that 'While the emperor still lived and ruled, the great *droungarios* took over the monastery. He was from the great city (Constantinople), a good man whose life was ornamented by holy virtue, bursting with much wealth, and honoured no less by the emperor (Nikephoros III Botaneiates) than any other lord. He sought the emperor's permission to leave the world and become a monk'.[33] Little is said about the fact that Symeon is a eunuch, although tradition forbade the residence of a eunuch on the Holy Mountain. The text simply says 'Inasmuch as upon the earth he had been deprived of his genitals and was a eunuch, in that place (Athos) he would lead the angelic life'.[34] With the emperor's help, Symeon took over the monastery of Xenophon, and with a large sum of money set about restoring its buildings, beautifying its church and improving its agricultural holdings. He was tonsured and changed his name from Stephon to Symeon.

Unfortunately, Symeon brought with him three beardless boys from his household, Eusebios, Candidos and Hilarion, and sponsored their entry into the monastic life.[35] The restoration went well and the monastery attracted new monks. Yet, for reasons that are not totally clear, though they seem to suggest that Symeon's three followers acted in a manner that the older monks considered to be arrogant, when the Athonite monks met for their general meeting, they expelled Symeon and the three boys from the Holy Mountain. The charge against Symeon was the introduction of beardless boys onto Athos.[36] Symeon and his followers left the mountain, perhaps journeying to Thessalonike where they may have established a monastery for eunuchs.[37]

When Alexios Komnenos became emperor in 1081, Symeon approached him to plead his case against expulsion from Athos. He asked for and obtained a royal decree signed by the emperor that forced the monks of

---

[33] D. Papachryssanthou, ed., *Actes de Xenophon* (Paris, 1986), 70.19.

[34] *Actes de Xenophon*, 70.23.

[35] It is unclear whether these boys are eunuchs or prepubescent. In this period, eunuchs are not usually referred to as 'beardless boys', especially in a text which talks of the two as distinct categories. In his *Defence of Eunuchs*, Theophylact discusses Symeon and his monastic foundations. The passage can be interpreted to indicate that Symeon founded a monastery for eunuchs in Thessaloniki or on Mount Athos or both. See *Defence of Eunuchs*, 329.4, and Gautier's comments, 116–17.

[36] D. Papachryssanthou, ed., *Actes du Protaton* (Paris, 1975), section 21, 1.101–106. The typikon also forbids the introduction of eunuchs on to the mountain but this does not seem to have been the reason for Symeon's expulsion.

[37] Morris, *Monks and Laymen*, 279.

Athos to reinstate him and his three followers. The emperor even sent his own personal representative to see that the decree was carried out.[38] Despite Symeon's apparent victory, however, it was agreed that this would be a singular exception to the traditions of the Holy Mountain and that no other beardless boys would be admitted. Nothing is said directly about eunuchs, but the act of 1089, in which this imperial decree is embedded, concludes by reiterating the traditional regulations of Athos: eunuchs, beardless boys and women cannot be admitted.

This vignette, set in the heart of the most rigidly ascetic part of the Byzantine world, reflects both old and new attitudes to eunuchs. Eunuchs, like beardless boys, can still be feared as objects of sexual desire and as individuals who blur the boundaries between sanctity, maleness and femaleness. Court eunuchs also bear the burden of years of active participation in the secular life and their worldliness made them the object of suspicion within a strict monastic community. On the other hand, eunuchs can be perceived as men of great spiritual power who in addition often have the resources to enrich a monastery. A court eunuch like Symeon used his political connection to acquire and hold on to his monastery, to enrich and endow his house. The fact that he managed to establish himself on Athos, even as an exceptional case, reflects significant changes in the status of the eunuch.

These historical and hagiographical sources, like Theophylact's essay, support the hypothesis that by the twelfth century the gender construct for castrated eunuchs was very different from that of the fourth century. Castrated eunuchs of the twelfth century were often the offspring of well-established families. They were highly educated and dedicated to a life of perfect, loyal service within the aristocratic family, at court or in the church. They were assumed to have a refined, elegant, graceful demeanour, and were accepted as ornaments to an aristocratic lifestyle. There is good evidence that since castration was carried out while these individuals were quite young, they developed distinctive physiological characteristics that marked them out as eunuchs, characteristics probably admired within their own culture. In both church and state, they played mediational roles and were specially charged with the care and protection of women and children.[39] At court they controlled a complex structure of spatial sanctity that surrounded the emperor and regulated court ceremonial.[40] Indeed, this special access to the emperor was often deeply and loudly resented by aristocrats.

---

[38] *Actes de Xenophon*, 1.48–52.
[39] Ringrose, 'Eunuchs as cultural mediators'.
[40] I am preparing a paper on this topic.

By the twelfth century, therefore, the gender construct of eunuchs included a number of special intellectual and spiritual powers. In literary sources, eunuchs often served as intermediaries between men and angels. This spiritual status was certainly connected, in a positive way, with their assumed celibacy, a connection actively fostered by wealthy, powerful court eunuchs who sponsored monasteries and contributed generously to the church. By the twelfth century, as Theophylact acknowledges, there were still eunuchs who were worthy of all the old negative stereotypes, but there were also worthy eunuchs who had earned their sanctity through work in the community, church and monastery, and through their acts of charity. The nature of the effort to reach sanctity had been broadened and could be achieved by holy eunuchs despite their inability to confront the whole man's struggle to achieve celibacy.

Finally, and this assertion is tentative and requires more discussion, I believe that the cultural boundaries of 'nature' and the way in which the human body was situated within the realm of 'nature' had changed. For the late antique world, the human body and its condition reflected the inner worth of the individual soul. Castration upset the body's natural condition and spoiled it for future perfection, interior or exterior. Writing in the twelfth century, on the other hand, Theophylact's attitude to castration was quite different. The soul and body were separate in the sense that the body was nothing more than a container for the soul. God had a plan for each soul. If a cultural practice, such as castration, made it easier for an individual to achieve perfection, then it was a useful and acceptable way of helping him to live 'beyond nature' as a valuable member of the earthly and heavenly kingdoms. All of this argues for a society that included several gender groups. Despite the reiteration of late antique tropes in some of the sources, middle Byzantium had moved a long way from Classical assumptions about gender bi-polarity. From unnatural de-gendered beings decried as tools of the devil, eunuchs had become a class of individual with a distinctive assortment of positive gender attributes that included the capacity for true sanctity.

13. In denial: same-sex desire in Byzantium[*]

Dion C. Smythe

There were no queens[1] in Byzantium. The evidence for same-sex desire in Byzantium is sparse, and its interpretation relies on the recognition of possibilities rather than identifying certainties, but to ignore same-sex desire in a volume on *Desire and Denial* would be to be 'in denial' indeed.[2]

---

[*] This paper is dedicated, with thanks, to James Hodgson.

[1] *Oxford English Dictionary*, 2nd edn (Oxford, 1989), sv 'queen' 12; 'quean' 3. A major problem writing about same-sex desire is what to call the people who did the desiring. Mary MacIntosh's article 'The Homosexual Role', *Social Problems* 16 (1968), 182–92, proposed a historical study of the origin and content of the 'homosexual role'. For David Greenberg this has led to a 'reconstruction of subcultures, identities, discourses, communities, repression and resistance', though he adds that 'it is doubtful that homosexuals were a distinct social group with a definite status before homosexuality became deviant', D.F. Greenberg, *The Construction of Homosexuality* (Chicago and London, 1988), 5 and 8. To use 'gay' is seen as 'advocacy history' by its opponents, whilst its proponents use the term to distinguish people who are self-aware and self-identifying in their difference ('gay' as a cultural marker). 'Homosexual' is seen as value-neutral by its supporters, but as highly negative and damaging by gay men and women who have encountered the medical establishment's attempts to pathologize and 'cure' homosexuality. Furthermore, the term's nineteenth-century origins place it within the construct of 'sexuality', something that people had that essentially defined and explained what they did and what they were: J.N. Zita, 'Male Lesbians and the Post-Modernist Body', *Hypatia* 7,4 (1992), 108–9. Furthermore, should people who experience same-sex desire, but who do not act upon it, be classified in the same way as people who experience same-sex desire and act upon those desires? The Byzantine world-view did not include sexuality which explains the objects of desire. Rather they saw individuals tempted by lust and the devil into sin; they were men who had sex with men, for example, A.P.M. Coxon, *Between the Sheets: Sexual Diaries and Gay Men's Sex in the Era of AIDS*, (London, 1996), 16–17; W. Johansson and W.A. Percy, 'Homosexuality', in V.L. Bullough and J.A. Brundage, eds, *Handbook of Medieval Sexuality*, (New York and London, 1996), 156–9; J. Murray, 'Twice Marginal and Twice Invisible: Lesbians in the Middle Ages', in Bullough and Brundage, eds, *Handbook of Medieval Sexuality*, 191–3.

[2] The conception of being 'in denial', derived from psychiatry, is one of the recognized defence mechanisms. If something is very painful or difficult for the personality to accept – for any number of reasons, which need not concern us here – then the individual denies that

If it is possible to be in denial about the source material, it is also possible to be in denial about the intellectual feasibility of undertaking the study. There is the argument that if one studies or writes about homosexuality, it is because one is homosexual and therefore is writing 'advocacy history' precluding scientific objectivity.[3] The contrary view is that if one is not 'X', then study of 'X' will be impossible, as no amount of empathy will compensate for the lack of 'experience of the life lived'.[4]

Desire

The homophonic concept of Kazhdan's *homo byzantinus* is an obvious starting point; writing about the 'ordinary' Byzantine, he rhetorically asks: 'Were the desires and passions of the Byzantines not like those of other people throughout the history of mankind?'[5] Kazhdan argues that they were largely the same and thus we have a point of contact with Byzantine people; yet they were also different, isolated from us in time and space. Presenting the common attributes of the ordinary Byzantine Kazhdan writes, 'No-one will deny that *homo byzantinus*, like people of all times, had two legs, needed food, married and raised children'.[6] However, by two of his four criteria Kazhdan renders as 'queer' monks, nuns, bishops and the childless,[7] who obviously are not numbered among his 'ordinary Byzantines'. Defining 'normal desires' to include getting married and having children, Kazhdan excludes what Kinsey reckoned to be one in ten of the population.

I define 'desire' drawing on the work of Michel Foucault, who located desire in the discourse of power over sexuality. Foucault's project in his *History of Sexuality* was a 'historical and critical study dealing with desire

---

such a thing is, or indeed could be. Rather than dealing with what may be uncomfortable, the individual – or indeed the society – denies that such a thing could be possible, and acts as if it did not exist. In its extreme forms, 'denial' may be a reaction formation: existent desire, denied expression by the superego, is manifest as dread, anger and loathing of the suppressed/denied desire. D. Brizer, *Psychiatry for Beginners* (London, 1993), 96; D. Brown and J. Pedder, *Introduction to Psychotherapy* (Tavistock, 1979), 26.

[3] J. D'Emilio, 'Not a simple matter: Gay History and Gay Historians', *Journal of American History* 76,2 (1989), 436–9; Greenberg, *Construction*, 2 and 5; D. Halperin, *Saint Foucault: Towards a Gay Hagiography* (Oxford and New York, 1995), 7–13; J. McNeil, *The Church and the Homosexual*, 4th edn (Beacon Press, 1993), 223.

[4] In the original formulation, 'X' was Orthodox monasticism, but one can easily insert homosexuality, or black history, or women's history with the same outcome. R. Morris, personal communication.

[5] A. Kazhdan and G. Constable, *People and Power in Byzantium: An Introduction to Modern Byzantine Studies* (Washington DC, 1982), 16–17.

[6] Kazhdan and Constable, *People and Power*, 22.

[7] Basil II leaps to my mind, M. Arbagi, 'The Celibacy of Basil II', *Byzantine Studies/Etudes Byzantines* 2 (1975), 41–5.

and the desiring subject',[8] where he saw desire as expressing the subject's individuality, history and identity as a subject.[9] Foucault criticized the notion of 'desire' because of its inherent medical and naturalistic connotations:

> That notion has been used as a tool, as a grid of intelligibility, a calibration in terms of normality: 'Tell me what your desire is, and I will tell you who you are, whether you are normal or not, and then I can validate or invalidate your desire'.[10]

'Desire' in this context is not an event but a permanent feature of the subject: it is a hook onto which is attached medical definitions of sickness and degeneracy, religious definitions of gross moral turpitude, sinfulness and guilt, and legal definitions of illegality and conduct 'liable to corrupt or deprave'.[11] Foucault, defined primarily in his early career as a psychologist, reacted against this notion of 'desire' that defines individuals by whom they desire.

> What this amounted to, in effect, was that desire and the subject of desire was withdrawn from the historical field and interdiction as a general form was made to account for anything historical in sexuality.[12]

Because of desire's role in controlling individuals ('Tell me what your desire is, and I will tell you ... whether you are normal or not') Foucault preferred to explore the notion of 'pleasure':

> The term 'pleasure' on the other hand is virgin territory, unused, almost devoid of meaning. There is no 'pathology' of pleasure, no 'abnormal' pleasure. It is an event 'outside of the subject' or at the limit of the subject, taking place in that something which is neither of the body, nor of the soul, which is neither inside nor outside – in short a notion neither assigned nor assignable.[13]

Though rejecting desire as a central object of study in favour of pleasure, Foucault nevertheless located 'desire', 'act' and 'pleasure' in an interlocking net, each distinguishable from the other, but unintelligible without the other.[14] Furthermore, Foucault noted with approval the Classical formulation, after Aristotle, that 'nature intended ... that the performance of the act be associated with a pleasure, and it was this pleasure that gave rise to ἐπιθυμία, to desire, in a movement that was naturally directed

---

[8] M. Foucault, *The Use of Pleasure: The History of Sexuality*, tr. R. Hurley (London, 1992), 2, 5.

[9] Halperin, *Saint Foucault*, 95.

[10] Halperin, *Saint Foucault*, 93.

[11] Halperin, *Saint Foucault*, 93.

[12] Foucault, *The Use of Pleasure*, 2, 4.

[13] Halperin, *Saint Foucault*, 93.

[14] Foucault, *The Use of Pleasure* 2, 42.

toward what 'gives pleasure'.[15] A study of 'desire' in Foucaultian terms, therefore, should take note of the 'act' and the 'pleasure' that arises from the action. However neither the acts involved nor the pleasure derived from them leave any historical trace.

A definition of 'same-sex desire' is needed. Is a study of 'homosexuality in Byzantium' the examination of acts or of desires? Are gay people defined by what they do or by what they think? If one focuses on acts, one sees largely what was forbidden: one sees the structures of power – secular and sacred law – mobilized against same-sex acts. Conversely, focus on same-sex intimacy has within its remit both platonic and erotic friendships. Neither is the complete picture. To concentrate on 'the act' comes close to voyeurism and ignores 'situational' homosexuality.[16] To concentrate on the intellectual-emotional component seems to ally oneself with the social-constructionists[17] and to suggest that anyone can be homosexual, that it is a 'choice'.

Legal and quasi-legal medieval sources focus on what people did, not what they might have been, or what they thought. Thus grounded in the

---

[15] Foucault, *The Use of Pleasure* 2, 43.

[16] Men who have sex with men because it is the only or easiest sexual outlet, but who are primarily heterosexual in their orientation. These 'situations' are usually identified as the military and the prisons. See also Greenberg, *Construction*, 69 and 110.

[17] Social constructionists argue that no sexualities exist outside of culture – that indeed, following Foucault, the very concept of 'sexuality' is a product of our scientific-rational culture. The individual's sense of self, and understanding of the world and how he or she fits into the scheme of things is generated by the experience of culture in interaction with others (D. Bell and G. Valentine, eds, *Mapping Desire: Geographies of sexuality* [London, 1995], 23; Halperin, *Saint Foucault*, 3–4 and 78). This social constructionist view is linked with lesbian–feminist theories of sexual identity as a matter of choice in the early 1970s. By contrast, the essentialists proclaim the idea that there is something that 'essentially' makes people homosexual. Being homosexual is proclaimed as a 'natural fact', something one is born with, as something that should not be viewed as pathological and as 'something that cannot be changed (no matter how many 'therapeutic' interventions are deployed)' (Bell and Valentine, *Mapping Desire*, 22). Essentialists are to be found among the biological scientists working on the human genome project and the studies of variation in male hypothalmus size, and among historians who search for 'gay people in history', convinced (as they are) that there have always been 'people like us'. These two perspectives are responses to the bipolarity inherent in modern western societies: a human being is a man or a woman, is heterosexual or homosexual. This bipolarity is an attempt to render simple what are much more complex issues. Science provides additional questions but few satisfying answers. For example, all bodies are sexed, but what it means to be a sex or to have a sex has shifted across time and place. The homosexual is no longer the 'woman trapped in a man's body' or 'the man trapped in a woman's body'; questions of gender assignment mean that one must now differentiate between the transvestite, the transgendered and the transexual (both pre- and post-operative). Additionally, advances in paediatric care of intersexed neonates with the associated greater chances of survival mean that doctors make social, not medical decisions (J. Cream, 'Re-solving Riddles', in Bell and Valentine, eds, *Mapping Desire*, 31–4).

sources, historical analysis has attempted to trace the development of responses to one specific act – male–male anal intercourse.[18] Ironically, such a concentration is a very 'gay' way of looking at the world: many gay men see willingness to engage in anal intercourse as the significant marker of gay identification; HIV-prevention agencies focus on unprotected male–male anal intercourse as the highest risk behaviour. However as the SIGMA research indicates, it is simplistic to equate all homosexual activity with anal intercourse.[19] Nevertheless, a starting point for many treatments of the deed of homosexuality is the Roman law codes. Eva Cantarella provides an outline of the stages of imperial repression of homosexual practice:

> in 342 Constantius and Constans stated that the law must arm itself with an avenging sword and punish passive homosexuality with a specially decreed penalty – presumably castration. In 390 Theodosios I decreed that passive homosexuals who prostituted themselves in brothels should be burned alive. In 438, the Theodosian law code extended the penalty of burning alive to all passive homosexuals. With Justinian, lastly, the condemnation was extended to all active homosexuals, and the penalty for all was death (although we do not know in what form).[20]

The very phrasing of Cantarella's summation points to another problem: the Roman legislation clearly differentiates – at least at the beginning – between the 'active' and 'passive' participants in anal intercourse. Punished first and with increasing severity were men who, as the receptive partners, were taking the 'woman's' role. As with the Judaeo-Christian tradition, one basis for the Roman antagonism to male–male sexual intercourse was the damage done to the gender bipolarity. In the *Ecloga*, (17:38) male homosexual acts are the result of an excess of licence (ἀσέλγεια).[21] The *Ecloga* and the law codes derived from it punished bestiality by castration, male–male sex by death.[22]

In writings from the Christian perspective, the various modalities of male–male sex are treated as the 'sin against nature' together with bestiality and are catalogued and accorded penalties of varying severity – fifteen years excommunication according to St Basil, eighteen years according to St

---

[18] Frequently this appears in the historical analyses as 'sodomy' though all non-reproductive sexual acts (oral sex irrespective of the gender of the participants, male–female anal intercourse) were so termed in the medieval period.

[19] Coxon, *Between the Sheets*, 73 and 175; P.M. Davies, F.C.I. Hickson, P. Weatherburn and A.J. Hunt *et. al.*, *AIDS: Sex, Gay Men and AIDS* (London, 1993), 106–10.

[20] E. Cantarella, *Bisexuality in the Ancient World*, tr. C. O'Cuilleanain (New Haven and London, 1992), 186; Greenberg, *Construction*, 229–35.

[21] A.E. Laiou, *Mariage, Amour et Parenté à Byzance aux XIᵉ–XIIIᵉ Siècles*, Travaux et Mémoires Monographies 7 (Paris, 1992), 71.

[22] Laiou, *Amour*, 73.

Gregory of Nyssa.[23] Homosexual activity was not a constant preoccupation of the church authorities. At times, when it came to notice – especially as a cause of outrage in monasteries – action would be taken; but as is usually the case with Byzantium, the legal evidence provides an idealized view of aspiration not of fact. Twelfth-century canonists comment carefully on canons dealing with homosexuality, but without the contemporary examples that illustrate their exegesis of the canons on incest, multiple marriages or even the practice of magic.[24] The term most commonly used to signify homosexuality was ἀρρενομανία or 'man-madness'. Laiou significantly remarks however, that though the disapproval is marked it appears that a certain 'economy' was observed in actually carrying out the punishments.[25] She further suggests that after being a preoccupation in the sources from the fourth to fifth centuries, homosexuality is then rarely mentioned – with the exception of some saints' lives. Laiou suggests that for all the zeal in normative prohibition, Byzantine society tolerated homosexuality as long as it was not a cause for scandal: in effect, that Byzantium was the first closet society.[26]

The homosexuality mentioned in the sources is usually male–male sex. One mention of lesbianism is in the *Life of Basil the Younger*, described as γυναικομανία – woman-madness.[27] And where it is mentioned, female homosexuality is expressed in terms of young girls sharing a bed.[28]

The second means of examining same-sex desire in Byzantium is to look at emotional intimacy.[29] In many ways, this is a subversive activity: talking about male–male anal intercourse – or even mentioning brachio-proctal intercourse – is 'safe(r) sex' because it is distant; talk about emotional intimacy and all bets are off, as the line between 'just good friends' and 'boyfriends' becomes ever harder to draw. Since the eighteenth century, close friendships between men have been suspect, and the term 'homosocial' has been coined in an attempt to restore the idea that close, emotionally

---

[23] Laiou, *Amour*, 72 and note 24.

[24] Laiou, *Amour*, 76.

[25] Laiou, *Amour*, 77.

[26] Laiou, *Amour*, 78; E. Sedgewick, *Epistemology of the Closet* (Hemel Hempstead, 1991). Furthermore, Arethas's scholion to Clement of Alexandria's *Paidagogos* 3.3.21.3 being 'the earliest known attestation of 'Lesbian' (literally, 'a female inhabitant of Lesbos') for a woman erotically oriented toward other women', see B. Brooten, *Love Between Women: Early Christian Response to Female Homoeroticism*, (Chicago, 1996), 5 and note 9, seems to position Byzantium clearly at the 'queer' end of the spectrum.

[27] Laiou, *Amour*, 75.

[28] Laiou, *Amour*, 82. For a fuller treatment of some of the issues of female homosexuality, see Brooten, *Love between Women*.

[29] H. Bech, *When Men Meet: Homosexuality and Modernity*, T. Nesquit and T. Davies, trs (Cambridge, 1997); G. Jackson, *The Secret Lore of Gardening: Patterns of Male Intimacy* (Toronto, 1991).

powerful friendships are not always erotically charged. Michel Foucault has pointed out directly the connection between modern Western-European society's fear of homosexuality and ambivalence towards friendship between men.[30] Alexander Kazhdan's formulation of friendship in the Byzantine world focuses strongly on Kekaumenos, using the Byzantine's attitudes to prove Kazhdan's theory of 'individualism without freedom' as the identifying characteristic of Byzantine society and the *homo byzantinus*.[31] One leaves Kazhdan's book with the impression of Kekaumenos's views life as nasty, brutish, short and friendless:

> First, Kekaumenos was obsessed by fear of natural dangers, such as poisonous mushrooms or rocks that might fall and destroy his house. Second, he was frightened of political forces and of any kind of authority – the emperor, the department head, and even lower officials – including the mob ready to riot. Finally he was afraid of social life and this fear is interwoven in his mind with his fear of authority.[32]

Kazhdan sees friendship – the most weakly defined of the Byzantine social relationships – as a major problem in the organization of Byzantine social relationships.[33] However Kazhdan overstates his case when he connects Kekaumenos's fear of being taken advantage of by friends with a more generalized fear of authority. It is a strange 'friendship' that is co-terminus with 'authority'. Averil Cameron has pointed out that Foucault was interested in the developing discourse of Christianity because, as Foucault saw it, 'it was both totalizing and individualist.'[34] Similarly, Giles Constable has formulated Kazhdan's theory of individualism without freedom as where 'the *homo byzantinus* was isolated, fearful and helpless before authority'.[35] Kazhdan believed '[s]ubmission and entreaty were the only possible attitudes toward power and the only hope of man',[36] that power was an alien superimposed force and that resistance is futile; Foucault sees resistance as the automatic outcome of the exercise of power, power a vectored force transmitted along a human relation will be met by an equal and opposite vector – resistance.[37]

---

[30] D. Eribon, *Michel Foucault*, tr. B. Wing (Cambridge MA, 1991), 316.

[31] Kazhdan and Constable, *People and Power*, 26.

[32] Kazhdan and Constable, *People and Power*, 26.

[33] Kazhdan and Constable, *People and Power*, 29–30.

[34] A.M. Cameron, 'Redrawing the Map: Early Christian Territory after Foucault', *JRS* 76 (1986), 266–71.

[35] Kazhdan and Constable, *People and Power*, ix and 34.

[36] Kazhdan and Constable, *People and Power*, 125.

[37] Halperin, *Saint Foucault*, 17.

Adelphopoiia

Any survey of same-sex desire in Byzantium must refer to *adelphopoiia*. Ruth Macrides defines *adelphopoiia* as 'the adoption of a brother or a sister', and cross-refers the reader to her articles on adoption and godparents.[38] *Adelphopoiia* had much in common with other relationships created by the prayers of a ritual – adoption, godparenthood or *synteknia*, and marriage. It is *adelphopoiia*'s similarities to and differences from marriage that earn it a place in the discussion of same-sex desire in Byzantium.[39]

In a paper published ten years before the appearance of his monograph on *adelphopoiia*, Boswell described *adelphopoiia* as 'basically a gay marriage ceremony for the Greek Church'.[40] In his scholarly publication, he described it more neutrally as a rite that created a same-sex union. In overtly drawing attention to the similarities between *adelphopoiia* and marriage, Boswell stirred up a hornets' nest. Rapp emphasizes the similarity between godparenthood and *adelphopoiia*, places more distance between *adelphopoiia* and marriage.[41]

A synthesis of the work of these three scholars provides the following. *Adelphopoiia* was a social relationship, created by a church rite that connected two individuals. *Adelphopoiia* was part of a spectrum of Byzantine social relationships 'by arrangement' that stretched from blood-kin, through marriage, adoption, godparenthood and *adelphopoiia* to friendship and acquaintance.[42] In the actual rite that created the social relationship of *adelphopoiia* there are many parallels with marriage. However, there are differences: *adelphopoiia* was intended as a relationship between equals;[43]

---

[38] R. J. Macrides, *ODB*, 1:19–20, s.v. 'Adelphopoiia'. *ODB*, 1:22, s.v. 'Adoption' (with Anthony Cutler, presumably for the paragraph on visual representations of adoptions); and 2:258, s.v. 'Godparents'. Interestingly, the links are reciprocal between adoption and godparents, but in neither case is the reader referred to *adelphopoiia*.

[39] There are two extensive studies of Byzantine *adelphopoiia*: J. Boswell, *Marriage of Likeness: Same-Sex Unions in Pre-Modern Europe* (London, 1995); and C. Rapp, 'Ritual Brotherhood in Byzantium', *Traditio* 52 (1997), 285–326.

[40] J. Boswell, *Rediscovering Gay History: Archtypes of Gay Love in Christian History*, Michael Harding Memorial Address (London 1982, reprinted 1985), 5–21.

[41] Rapp, 'Ritual Brotherhood', 326.

[42] R. Macrides, 'Kinship by Arrangement', *DOP* 44 (1990), 109.

[43] Using *adelphopoiia*, a man and a woman could form a caring partnership that had some recognition, but which would not involve the subjugation of the woman's property to the man. This apparently was the reason for the long popularity of the rite in Romania. Boswell, *Marriage of Likeness*, 267 note 24. Rapp's stress on *adelphopoiia* as creating a 'horizontal bond' ('Ritual Brotherhood', 286) links any possible homosexual aspect to modern constructions of gay partnerships but away from the classical model where transgenerational models were the norm.

it did not create rights of inheritance;[44] it did not create impediments to marriage.[45]

Rapp has succeeded in her stated aim of collecting and presenting the evidence of *adelphopoiia*.[46] Hagiographical texts provide four examples: St Theodore of Sykeon and Thomas, patriarch of Constantinople; John the Almsgiver, patriarch of Alexandria and Niketas, governor of Egypt; Symeon the Fool and John the Syrian; and Nikolaos, patriarch of Constantinople and Leo VI. The complex *adelphopoiia* relationships of Basil I with John the son of Danelis and/or with Nikolaos, caretaker of the Church of Diomedes are followed by a treatment of Basil I's *adelphopoiia* with Symbatios and three others.[47] Romanos IV Diogenes and Nikephoros Bryennios are followed by John III Doukas Vatatzes and Demetrios Tornikes and John VI Kantakouzenos and Andronikos III Palaiologos. This wealth of evidence provided by Rapp shows the 'pervasiveness of non-biological 'brotherhood', and especially of *adelphopoiesis*, in Byzantine society'.[48] The many prohibitions against *adelphopoiia* stand witness to its continued popularity and also the vague feeling that it was the occasion for 'many sins'.[49]

Conclusions

Adelphopoiia was a form of ritual kinship, that was common in Byzantium, but which was frowned upon by the Church, though the Church itself provided the ritual by which it was created. *Adelphopoiia* gave formal expression to friendship, or created a situation in which friendship might develop. It was a means whereby members of the opposite sex who were not connected by other ties of kinship could gain access to one another. It could have been used by people who were conducting an illicit sexual relationship – either heterosexual or homosexual – to conceal their relationship under the guise of friendship.[50] *Adelphopoiia* should be placed

---

[44] If inheritance was the primary goal, then adoption was the favoured route. A possible problem with adoption was the inequality involved: there is difference of opinion whether adoption created *potestas patria* over the adoptee. What is accepted by both sides in this argument is that such a power relationship was not created by *adelphopoiia*.

[45] Macrides and Rapp record the statement from the *Peira* (49:11) that *adelphopoiia* creates a marriage impediment to the individuals involved in the ritual siblinghood (thereby implying that *adelphopoiia* could be contracted by a man and a woman) but not to their relations. Rapp, 324–325, refers to a 'rather cryptic passage' in John Pediasimos's treatise *On Marriages* which implies that a preceding unrevealed [unconfessed?] *adelphopoiia* prohibits a nuptial blessing because the blessings involved in *adelphopoiia* and marriage are too similar.

[46] Rapp, 'Ritual Brotherhood', 286.

[47] For a further interpretation on the strange career of the 'quare fellow' Basil I, see the article by Shaun Tougher, in this volume.

[48] Rapp, 'Ritual Brotherhood', 289.

[49] Macrides, 'Kinship by Arrangement', 110; Rapp, 'Ritual Brotherhood', 319 and 323.

[50] Macrides, 'Kinship by Arrangement', 110.

in the context of other binary fictive kinships, to use Macrides's term. These could be same-sex or different-sex; mutual and supportive or inequal and exploitative; coeval or transgenerational. There are many parallels with the heterosexual marriage ceremonies of the Church, which cause problems when the ritual is discussed. Boswell emphasizes the same-sex element of the ritual; Macrides tends to conceal it. The relationship created by *adelphopoiia* may indeed have been a non-erotic 'simple' friendship. Rapp describes one account of an *adelphopoiesis* between Symeon and John as 'a moving description of an intimate relationship' adding 'but what is the exact nature of this relationship and how was it created?'[51] I do not suggest that this is the record of a homosexual relationship between Symeon the Fool and John the Syrian, but as Rapp states earlier in her article, what is needed is careful reading of the sources and notice being given where 'brother' terminology is used. The relationship between individuals created by *adelphopoiia* has no single modern counterpart. Boswell has pointed out 'heterosexuals will be more inclined to assume [simple enduring friendship] as the most likely interpretation, while gay people will only consider it one of two distinct possibilities.'[52]

This leads to my final conclusion. Can we prove the existence of homosexual desire or its fulfilment in Byzantine society? Can we produce a check-list of criteria by which to identify the existence of same-sex desire? No, we cannot. It remains notoriously difficult in our own society to determine someone else's sexual orientation (should one be so crass as to want to know) unless they choose to self-identify as 'out' and 'gay'; grey areas abound. However, this is not the same as saying that all Byzantines were straight. When we read our sources, we should be alive to the possibility that there may be a 'queer' reading available.[53] We may be reading the coded outpourings of a heart attracted to another, constrained by the strictures of the society that brought them forth; they may be just good friends; they may understand friendship at an erotic level, that might or might not have physical expression. To deny the possibility of such desire would be to be in denial indeed.

---

[51] Rapp, 'Ritual Brotherhood', 297.
[52] Boswell, *Marriage of Likeness* xxvii.
[53] L. Edelman, *Homographesis: Essays in Gay Literary and Cultural Theory* (London, 1994); J. Goldberg, ed., *Queering the Renaissance* (Durham NC, 1994); A. Sinfeld, *Cultural Politics – Queer Reading* (London, 1994).

14. Michael III and Basil the Macedonian: just good friends?

Shaun Tougher

A Byzantine case of 'just good friends' is that of the ninth-century Emperor Michael III (842–67) and his ultimate successor Basil the Macedonian; it has been hypothesized, primarily by Romilly Jenkins, that these two men had a homosexual relationship with each other.[1] Given the theme of the conference which inspired this book, it seemed appropriate to refocus attention on this case. I will provide background information on the lives of the two men, touch on the more familiar heterosexual aspect of their story, then I will examine the case of the homosexuality of the two men separately before addressing the question of their relationship with each other.[2] I will be particularly concerned to assess the evidence of the sources and its nature, and aim to reach a conclusion on where these reflections concerning the question of the sex lives of Michael and Basil take us, as far as the issues of desire and denial go.

Prime sources for the lives of Michael and Basil are the chronicle of the Logothete tradition and the *Life of Basil*, and it is these texts that I shall be particularly concerned with. Both texts date to the mid-tenth century, but are of very different character. The biography is a panegyrical account of the *Life of Basil* the Macedonian commissioned by Constantine VII, Basil's grandson (whose accession to full power was impeded by Romanos Lekapenos and his family), whilst the chronicle has a marked anti-Macedonian streak, reflecting a Lekapenid bias.[3]

---

[1] See R.J.H. Jenkins, 'Constantine VII's Portrait of Michael III', *Bulletin de l'Académie Royale de Belgique. Classe des lettres et sciences morales et politiques*, fifth series, 34 (1948), 71–7, esp. 76, repr. in *Studies on Byzantine History of the 9th and 10th Centuries* (London, 1970), I, and also his *Byzantium. The Imperial Centuries AD 610–1071* (London, 1966), 165.

[2] I use the terms homosexual and heterosexual merely for convenience; I do not wish to imply anything about Byzantine sexual self-awareness. See Dion Smythe's paper in this volume for a discussion of the problems of terminology.

[3] For the text of the *Life of Basil*, which forms Book V of the chronicle of Theophanes Continuatus, see Theophanes Continuatus, ed. I. Bekker CSHB (Bonn, 1838), 211–353. For

These texts provide narratives from which we construct our own. Michael III was still a minor when his father the Emperor Theophilos died in 842. For a time power was in the hands of a regent, Michael's mother Theodora. It was during the period of this regency that Michael was married to Eudokia Dekapolitissa, though, according to the chronicle, his preference was for another Eudokia, Eudokia Ingerine. Theodora was ousted from power in 856 by her brother Bardas, who himself became a leading figure of Michael's reign. It was around this time that Michael III first came into contact with Basil, a man probably of similar age to the emperor, who had come to Constantinople to make his fortune.[4] The context of their first contact was said to be the taming of a horse of the emperor. On witnessing Basil's equine skills Michael entered him into his service, in which Basil rose, ultimately becoming co-emperor. By 865 Basil had reached the position of *parakoimomenos* and had married Eudokia Ingerine, whom the chronicle says remained the mistress of Michael; it also says that this arrangement necessitated the separation of Basil from his wife Maria and the granting of Michael's sister Thekla to him as a partner. In 866 he participated in the assassination of Bardas, and afterwards became Michael's co-emperor and adopted son. In the following year however, after Michael had threatened to take a man called Basilikinos (or Basiliskianos)[5] as his co-emperor, Basil planned and effected the assassination of Michael.

Of these details, most people's minds have been concentrated on the so-called 'ménage à trois' between Michael, Basil and Eudokia, for it has a bearing on the paternity of the Emperor Leo VI (886–912).[6] To use the term ménage à trois however is to ignore the exact detail of the chronicle which makes clear that Basil was husband of Eudokia in name only and was

---

comment on the nature of the life see for example R.J.H. Jenkins, 'The Classical Background of the Scriptores Post Theophanem', *DOP* 8 (1954), 13–30, repr. in *Studies on Byzantine History*, IV. Note that the chronicle of Theophanes Continuatus also contains an account of the reign of Michael III (Book IV), Theophanes Continuatus, 148–211. For a bibliography on the Logothete tradition and its complexities see A. Markopoulos, 'Sur les deux versions de la chrono-graphie de Symeon Logothete', *BZ* 76 (1983), 279–84, 279 note 1. Here I will refer to the chronicle of Georgius Monachus Continuatus as a representative of the Logothete tradition, in Theophanes Continuatus, ed. Bekker, 761–924. For interest see also P. Karlin-Hayter, 'Le *De Michaele* du logothète. Construction et intentions', *B* 61 (1991), 365–95. For the reign of Michael III we also have the account of Genesios; see A. Lesmueller-Werner and H. Thurn, *Iosephi Genesii Regum Quattuor*, CFHB 14 (Berlin and New York, 1978). For interest see P. Karlin-Hayter, 'Études sur les deux histoires du règne de Michel III', *B* 41 (1971), 452–96, repr. in *Studies in Byzantine Political History* (London, 1981), IV.

[4] For issues of the chronology of Basil's life see for example E. W. Brooks, 'The Age of Basil I', *BZ* 20 (1911), 486–91; N. Adontz, 'L'âge et l'origine de l'empereur Basile I (867–86)', *B* 8 (1933), 455–500.

[5] The *Life* gives Basilikinos, whilst the Logothete tradition gives Basiliskianos.

[6] For recent discussion see P. Karlin-Hayter, 'L'enjeu d'une rumeur', *JÖB* 41 (1991), 85–111; S. Tougher, *The Reign of Leo VI (886–912)* (Leiden, New York, and Cologne, 1997), chap. 2.

to find solace with Thekla; the chronicle creates two partnerships, not one with three corners. That Thekla was an essential element of this arrangement is stressed again by the chronicler when he reports that in the course of his own reign Basil discovered that she had a lover and had the man tonsured, whilst Thekla was beaten and deprived of her wealth.[7] These indications of heterosexual relationships are provided solely by the Logothete tradition. They need not be a bar to the possibility of homosexual relationships however, and certainly marriage alone is no guarantee of heterosexuality.

A homosexual relationship between Michael III and his obscure favourite Basil the Macedonian was first hypothesized by Romilly Jenkins in his 1948 article 'Constantine VII's portrait of Michael III'. Jenkins suggests that the image of Michael in the *Life of Basil* was influenced by Plutarch's lives of Antony and Nero, and remarks that:

> It is notable that almost the only vice which Constantine does not emphasize in his portrait of Michael is that of sexual excess or perversion although ample material of this nature was discoverable in the lives of Antony and Nero. The omission is suggestive. Michael's Poppaea was Constantine's grandmother, Eudocia; his Pythagoras and his Sporus were – dare one suggest it? – Basil and Basiliscinus![8]

By 1966 Jenkins was rather more certain of his hypothesis, and rather more repelled by it as well. He states:

> The intimate friendship between the Emperor Michael and the Armenian groom [Basil] is a circumstance which suggests reflexions of a not very pleasing nature. Bad as Michael's character was – weak, drunken, faithless – it seems that we must also credit him with homosexualism: and this is confirmed, both by his making Basil his bedfellow, and by his choice, when he grew tired of Basil, of a pretty boy to succeed him as favourite. Michael's character was of course known to his family, who regarded him with well deserved contempt.[9]

Jenkins's lead appears to be followed by Margaret Mullett; discussing Byzantine friendship she refers to the relationships between Basil and Michael III and Constantine IX and an actor, and finds 'suggestions of homoeroticism' in the source material.[10] She comments 'There is no reason to doubt that homosexual relations existed in Byzantium'.[11] Recently the relationship between Michael and Basil has been referred to again, this time

---

[7] Theophanes Continuatus, 842, chap. 8. It is possible to read these actions as politically-motivated, but it could have a personal dimension.

[8] Jenkins, 'Portrait', 76.

[9] Jenkins, *Imperial Centuries*, 165. See also *Imperial Centuries*, 198–9 for Jenkins's comments on Michael's childlessness.

[10] M. E. Mullett, 'Byzantium: A Friendly Society?', *Past and Present* 118 (1988), 3–24, esp. 10–11.

[11] Mullett, 'Friendly Society?', 11 note 41.

by John Boswell in his *The Marriage of Likeness*.[12] His main concern however is the phenomenon of *adelphopoiesis*, the rite of entering into a same-sex bond; Michael and Basil did not enter into such a bond together. Jenkins's hypothesis has not won sanction in all quarters however. Certainly Patricia Karlin-Hayter does not lend it much credence.[13] She asserts that there is a lack of evidence to support it, and comments 'Another hypothesis presents itself equally well: perhaps, for the young emperor, he just represented someone to trust'.

Given these rather varied approaches a fresh examination of the evidence is called for. I will look at the cases of Michael and Basil separately before considering their relationship together, for the picture is wider than the unit of 'Basil and Michael'. Starting with Michael III, contrary to Jenkins's belief, I would suggest that we do find in the *Life of Basil* broad hints, if not explicit statements, concerning the emperor's 'perversion'. Significantly Gibbon embarks on his account of Michael III with the comment 'Among the successors of Nero and Elagabalus, we have not hitherto found the imitation of their vices, the character of a Roman prince who considered pleasure as the object of life, and virtue as the enemy of pleasure',[14] whilst Cavafy alludes to 'the wanton times of Michael the Third' in his poem *Imenos*.[15] It seems likely that both these authors were influenced by the account of the *Life of Basil*. The panegyrical biography of Basil refers to Michael breaking the laws of nature and to his impious desires, which could be references to homosexual practices.[16]

That these allusions are contained in the section describing the crimes of Michael which precedes Basil's murder of the emperor and serves as a justification for the act implies that the perversion of the emperor was another good reason for his death. A very direct suggestion of the homosexual practices of Michael seems to be found when the author of the *Life of Basil* describes Michael's introduction of his new favourite Basilikinos to the senate.[17] Basilikinos is initially described as 'common and coarse, both effeminate and fond of revelry'. It is said that Michael once decked out

---

[12] J. Boswell, *The Marriage of Likeness: Same-Sex Unions in Pre-Modern Europe* (London, 1995), esp. 231–9.

[13] See Karlin-Hayter, 'Rumeur', 88, and 88–9 note 9.

[14] E. Gibbon, *The History of the Decline and Fall of the Roman Empire*, vol. 5, chap. 48 (vol. 3 [London, 1994], 47–8). Note however that Gibbon also states: 'The unnatural lusts which had degraded even the manhood of Nero, were banished from the world; yet the strength of Michael was consumed by the indulgence of love and intemperance.'

[15] For a translation of the poem see *The Complete Poems of Cavafy*, tr. R. Dalven (London, 1961), 95.

[16] Theophanes Continuatus, 243, chap. 20.

[17] Theophanes Continuatus, 250–51, chap. 25. A simpler version of this story is also found in the chronicle of Theophanes Continuatus Book IV: Theophanes Continuatus, 208, chap. 44. Note that Boswell, *Marriage of Likeness*, 238 note 93, misidentifies the 'pretty boy' as Gryllus.

Basilikinos in full imperial regalia and led him by the hand to the senate 'as that Nero did the notorious Eros long ago'; there he stated that Basilikinos was worthy to be emperor. Jenkins comments that Eros is unknown to us but probably featured in the lost life of Nero by Plutarch; he also comments that Eros 'was no doubt of the same kidney as Sporus'.[18] This Sporus was a freedman whom Nero had castrated, used like a wife, and later married; the emperor was also married to Pythagoras, who played the part of husband to that of Nero's wife.[19] This episode where Michael and Basilikinos are likened to Nero and Eros is one of the key elements in Jenkins's construction of a homosexual Michael. Karlin-Hayter, recognizing Basilikinos as Jenkins's 'pretty boy', views the scene however as a suspect literary creation of the *Life of Basil*.[20] She thus dismisses its reliability as evidence given the fact that it is conjured up by an author whose aim is to blacken Michael to the point where his death will be seen as deserved; yet the important point is that it must be acknowledged that the reader is forced to associate homosexuality with Michael, whether or not the emperor was in reality a man who had sex with another man.

A comparable scene, without the sexual undercurrent however, is found in the chronicle,[21] where Basiliskianos (identified as a patrician) is ordered by Michael to put on the imperial boots in the aftermath of horse-racing at St Mamas, much to the consternation of Basil; Michael then explicitly states his wish to make Basiliskianos his co-emperor. In discussions of the sexuality of Michael III it is not often noted that Basiliskianos also appears in the chronicle on the night of Michael's murder. The scene is Michael's palace of St Mamas, which is quieter than usual as Michael has sent his servants, led by the protovestiarios Rentakios, on an errand to his mother. The significance of the absence of several staff from the palace might be that it explains why Basil chose this moment to put his plot into action, but Michael may have had his own reasons for a quiet night; in his bedroom that evening was the chamberlain Ignatios, doing what eunuch chamberlains usually do, but also, sleeping in Rentakios's bed, Basiliskianos. Whilst it is possible to see significance in this detail, it is important to remember that the *Life of Basil* and the chronicle are two very different sources, and the chronicle has given its reader no reason to ponder on the nature of the relationship between Michael and Basiliskianos. Indeed the chronicle states explicitly that Basiliskianos had been ordered by the emperor to sleep in the bedroom so that he could act as his guard.

---

[18] Jenkins, 'Portrait', 75 and note 8.

[19] See for instance Cassius Dio, *Epitome* of Book LXII, 28. 2–3, tr. E. Carey, *Dio's Roman History*, vol. 8 (London and Cambridge MA, 1968), 134–7; Suetonius, *Nero*, XVIII and XXIX, tr. J. C. Rolfe, *Suetonius*, II (London and Cambridge MA, 1950), 130–33.

[20] Karlin-Hayter, 'Rumeur', 88–9 note 9.

[21] Theophanes Continuatus, 835–6, chap. 33.

Turning to Basil now, the sources are more ambiguous. It is clear from both the *Life of Basil* and the chronicle that part of Basil's attraction for those he met was his physique, his strength and size. In the chronicle the doctor brother of the keeper of the church of St Diomedes marvels at Basil's size and virility,[22] whilst the *Life of Basil* indicates that Theophilitzes employed Basil as he was keen to be surrounded by noble, good-looking and well-built men; and since Basil surpassed the other men in Theophilitzes's service in respect of his physical strength and spiritual manliness, he was appointed protostrator, and 'day by day he [Basil] was loved more by him'.[23] Boswell certainly finds the enthusiasm of Theophilitzes telling, and comments that Basil 'made the most of the appeal [his hunkiness] exercized for some of his contemporaries'.[24] One wonders though how much can be made of this reaction that Basil is said to induce in those around him; this perhaps raises the question of the appreciation of masculinity by men in the Byzantine world rather than the specific question of homosexuality, and in the case of Theophilitzes it is indicated that it was his pride that motivated his desire to have hunks around him, making him a somewhat absurd figure.

Boswell is however most concerned with the cases where Basil the Macedonian underwent the debated and controversial rite of *adelphopoiesis*, a rite of same-sex bonding.[25] Boswell identifies two cases of this in the sources, one in the *Life of Basil*, the other in the chronicle. The case in the former is where the rich Peloponnesian widow Danelis, hearing from a monk that Basil will one day be emperor, acts as his benefactor and forges a 'ceremonial union' between him and her son John, though the term *adelphopoiesis* is not used but the phrase 'the bond of spiritual brotherhood'.[26] Boswell sees added significance in the fact that John was summoned to Constantinople when Basil became emperor and honoured John with the title of *protospatharios* and intimacy (παρρησία) with the emperor; Boswell gives this 'intimacy' a marriage context. Boswell also argues that when Danelis visited Constantinople herself the gifts she presented were for Basil and her son. This reading of the episode feels rather forced. Concerning John's reception in Constantinople, Basil simply appears to be fulfilling his part of the bargain struck at Patras; regarding 'intimacy', this could just mean access to, and freedom of speech (the regular meaning of the word) with the emperor; the case of Danelis's gifts can be read as being given to her son and emperor, meaning Basil in both cases. Most significant of all, Boswell shows little consideration for the nature of his source, a panegyrical

[22] Theophanes Continuatus, 820, chap. 10.
[23] Theophanes Continuatus, 224–5, chap. 9.
[24] Boswell, *Marriage of Likeness*, 234.
[25] For a discussion of this rite, see Dion Smythe's paper in this volume.
[26] Theophanes Continuatus, 226–8, chap. 11.

life commissioned by a dynasty member; it seems unlikely that Constantine VII would tolerate implications of homosexuality about his grandfather.

The second case of *adelphopoiesis* is found in the chronicle,[27] though Basil's connection with the partner here, Nikolaos, also features in the *Life of Basil*. The context is Basil's journey to Constantinople to seek his fortune. He arrives at the city at sunset, and passing through the Golden Gate decides to spend the night in the porch of the church of St Diomedes. The keeper (*prosmonarios*) of the church, Nikolaos, is instructed by 'the divine voice' to go and bring in the emperor. This happens three times,[28] and only on the third occasion does Nikolaos realize that the man meant is the one he took to be a pauper. Nikolaos brought Basil in, 'and on the following day going with him to the bath he bathed and changed him, and going into the church he effected the rite of *adelphopoiesis*, and they rejoiced in each other'. Boswell notes 'The odd final phrase' which he suggests 'would probably recall to a Christian Greek reader the biblical 'Rejoice with the wife of thy youth''. Boswell sees the relationship as one 'undertaken for personal reasons', and notes that both Basil and Nikolaos already had brothers. He argues that the conclusion of the story is evocative of a wedding 'followed by jubilation and a shared life'. Boswell recognizes that from the point of view of the source Nikolaos enters into the relationship as he expects to find his reward when Basil becomes emperor (and indeed the chronicler records that he and his brothers were much rewarded in Basil's reign),[29] but Boswell also stops to wonder what sort of relationship it was; he finds a clarification by Basil's subsequent career with the hunk-approving Theophilitzes.

In his interpretation of the relationship between Basil and Nikolaos, Boswell does seem on firmer ground; we have the explicit mention of the rite of *adelphopoiesis*, and the indication of an intimate relationship between the two men. I would suggest that there is a further element in the text supporting this interpretation of the relationship. Boswell notes that when Basil arrived in Constantinople he possessed nothing but a staff and knapsack, and reads this as an indication that Basil was 'a young man from the provinces with no connections in the capital'. However he does not note that this detail is supplied only by the Logothete tradition. Its absence from the *Life of Basil* seems puzzling; why should such a seemingly uncontroversial element be lacking in its version? Further the chronicle puts a great amount of stress on the element of the staff and knapsack both in terms of

---

[27] See Theophanes Continuatus, 819–20, chap. 9. For Boswell's discussion of the episode see *Marriage of Likeness*, 231–4.

[28] Note that the version of Leo the Grammarian has only two trips to the porch, which feels less satisfying, Leonis Grammatici, *Chronographia*, ed. I. Bekker, CSHB (Bonn, 1842), 233–4.

[29] See Theophanes Continuatus, 842–3, chap. 10.

phrasing and context. They appear only at the moment of the decisive third
trip to the porch; Nikolaos is said to have found Basil with his knapsack
and staff. This emphatic treatment of this element of the story seems to call
for an explanation; the answer I suggest is that the author includes these
details as a *double entendre*. Certainly in the classical world the words πήρα
(knapsack/purse/leather bag) and ῥάβδος (staff/rod/wand) can have the
meanings of scrotum and penis respectively.[30] Whether Byzantium
continued to be aware of these meanings and use the words in this sense
is not so clear, but I would argue that amidst the tone of sexual ambiguity
of the chronicle's description of the relationship between Nikolaos and Basil
and the emphatic stress on the words such a reading would make sense;
Nikolaos's decision finally to admit Basil is thus reached not simply by a
realization of the truth but the sight of Basil's genitalia.

Thus in the case of the relationship between Nikolaos and Basil as found
in the chronicle I would argue that there are implications of homosexuality,
as Boswell suggests. However it is clear that Boswell fails to appreciate the
character of his source material. Commenting on the case of Basil and
John in the *Life of Basil* and that of Basil and Nikolaos in the chronicle
Boswell notes:

> The two stories about Basil are similar: in each there is a divine revelation, to
> a cleric or monk, about Basil's future greatness; in each the relationship
> established is to Basil's material advantage. It is possible that in imperial
> circles it was later known that Basil had profited substantially as a young man
> from a formal relationship with another male, and different chroniclers simply
> supplied different details.[31]

By this rationalizing approach (though he concedes that it is possible that
Basil was united with both men), Boswell fails to grasp the different
characters of the two sources, fails to realize that the *Life of Basil* and the
chronicle have different agenda; there is no reason why these two different
texts should be rationalized together. The *Life of Basil* creates an uncontroversial relationship between John and Basil in the context of explaining
how Basil was provided with much of his wealth and property by Danelis.
However it also presents the relationship between Nikolaos and Basil,
though in very different terms.[32] Nikolaos is not a simple keeper, but
abbot of the monastery of St Diomedes;[33] there is no mention of the staff
and knapsack, the bathing, dressing, *adelphopoiesis* or rejoicing. Boswell's
comment that 'it is striking that in [the] tradition about this relationship in
which Nicholas is identified as a monastic, the ceremonial union is not

---

[30] See J. N. Adams, *The Latin Sexual Vocabulary* (London, 1982), 14–15, 75
[31] Boswell, *Marriage of Likeness*, 236.
[32] See Theophanes Continuatus, 223–4, chap. 9.
[33] As C. Mango, 'Germia: A Postscript', *JÖB* 41 (1991), 297–300, esp. 299, points out.

mentioned' seems to miss the point.[34] It is not a question of the choice of one or the other, but of the manipulation of the stories to serve different ends.

Turning at last to consider the case of 'Michael and Basil', it is we as historians who have to put the case together. The sources agree that Basil had a powerful effect on his patrons, and Michael too is presented as showing particular attachment to Basil.[35] In the *Life of Basil*, Michael is initially impressed by Basil, and promotions duly follow. But then the author has to dissociate the two men, for part of his justification for the murder of the emperor is the crimes that Michael and his company of unsavoury favourites perpetrated; it would not do for Basil to be mistaken as one of this crew. The chronicle is less constrained. It remarks succinctly that 'the toils and the brave deeds against the enemy were for others; whilst the love of the emperor for Basil was profuse, and this man alone was his attendant'.[36] Boswell draws particular attention to Michael's speech at the coronation of Basil in the aftermath of the assassination of Bardas, recorded by the chronicle. Michael explains that he is making Basil co-emperor because the latter had saved him from assassins and on account of 'the great love [he] has for me'.[37] Boswell notes that the word for love here is *pothos*, which he says 'usually means "longing" or "desire" ... and is the word that Fathers of the Eastern church used specifically of sexual desire between husband and wife'.[38] Basil's holding of the office of *parakoimo-menos* can also be seen as significant; it is surely this post on which Jenkins bases his assertion that Basil became the emperor's bedfellow. Certainly the literal name of the office conveys close physical proximity. Karlin-Hayter is quick to point out that the holder of the office did not necessarily share the emperor's bed, but she misses the point that the very granting of the office has significance, for it was a position that was meant to be reserved for eunuchs alone. Boswell does realize the import of this, commenting 'That eunuchs were used for sexual purposes was axiomatic in antiquity ... and apparently still widely believed in medieval Byzantium'.[39] Also worth noting is that Michael's new attachment to Basiliskianos agitated Basil, though this could be interpreted in political terms rather than meaning that he felt spurned (or indeed as both). Finally Mullett finds homoeroticism in the chronicle.[40] The specific episode she refers to is the account of Basil's actions immediately prior to the murder of Michael III. Basil excuses

---

[34] Boswell, *Marriage of Likeness*, 233.

[35] See also the indications in Liudprand as noted by Boswell, *Marriage of Likeness*, 238.

[36] Theophanes Continuatus, 825, chap. 18.

[37] Theophanes Continuatus, 832, chap. 30. Note however the absence of this phrase in the version of Leo the Grammarian, *LG*, 246.

[38] Boswell, *Marriage of Likeness*, 237 and note 91.

[39] Boswell, *Marriage of Likeness*, 237 and note 87.

[40] Mullett, 'Friendly Society?', 11 note 41.

himself from the dinner table, goes to the emperor's bedroom and bends the locking bar so that it will no longer work, and later kisses Michael's hand as he retires to bed for the last time. Mullett however does not account for her reading of homoeroticism; betrayal is what springs to my mind, as it does to Karlin-Hayter's.[41]

Having considered the source material and the comments on it, it is time for some conclusions. The question about a sexual relationship between Michael III and Basil the Macedonian seems to be, in reality, a question about texts. At one level we have the question of interpretation – of reading the texts and responding to them. This carries the danger of reading things in that the author perhaps did not intend. At another level we have to appreciate the individuality of the texts, their different characters and purposes, and also the logic of their own stories. Bearing these issues in mind, I would argue that in the chronicle of the Logothete tradition we can detect ripples of homosexuality surrounding Basil, and perhaps Basil and Michael as a unit, whilst in the *Life of Basil* we find implications about Michael, implications which Basil is kept firmly away from. One might suggest that the very sensitivity of the *Life of Basil* in this respect is telling, but it could be that it is merely responding to the image of Basil that the chronicle had created. Ultimately these sources are hardly concerned with the historical reality of Michael and Basil; they can manipulate their narratives to suit their own agendas. What emerges clearly is that we as readers have our own part to play in the detection of desire, or in its denial.

---

[41] Karlin-Hayter, 'Le *De Michale*', 391.

Section V

Byzantine Erotica

15. Ninth-century classicism and the erotic muse

Marc Lauxtermann

Ninth-century classicism is a short-lived cultural movement centred around the enigmatic figure of Leo the Philosopher, which lost its impetus after the death of this scholar (c. 870) and dwindled thereafter. We do not know much about Leo the Philosopher, but the little we do know is proof enough that he was a scholar of true genius versed in almost every branch of science and the liberal arts. The story goes that his universal erudition was being sought after even by the Arab caliph; on hearing that Leo had been offered an opportunity to teach in Baghdad, the emperor Theophilos wisely decided that the Byzantine empire could not afford to give away its intellectual potential to the enemy and subsequently appointed Leo to a high position. This is almost certainly an apocryphal story, but it indicates that Leo's talents must have been extraordinary. Leo was archbishop of Thessalonike in the last years of the iconoclastic controversy, from 840 to 843. Some years later he was appointed head of the imperial institution of higher education at the Magnaura palace founded by Bardas Caesar. At the Magnaura school Leo lectured on philosophy and he is known to have studied and annotated philosophical texts, mainly Plato and the neoplatonic corpus. He also wrote on mathematics, geometry, astronomy and natural sciences.[1]

One aspect of Leo's various scholarly pursuits appears to be little known: epigrams. The text tradition of the *Greek Anthology*, at least in its present, Byzantine form, starts with Cephalas. Around 890–900 Constantine Cephalas put together an anthology of mainly ancient and late antique epigrams. The anthology itself is lost, but fortunately we do possess a fairly reliable copy, the *Palatine Anthology*, dating to c. 950, which (along with the *Planudean*

---

[1] This brief biography is based upon the classic study of P. Lemerle, *Le premier humanisme byzantin* (Paris, 1971), 148–76.

Anthology and the so-called *syllogae minores*) enables us to reconstruct the original Cephalas in broad outline. For his anthology Cephalas made use of various sources, ancient, Late Antique and Byzantine, that disappeared precisely because they ended up in Cephalas' vast anthology. Nowadays, because of the tremendous success of Cephalas's anthology, there is only one manuscript in which pre-Cephalan material can be found. But if one studies the structure of the *Palatine Anthology* and the order of the epigrams in it attentively, one can detect traces of a mid ninth-century sylloge, which I have labelled the *Palladas Sylloge*, transliterated and edited by Leo the Philosopher.[2] The original sylloge itself dates to the fifties of the sixth century: it contained Palladas, some Lucian, and a fair number of Late Antique epigrams. Leo copied this sylloge, or had it copied, adding some epigrams of his own: *AP* 9.200–203, 214 and 578.[3] Leo's copy of the *Palladas Sylloge* is one of the main sources used by Cephalas for his anthology (along with Meleager, Philip, Diogenian and Agathias). Leo's name is attached, incorrectly, to a fragment of an epic poem (*AP* 9.579 on the Arethousa source of Sicily[4]) and to a Homeric cento (*AP* 9.361[5]), both dating from late antiquity. The reason for these false ascriptions is obvious. Cephalas found the epic fragment and the cento in the *Palladas Sylloge* together with poems by Leo the Philosopher and inferred that they had to be the work of the same author. One of the *syllogae minores*, the so-called *Euphemiana*, contains a satirical poem by Leo, in which he makes fun of his doctor who prescribed a regime of cold water despite the winter snow and frost.[6] Leo's satirical epigram on a stammering student of his coins the word τραυλεπίτραυλος, which is formed by analogy with the neologism φαυλεπίφαυλος found in *AP* 11.238.[7] The inclusion of Leo's satire in the *Sylloge Euphemiana* and the literary reminiscence of *AP* 11.238, once again, indicate that Leo the Philosopher is somehow connected with the fashionable revival of the epigram in the ninth century. It is quite likely that it was Leo who initiated this revival, not only because of his contribution to the

---

[2] M.D. Lauxtermann, 'The Palladas Sylloge', *Mnemosyne* 50 (1997), 329–37; see also my Ph.D. thesis, *The Byzantine Epigram in the Ninth and Tenth Centuries* (Amsterdam, 1994), 244–6.

[3] See L.G. Westerink, 'Leo the Philosopher: *Job* and Other Poems', *Illinois Classical Studies* 11 (1986), 193–222; see also B. Baldwin, 'The Epigrams of Leo the Philosopher', *BMGS* 14 (1990), 1–17.

[4] Cf. the fragments of the Metamorphoses by Nestor of Laranda, *AP* 9.128–9, 364 and 537, which also deal with rivers and sources.

[5] Cf. *AP* 9.381–2 and Appendix Barberino-Vaticana no. 7 (Alan Cameron, *The Greek Anthology from Meleager to Planudes* [Oxford, 1993], 172) – all three of which are centos dating to late antiquity.

[6] Westerink, 'Leo the Philosopher', 200.

[7] Westerink, 'Leo the Philosopher', 200–201. A word-for-word paraphrase of *AP* 11.238, substituting the Armenians for the Cappadocians, is attributed to Kassia, but dates to a later period, see Lauxtermann, *The Byzantine Epigram*, 198–9.

Palladas Sylloge, but also on account of the significant role played by two of his students in the transmission of erotic epigrams.

The *Sylloge Parisina* (found in Par. suppl. gr. 352 as well as in its direct copy Par. gr. 1630[8]) consists of two parts, divided the one from the other by the ᾠδάριον ἐρωτικόν of Constantine the Sicilian.[9] The first part contains excerpts of Cephalas's anthology. The second part exclusively consists of pederastic epigrams, derived from various sources such as Meleager and the *Boyish Muse* of Strato of Sardis. Its closest equivalent is Book 12 of the *Palatine Anthology*, a direct copy of Cephalas's compilation of paederastica. However, as the second part of the *Sylloge Parisina* contains many epigrams that cannot be found in Book 12, the former is likely to derive from a source other than the anthology of Cephalas. This source I will call henceforth *PCP* (Parisian Collection of Paederastica).

Alan Cameron does not agree with this point. In his splendid study on the *Greek Anthology* he assumes that Cephalas did all the work and that no Byzantine scholar, either before or after Cephalas, was involved in collecting and compiling ancient epigrams. It is for this reason that Cameron supposes that the additional epigrams of *PCP*, too, could be found in Cephalas's anthology and that the exemplar used by the scribes of the *Palatine Anthology* simply missed some folios.[10] It is a fact that this exemplar had a major lacuna, in Book *AP* 9, due to the loss of three quaternia. But these three missing quaternia are located at one and the same point (between 9. 583 and 584) and not throughout the whole of *AP* 9. If we are to believe Cameron, throughout *AP* 12 several pages were missing in the exemplar used by the Palatine scribes. This would be the only instance where the Cephalan manuscript used by the Palatine scribes had that many loose pages missing.

Furthermore, he avers that the *Sylloge Parisina* shows the same sort of silly mistakes in distinguishing hetero- from homoerotic epigrams as Cephalas does. To prove his point, Cameron adduces as evidence of misclassification three epigrams: *AP* 12.50, *Cougny* III. 169 and 170.[11] *AP* 12.50 by Asclepiades is indeed misclassified: it is a self-address, not advice addressed to another male to drown the sorrows of love in drink. A 'stupid' error, no doubt, but not an error related to gender, for after all the person who is addressed, Asclepiades himself, is a male and the endings of the adjectives are masculine. Epigram III. 170, a poem on the power of Eros, is not explicit in its sexual orientation: it could equally be homo- or heteroerotic. The text of III. 169 is incomplete and badly damaged. It is heteroerotic only in the version of Cameron, who arbitrarily adds the word 'breasts' and changes

---

[8] Lauxtermann, *The Byzantine Epigram*, 137–40.
[9] Described in detail by Cameron, *The Greek Anthology*, 217–45.
[10] Cameron, *The Greek Anthology*, 224.
[11] Cameron, *The Greek Anthology*, 238–9 and 242.

the masculine participle σαλευόμενον into the feminine σαλευομένης. However, he faithfully translates the second verse: 'What fresh bloom hangs from the tips of the loins'. It does not require much imagination nor much knowledge of the human anatomy to understand what is hanging from the tips of the loins.

In fact, the main difference between Cephalas and *PCP* is that the latter actually does not confuse gender. It contains, for instance, two distichs, *AP* 11.51 and 53, of a pederastic nature that is not clear at first sight, and which Cephalas therefore mistakenly put among the gnomic epigrams. The redactor of *PCP*, however, had no problem at all in grasping the sexual innuendo of these two poems and rightly recognized that they are pederastic. *PCP* also contains Plato's famous epigram on Agathon: 'I stayed my soul on my lips kissing Agathon. The rascal had come to cross over to him'. Whereas one might question the ascription to Plato, no one in his right mind would doubt that this epigram is homoerotic. But not so Cephalas, who misclassified it in his heteroerotic section (*AP* 5.78). Cephalas often seems to have been at a loss in matters of gender, especially when dealing with female names on -ιον, such as Φανίον or Τιμαρίον, which he thought to refer to boys. In his heterosexual section there are many pederastic epigrams and *AP* V.78 is only one of many instances where Cephalas, for one reason or another, failed to understand the precise erotic nature of an epigram. However, *PCP* put Plato's epigram on Agathon among the paederastica, where indeed it belongs. Seeing that *PCP* does not confuse gender as Cephalas did and that it contains many paederastica not found in *AP* 12, it is obviously not Cephalan.

Since the anthology of Cephalas was such a tremendous success that after its publication Byzantine scholars seem to have stopped looking for new material, *PCP* must date to a stage of anthologizing prior to Cephalas. The scholar to whom we owe this pederastic sylloge is Constantine the Sicilian, whose ᾠδάριον ἐρωτικόν forms the first poem of *PCP*. No, says Cameron: Constantine is not a ninth-century scholar as is generally assumed, but his *floruit* falls in the first half of the tenth century, for which he adduces as evidence the use of the word μακάριος, 'late', in the lemma of *AP* 15.13. In his view this word indicates that Constantine was recently dead when the lemma was written (after 944).[12] That is reading too much in too little. Μακάριος simply implies that Constantine was dead and that the lemmatist paid his respects to a scholar of an older generation.[13] *AP* 15.13 fits into a

---

[12] Cameron, *The Greek Anthology*, 245–53.

[13] The lemmatist, scribe J, is none other than Constantine the Rhodian (see Cameron, *The Greek Anthology*, 300–307). As Constantine the Rhodian was born c. 880 (see G. Downey, 'Constantine the Rhodian: his life and writings', in *Late Classical and Medieval Studies in Honor of Albert Mathias Friend Jr.* [Princeton, 1955], 212–21), he may well have personally known Constantine the Sicilian who was born some fifty years earlier (see below, note 27).

series of three epigrams: 15.12 by Leo the Philosopher, 15.13 by Constantine the Sicilian and 15.14 by Theophanes the Grammarian. We find the same sequence of scholars in Barb. gr. 310, an early tenth-century collection of anacreontics and alphabets,[14] which has lost most of its pages, but not its index which tells us what the manuscript used to contain.[15] The index brackets together groups of poets: items 1–26 Sophronios and other Palestinian authors; 27–39 Ignatios the Deacon, Arethas and Leo Choirosphaktes; 40–57 the sixth-century poets John of Gaza and George the Grammarian; 58–64 Leo the Philosopher and others; and 65–80 ancient anacreontics. The group 58–64 contains Leo (nos 58–9), Sergios and Leontios the Grammarians (60-61), Constantine the Grammarian (62–3) and Theophanes the Grammarian (64). Item 63 is the erotic anacreontic with which *PCP* begins. Constantine is given the sobriquet 'the grammarian' because he held a professorial chair, as he proudly tells us in *AP* 15.13. Theophanes, too, seems to have been a teacher, seeing that in his reply on Constantine's pompous epigram a touch of professional envy shows through (*AP* 15.14). It can be hardly a coincidence that *AP* and Barb. gr. 310 bracket together the same three scholars, even in the same order of appearance. Then there is another piece of evidence: a set of poems in which a former student of Leo the Philosopher, Constantine, accuses his teacher of poisoning the minds of young people with hellenism and pagan ideas.[16] Whatever one may think of this kind of spiritual patricide (some of Constantine's contemporaries at least were not much pleased with it), the poems bear witness to Constantine's learning and level of education. Leo the Philosopher would have been proud to see the intellectual progress of his student: impeccable metrics, highbrow Greek, fine rhetoric, literary reminiscences – although he might have questioned his pupil's ethics. Constantine the Sicilian's anacreontics show the same literary qualities and standard of education as Leo's pupil displays; in all our sources he is associated with Leo the Philosopher; and his conceit and puffery, which was criticized by Theophanes, also marks the invectives against Leo. There is no good reason to doubt that Constantine the Sicilian is the same person

---

[14] The ms. dates to the end of the tenth century (see M.L. Agati, *B* 54 (1984), 615–25), but as it is primarily meant to be a collection of contemporary poems and as its latest dateable poem was written in 919 (item 39), it follows that the collection was compiled shortly after 920. Incidentally, this implies that the ancient anacreontics it contained (nos 65–80) were copied before the similar collection in the Palatine Anthology.

[15] Published by C. Gallavotti, 'Note su testi e scrittori di codici greci. VII–XII', *RSBN*, n.s., 24 (1987), 29–83, with an extensive commentary. I follow Gallavotti's numbering of the index.

[16] M.D. Spadaro, ed., 'Sulle composizioni di Constantino il Filosofo del Vaticano 915', *Siculorum Gymnasium* 24 (1971), 200–202. As the title indicates, Spadaro identifies Constantine with the homonymous missionary to the Slavs, who, if he were the author of poems written after 869, would have performed a posthumous miracle.

as Leo's ungrateful pupil. The *onus probandi* rests with those who wish to maintain otherwise.

The anacreontic poem with which *PCP* begins describes how Constantine once saw Eros taking a bath together with water nymphs; struck by the arrows of love the poet chases the winged creature through flowery meadows and shady woods, but in vain alas; when he finally gives up all hope of catching the little devil, Eros turns around and 'shooting his last arrow hit me below the waist'. Not knowing where to turn for help or what to hope for, the poet begs the chorus of his companions to join in the singing: 'My friend, spend sleepless nights like Achilles singing in sweet harmony with the warbling nightingales. I have learned the charms of love, but I do not find anywhere the way out; give me a companion along the paths of song, to sing with me of Eros'. The poem seems quite appropriate as an introduction to a collection of pederastic epigrams, for each of these epigrams in a certain sense celebrates Eros, just as requested by Constantine the Sicilian: 'let someone share the paths of song and sing with me of Eros'. As the lemma itself states, Constantine's anacreontic is a playful scherzo written in his youth: ἐν νεότητι παίζων, οὔτι σπουδάζων. The erudition of this young man should not be underestimated: there are numerous borrowings from Moschus's *Runaway Love*, from Longus's *Daphnis and Chloè* and from Late Antique epithalamia.[17] This is certainly not the kind of run-of-the-mill erudition of the average Byzantine scholar. It is not totally clear how widely read Moschus's *Runaway Love* and Longus's *Daphnis and Chloè* were in Byzantium. Moschus's delightful poem has come down to us through the *Greek Anthology* and it is reasonable to assume that Constantine the Sicilian read this poem in the *Garland* of Meleager. *Daphnis and Chloè* is only found in late Byzantine manuscripts, but the Greek romances seem to have been read by the circle of Leo the Philosopher. Leo himself is the author of an epigram on the novel of Achilles Tatios, in which he defends it from accusations of immorality (*AP* 9.203). It is a very decent story, so we are told, not at all improper to read, for in the end the hero and heroine are rewarded for their chastity with the pleasures of blessed marriage. If we compare this judgement with the shocked reaction of Photios[18] or the modern prudery of the Loeb edition in which the purple passages are translated into Latin, Leo's *nihil obstat* is a landmark of liberal thinking.

The index of Barb. gr. 310 mentions a (now lost) erotic anacreontic with the following title: 'anacreontics by Leontios the Grammarian, who, in love with a girl, suffered during the day, but was relieved from his

---

[17] See R.C. McCail, 'Did Constantine of Sicily read Daphnis and Chloè?', *B* 58 (1988), 112–22, and Cameron, *The Greek Anthology*, 249–52.

[18] H.-G. Beck, *Byzantinisches Erotikon* (Munich, 1986), 113–4.

lovesickness at night when he was asleep; early in the morning, when a swallow woke him up by flapping its wings, he lectured the bird as follows' (no. 61). Leontios must have been a member of the circle of Leo the Philosopher, as his name figures among the group of ninth-century grammarians headed by Leo (58–64). At first sight the subject of his poem seems to be a variation on the anonymous poem Anacreon 10 P., in which the lyrical subject reproaches a swallow for disturbing the pleasant erotic dream he had.[19] In Leontios' anacreontic, however, the swallow disturbs, not an erotic dream, but those precious moments of sleep when the poet is finally at ease and no longer tormented by love's anguish. The literary model Leontios imitates is doubtless *AP* 5.237, an erotic epigram by Agathias on the same theme – which, again, clearly shows that Leo the Philosopher and his colleagues knew the *Greek Anthology* intimately. Theophanes the Grammarian, another member of the circle of Leo the Philosopher, also seems to have indulged in the secret pleasures of the erotic muse. His anacreontic is entitled: 'how he loves his friend and how he is not loved in return because of his extreme affection' (no. 64). The anacreontic itself is lost, but there can be little doubt that it must have been of an erotic nature. The anthology of Cephalas contains an erotic epigram by the same author, which reads: 'If only I could be a white lily so that you may put me close to your nostrils and satiate me still more with your skin' (*AP* 15.35). Theophanes' poem is an imitation of two ancient erotic epigrams (*AP* 5.83–84), the second of which reads as follows: 'If only I could be a purple rose so that you may take me in your hand and put me between your snowy breasts'. Originally, in the anthology of Cephalas, Theophanes' epigram followed immediately upon *AP* 5.83–84[20], in the series of epigrams that ultimately goes back to the so-called *Sylloge Rufiniana* (traces of which can be detected in *AP* 5.2–103). This must have been a rather small sylloge of heteroerotic epigrams by the first-century poet Rufinus and a few contemporaries; since some of these contemporaries, such as Gaetulicus, Cillactor and Nicarchus, also appear in the second-century anthology of Diogenian, it is probably Diogenian who compiled this minor sylloge.[21] It is worth noticing that Diogenian's anthology of satirical epigrams also contains an epigram by Strato (*AP* 11.117).[22] This is the point where intriguing hypotheses arise. We see a sort of ping-pong effect: Strato of Sardis imitates Rufinus; the *Sylloge Rufiniana* contains Diogenianic poets; Diogenian's anthology has Strato. It is probably mere speculation, but I would suggest that the ἐπιγραμμάτων ἀνθολόγιον compiled by Diogenian

---

[19] M.L. West, *Carmina Anacreontea* (Leipzig, 1984), no. 10; see also the introduction, x.
[20] See Cameron, *The Greek Anthology*, 283–5.
[21] See P. Sakolowski, *De Anthologia Palatina Quaestiones* (Leipzig, 1893), 64–71.
[22] See Cameron, *The Greek Anthology*, 66–9.

consisted of three parts: (1) satirical epigrams by various poets, (2) the poems of Rufinus, to which he added some extra heteroerotic epigrams, and (3) the *Boyish Muse* of Strato of Sardis.

Whatever the case, the *Sylloge Rufiniana* appears to have been reedited by Theophanes the Grammarian in the ninth century. Since Cephalas's anthology is primarily a collection of ancient and late antique epigrams (*AP*, books 4–7 and 9–14), contemporary epigrams are to be found at the very beginning and the very end of this collection: *AP* 1 and *AP* 15, 28–40. There are two exceptions to this general rule: some epigrams by Leo the Philosopher in *AP* 9 and Theophanes' erotic epigram in the heteroerotic section. As for the epigrams of Leo the Philosopher, we know that they derive from his copy of the *Palladas Sylloge*. I would suggest likewise that Theophanes copied the second-century *Sylloge Rufiniana* with some reworking of his own. Cephalas used the editions of Leo the Philosopher, Constantine the Sicilian and Theophanes the Grammarian for his own anthology and, probably as a tribute to their scholarship, copied their epigrams along with the sylloges they had put together. Cephalas did not use Constantine's anacreontic because it was too long and not epigrammatic enough, but he incorporated Theophanes' and Leo's epigrams in his own anthology. If this hypothesis is correct, the interest shown by the circle of Leo the Philosopher in erotic epigrams is quite remarkable. Theophanes the Grammarian copied the heteroerotic epigrams found in the *Sylloge Rufiniana* and Constantine the Sicilian copied and enlarged the paederastica found in the *Boyish Muse* of Strato of Sardis. It is even possible that they collaborated on this project of editing erotic epigrams. It is often stated that the division between heteroerotic and homoerotic epigrams was introduced by Byzantine scholars, such as Cephalas or his late ninth-century colleague responsible for separating Theognis's collection into gnomic epigrams and paederastica.[23] But this division based on gender goes back to the second century, to Strato and Rufinus.[24]

The fundamental difference between the literary activities of the circle of Leo the Philosopher and Cephalas is their concept of gender and sexuality. Cephalas apparently was not entirely satisfied with the scholarly work of Constantine the Sicilian and Theophanes the Grammarian and decided that he could do better. So he rearranged the epigrammatic material found in his various sources. But while doing so, he committed a lot of silly mistakes regarding gender, perhaps as a result of Freudian inhibitions, perhaps because he was not as good a philologist as Leo, Constantine or

---

[23] M.L. West, *Studies in Greek Elegy and Iambus* (Berlin and New York, 1974), 44–5.

[24] Despite the odd pederastic epigram in the *Sylloge Rufiniana* (*AP* 5.28), which is the exception that proves the rule. The *Sylloge Rufiniana* is basically a collection of epigrams on girls, just as Strato's *Boyish Muse* exclusively talks about boys.

Theophanes. These three mid ninth-century scholars were genuinely interested in the erotic muse and had no problems in sorting out their material. 'Is it a boy or is it a girl?' is not the kind of question they found difficult to answer. It seems beyond any doubt that the circle of Leo the Philosopher enjoyed reading and studying romances, erotic epigrams whether on boys or on girls, epithalamia, and salient anacreontics. They composed erotic epigrams and anacreontics themselves as a result of this scholarly interest. To modern standards these poems are quite innocent, but it is fair to assume that in ninth-century Byzantium they must have seemed rather risqué. Around 850, when the circle of Leo the Philosopher indulged in the erotic muse, the anonymous *Epitome* of Hesychius mentions in its entry on Theognis: 'Theognis also wrote gnomic epigrams, but among these you may find disgusting love poems on boys and many other things that are repugnant to those who live a pious life'.[25] Some years later Photios expressed his indignation over the indecent contents of Achilles Tatius's novel.

In the end it was moral fundamentalism that won the day. No erotic epigrams or anacreontics were written between 870 and the beginning of the twelfth century. The late tenth-century poet John Geometres wrote some epigrams on the dangerous power of Eros, but only to express his hope that Christ may rescue him from the pitfalls of lust and desire.[26] Though Cephalas did admit ancient erotic epigrams in his anthology, he felt obliged to defend his choice to his probably shocked audience. Cephalas's prooemium on the *Boyish Muse* states that Strato of Sardis wrote his pederastic epigrams merely as a literary exercise in the epideictic genre and not because he was genuinely interested in boys. The first book of his anthology, containing the heteroerotic epigrams, begins with a prooemium in verse, which reads as follows: 'Warming the hearts of youth with learned fervour, I will make Love the beginning of my discourse, for it is Eros who lights the torch for youth' (*AP* 5.1). The key-words in this epigram are σοφός and λόγος. Though Cephalas is aware of the danger that his students may get aroused when they read erotic epigrams, he tries to make it clear that the erotic muse stimulates his students' zeal for learning. It advances their knowledge of learned Greek and ancient poetry; it helps them in learning how to compose a rhetorical discourse. It is obvious that Cephalas intends to study erotic poetry only as a means to acquire stylistic skills. His students are not supposed to read attentively *what* is said, but *how* it is said.

The erotic muse died with Leo the Philosopher. After his death Constantine the Sicilian wrote the two poems in which he accuses his teacher of having corrupted the minds of young people. Leo was the devil

---

[25] West, *Studies*, 44.
[26] Beck, *Byzantinisches Erotikon*, 120.

in disguise, Satan reincarnated, who loved to read and to study those perverted ancients – may he rot in hell! There is a third epigram in which Constantine claims to have found his salvation, albeit as an old man: now he knows that the Christian rhetoric of patriarch Photios is the only way leading to heaven.[27] Times have definitely changed: the young man who compiled a collection of paederastica and who wrote a very learned, but delightful erotic anacreontic, now feels the need to publicly denounce his former hellenism. The evil genius behind the scenes, the person who rooted out what could have been the beginning of a truly Byzantine form of humanism, is Photios. The two greatest scholars of the ninth century are Photios and Leo the Philosopher, but apart from the immense erudition they have in common, they are worlds apart.[28] Whereas Photios embraces a sort of christianized classicism, Leo does not have any scruples about studying the ancients on their own terms. It is much to be regretted, I think, that in the end Leo the Philosopher failed to persuade his fellow Byzantines of his vision of an enlightened hellenism.

The title of Lemerle's famous study of ninth- and tenth-century scholarship, *Le premier humanisme byzantin*, is well known. Unfortunately this title is only correct insofar as the literature of c. 840–870 is concerned. But after 870 there is no trace of humanism at all. There is no lack of classicism, true enough, but classicism in itself does not presuppose the openmindedness that one usually associates with the concept of humanism. The gratuitous imitation of forms and stylistic elements, as seen, for instance, in the famous Paris Psalter, leads to art without a soul – an art as meaningless as those pseudo-ancient columns one sees in Greek restaurants. To end with this sad note, one need only recall the prooemium of the collection of Christian epigrams (*AP* 1), which Cephalas placed before his anthology of ancient epigrams, in order to understand that the hellenism of Leo the Philosopher had died a silent death: 'Let the pious and godly Christian epigrams take precedence, even if the Hellenes are displeased'. This was not the climate in which the erotic muse could prosper.

---

[27] Spadaro, ed., 'Constantino il Filosofo', 202. Old age is of course a relative notion and the word γεροντοδιδάσκαλος with which Constantine refers to Photios is merely a literary reminiscence (Plato, Euthydemus, 272c). Since Constantine was a student of Leo the Philosopher and since Leo became head of the Magnaura school some years after 843, Constantine the Sicilian was born probably c. 825–30.

[28] See K. Alpers, 'Klassische Philologie in Byzanz', *Classical Philology* 83 (1988), 353–4, 356–8 and 360.

16. Erotic imagery on Byzantine ivory caskets

John Hanson

The title of this paper must seem like a punchline to one of those 'what-is-the-shortest-book-in-the-world?' jokes. People are generally surprised to hear that I have been researching erotic imagery in Byzantine art, as if the idea were unthinkable. Scholars who have written histories of erotic art, as it will perhaps not surprise the reader to know, have not included Byzantine art in the canon – not, that is, until the publication of the new Grove's *Dictionary of Art*, which cites the Veroli casket as a medieval example of erotic imagery.[1] In general, the medieval period is normally characterized as an interruption to the career of erotic art, a career which was well under way in the ancient period, for example on Athenian vases depicting sex acts, and not really taken up again until the Renaissance, when themes such as Susannah, or Venus and Adonis were taken up as pretexts for viewing the nude. This scenario bears a striking resemblance to the old historical view of the Middle Ages as a rest period between the two great peaks of cultural achievement. And, as with the case of cultural achievement, the blame is placed squarely on the shoulders of the repressive influence of the Church. Sexual motifs in church decoration or in the margins of illustrated books are usually interpreted as expressions of inhibited sexual urges, what Edward Lucie-Smith calls 'the open secret',[2] an explanation akin to Sigmund Freud's explanation of the artistic impulse as a sublimation of sexual desire.[3]

It is interesting to find that similar views were expressed in the last century, before the publication of Freud's theory of artists or any history

---

[1] P. Webb, 'Erotic art', in J. Turner, ed., *The Dictionary of Art* (London and New York, 1996), 10, 472–87, esp. 475.

[2] E. Lucie-Smith, *Eroticism in Western Art* (London, 1972), chap 3.

[3] S. Freud, 'The Path to the Formation of Symptoms', in J. Strachey, ed. and tr., *The Complete Introductory Lectures on Psychoanalysis* (New York, 1966), 375–7.

of erotic art, by the father of medieval ivory studies, Hans Graeven. Graeven undertook the formidable task of assembling a comprehensive catalogue of all known medieval ivory carvings, a project later completed by Adolf Goldschmidt, Kurt Weitzmann, Raymond Koechlin, Hans Swarenski and Ernst Kuhnel.[4] So, it was well before the corpus was assembled and only shortly after Byzantine art objects came to be appreciated in their own right, rather than as curious after-tastes of antique art, that Graeven published an essay on the Byzantine ivory caskets decorated with Adam and Eve cycles.[5] In this article, he makes a most interesting conjecture. He supposes that the reason that Adam and Eve is such a common theme on Byzantine caskets is that the customers had a penchant for nude figures on their caskets, and that Adam and Eve provided a biblical pretext for such displays of nudity (Figure 16.1). The vogue for nudity to which he refers is seen primarily in the imagery of the mythological caskets, which far outnumber the biblical caskets. He goes on to compare this lecherous use of biblical history to the preoccupation of 19th-century English sculptors with the same subject, exploiting the theme to voyeuristic ends, in a way virtually indistinguishable from pagan nudes.[6] On the surface, Graeven's suggestion appears absurd, but it is nevertheless an attractive starting point for a fruitful meditation.

The first order is to survey the erotic material in Byzantine ivories, second to ask whether Graeven's voyeuristic theory or Lucie-Smith's 'open secret' apply to the imagery, and, finally, to suggest some alternative avenues for understanding the imagery.

The majority of images on Byzantine ivory caskets are those that have been categorized, somewhat loosely, as mythological; 'loosely' because the repertoire of images includes genre images of Islamic origin, as well as various warriors relating to biblical military texts such as the Book of Joshua, in addition to the many Herakles, centaurs, Europas and other figures from ancient traditions.[7] Among the mythological images are a number of rape scenes. One example is the rape of Europa, familiar from

---

[4] A.Goldschmidt, *Die Elfenbeinskulpturen aus der Zeit der karolingischen und sachsischen Kaiser VIII–XI Jahrhundert*, 2 vols (Berlin, 1914, 1918), and *Die Elfenbeinskulpturen aus der romanischen Zeit XI–XIII Jahrhundert*, 2 vols (Berlin, 1923, 1926); A. Goldschmidt and K. Weitzmann, *Die byzantinischen Elfenbeinskulpturen des X–XIII Jahrhunderts*, 2 vols (Berlin, 1930, 1943); R. Koechlin, *Les ivoires gothiques*, 3 vols (Paris, 1924); H. Swarenski, 'Two Oliphants in the Museum', *Bulletin, Museum of Fine Arts*, Boston 60.320 (1963), 275–9; E. Kuhnel, *Die islamischen Elfenbeinskulpturen VII–XIII Jahrhundert*, 2 vols (Berlin, 1971).

[5] H.Graeven, 'Adamo ed Eva sui coffanetti d'avorio bizantini', *L'arte* 2 (1899), 5–23.

[6] One of these English sculptures is E.H. Baily's, *Adam and Eve*, formerly in the Bourne Collection, Grittleton House, Wiltshire (see J. Kenworthy-Browne, 'Marbles from a Victorian Fantasy', *Country Life* 190 [1966], 708–12, esp. 710, fig. 3).

[7] Goldschmidt and Weitzmann, *Byzantinischen Elfenbeinskulpturen* I, 16–19.

Fig. 16.1. Ivory Casket, Cleveland Museum of Art, detail: *Expulsion and Labours of Adam and Eve* (photo: The Cleveland Museum of Art, 1997. Gift of J.H. Wade, John L. Severance, W.G. Mather, and F.F. Prentiss, 1924.747).

Fig. 16.2. Ivory Casket, London, Victoria and Albert Museum, detail: *The Rape of Europa* (photo: Victoria & Albert Museum).

Fig. 16.3. Ivory Casket, Cividale, Museo Archaeologico, detail: *Rape of Lapith Woman* (photo: Museo Archaeologico, Cividale). [After Goldschmidt and Weitzmann, *Die Byzantinisehe Elf enbeinskulpturen des IX–XIIe fahrhunderts*. I. Kästen, Berlin, 1930.]

Fig. 16.4. Ivory Casket, London, Victoria and Albert Museum, detail: *Ares and Aphrodite; Erotes with Animals* (photo: Victoria & Museum).

Fig. 16.5. Ivory Casket, Sens, Cathedral Treasury, detail: *Joseph and Potiphar's Wife* (photo: Musées de Sens, L. De Cargouët).

the lid of the Veroli casket (Figure 16.2).[8] On one of the sides of the Veroli casket there is what was always assumed to be another version of the rape of Europa, but which Anthony Cutler has suggested to be not Europa but just one more of the many erotes that are seen at play around the casket.[9] He is not really being raped, merely playing at rape. Another theme which occurs on two extant examples is the rape of the Lapith women by centaurs (Figure 16.3).[10] In another case, the centaur has been replaced by a man for a variation on the theme.[11] Whether or not this is meant to be Achilles and Penthesilea, as has been suggested, is irrelevant. In intent, it is probably simply a generic rape scene among the various generic hunting and battle scenes which decorate so many caskets.

Lest the more sentimental reader despair, I hasten to point out that not all of the erotic images on the mythological caskets are violent. There are a number of panels depicting couples in tender gestures, including one on the Veroli casket possibly depicting Aphrodite and Ares (Figure 16.4).[12] Again, these are never easy to identify, and are better understood as generic depictions of lovers. Besides these various couplings, there are also many erotic scenes in the literal, eponymous sense of images of erotes at play, even if they do appear at times to be playing rape, either as a Lapith woman or as Ganymede. In Darmstadt, there is a series of plaques from a casket displaying widely eclectic themes, including the Ascension of Alexander from the Alexander Romance and, closer to the present theme, a scene of a nude man in bed apparently attempting to seduce a reluctant woman.[13]

So much for the erotic themes on the mythological caskets. As we turn to caskets with biblical imagery, we find that the predominant theme is, in a sense, erotic: that of Adam and Eve. I am classifying the theme of Adam

[8] Goldschmidt and Weitzmann, *Byzantinischen Elfenbeinskulpturen* I, no. 21, 30–32, pls 9, 10; cf. no. 23, 32, pl. 9.

[9] A. Cutler, 'On Byzantine Boxes', *Journal of the Walters Art Gallery* 42, 3 (1984–5), 32–47, esp. 44.

[10] Goldschmidt and Weitzmann, *Byzantinischen Elfenbeinskulpturen* I, no. 27c, 34 and pl. 13; and no. 28b, 34–5, pl. 15. The theme of the Lapiths and the Centaurs also appeared on a now lost octagonal casket known from two sources, 1) a drawing of the casket in the Codex Aschaffenburg (Aschaffenburg Hofbibliotek cod.14, f. 421v), in which the theme is strangely combined with Europa and the Bull; and 2) a seventeenth-century drawing from the Hallesches Heiligtum of a twelfth-century Western casket incorporating some of the plaques, and including one more Lapith scene. See Goldschmidt and Weitzmann, *Byzantinischen Elfenbeinskulpturen* I, nos 240, 241, 83–4, pl. 78.

[11] Goldschmidt and Weitzmann, *Byzantinischen Elfenbeinskulpturen* I, no. 41, 39–40, pl. 23.

[12] Goldschmidt and Weitzmann, *Byzantinischen Elfenbeinskulpturen* I, no. 21c, 30–32, pl. 9. They tentatively identified another couple as Ares and Aphrodite, this time entertained by musicians, in a drawing from the Hallesches Heiligtum and the metal copy in Agnani (I, no. 242d, 84–5, pl. 79); among other unidentified couples (I, nos 23, 32, pl. 9; 30d. 35–6, pl.15; and 31a. 36, pl. 17).

[13] Goldschmidt and Weitzmann, *Byzantinischen Elfenbeinskulpturen* I, no.125b, 66, 67, pl. 76.

and Eve as erotic because it is, after all, the story, not only of the origins of sin but also the story of the origins of gender and sexual union. The cycles are very much of a piece, following the story from the creation of Adam to the murder of Abel, and usually ending with Adam and Eve at the forge. Adam hammers iron on an anvil, while Eve works the bellows.[14] This scene is not biblical. In fact, this unusual iconography is found exclusively on ivory caskets and represented by many surviving examples of both caskets and fragments.[15]

Apart from Adam and Eve, there is very little among the biblical scenes carved in ivory that could be described as erotic, and what there is is very incidental to the main stream of the narrative, such as the attempt of Potiphar's wife to seduce Joseph (Figure 16.5) or the wedding of David and Michal.[16]

So, there it is. One can indeed assemble a body of erotic material from these ivory caskets, giving some credence to Graeven's hypothesis of a market for erotic themes on Byzantine caskets. This catalogue depends, however, on a definition of what might be considered erotic that is considerably broader than Graeven's. His references to nudity and to nineteenth-century sculpture indicate that he was thinking in terms of sensuality. Now although the Byzantines could be described as a sensual society, their practice of prayer, for example, being aided by sumptuous sensory experiences, especially aural and visual, it is by no means clear that such erotic imagery as I have presented had significant sensual appeal. This is perhaps best illustrated by the depiction of Joseph and Potiphar's wife (see Figure 16.5). On the level of representing the facts of the story, it would have to be seen as something of a failure. Contrary to the more conventional depictions of the same incident which shows Joseph running out of the door, on the Sens casket, it is Joseph who sits on the bed, while Potiphar's wife waits in the doorway. Her attitude is not one that could be described as seductive. Rather, she seems even to be pulling away from Joseph as she grabs hold of his cloak. The scene is so conspicuously lacking in what might be called sexual energy as to cause one to wonder whether the artist really understood the gist of the story. An alternative and more

---

[14] The Adam and Eve caskets are found in Goldschmidt and Weitzmann, *Byzantinischen Elfenbeinskulpturen* I, nos 67–82, 84, 86, 87, 89–93 and 118; 48–55, 61, 62; pls XLVII–LIII, LXVIII; and II, no. 237, 83, pl. LXXVIII. An example of Adam and Eve at the forge is I, no. 68c, 49–50, pl. XLIX.

[15] In all there are seven entire caskets and twenty-two fragments catalogued in Goldschmidt and Weitzmann, *Byzantinischen Elfenbeinskulpturen* II, nos 67–93, 48–55, pls 47–55; nos 115, 118, 61, 62, pls 67, 68.

[16] The episode of Joseph and Potiphar's wife is found on the Sens casket (Goldschmidt and Weitzmann, *Byzantinischen Elfenbeinskulpturen* I, no. 124k, 64–6, pl. 73) and David and Michal on the Palazzo Venezia casket (no.123e, 63–4, pl. 71).

probable explanation is that sexual energy was not considered an important part of the narrative. That is, perhaps seduction was interpreted as an act of treachery rather than a sexual act.

Graeven's sexual spin on the imagery falls equally short when we consider the issue of nudity. While the panels of the Veroli casket are carved, in accordance with its classicizing idiom, in celebration of the human anatomy in all its detail, the more common nude figure is much more generalized. Indeed, Adam and Eve are quite sexless (see Figure 16.1). Moreover, if the nudity found on the caskets was meant to have sexual appeal, as the nineteenth-century sculptures certainly were, it seems likely that the majority of nudes would be female, rather than male, assuming that the imagery originates from a male-dominated world view. So, while Graeven, in proposing erotic imagery as a category for these ivory carvings, has put his finger on an important piece of the puzzle, his discussion of nudity and sensuality must be taken as a piece of a different puzzle. Really, the way forward with this imagery is to take a creative and critical look at aspects of the erotic imagery other than the strictly sensual aspects.

One obvious place to start is with the prevalence of rape scenes. Sex and violence are easily the predominant thematic categories of the imagery on these caskets. One reaction to these themes has been to link them with the classical past. This is, of course, easily done, not only because many of the themes derive from ancient mythology, but also because the forms relate so closely to ancient traditions. Thus the imagery of the Veroli casket has been linked by Erika Simon to the *Dionysiaka* of Nonnus and by Kurt Weitzmann to a larger repertoire of hypothetical illustrated mythological manuals.[17] More recently, Anthony Cutler has rejected this rather stuffy interpretation in favour of a comedic reading, highlighting the many incongruities among the images, such as the unauthorized attack on Europa by a stone-wielding group, related compositionally to the imagery of the Joshua Roll.[18]

I would like now to introduce into discussion another class of objects closer in time to the antique models and, I believe, more relevant, namely ivory carving from France from the Gothic period. A wide range of ivory products, predominantly caskets and mirror cases, were decorated with themes of chivalric heroism and courtly love, like the Byzantine objects linking sex and violence.[19] A fairly common example is the Tower of Love. The women are enclosed in their fortified stronghold as the men try to

---

[17] E. Simon, 'Nonnos und das Elfenbeinkästchen aus Veroli', *Jahrbuch des deutschen archäologischen Instituts* 79 (1964), 279–336; K. Weitzmann, *Greek Mythology in Byzantine Art* (Princeton, 1951).

[18] Cutler, 'On Byzantine Boxes'.

[19] For a recent treatment of this material, with an extensive bibliography, see P. Barnet, ed., *Images in Ivory. Precious Objects of the Gothic Age* (Detroit, 1997), esp. nos 51–64, 217–48.

penetrate it, undaunted even by the bunches of roses that the women use as projectiles (Figure 16.6). Themes of rape, at least in the sense of abduction, are also present.[20] Even the theme of the couple portrait, with one caressing the other's chin, has examples both from Byzantium and the West (Figure 16.7 and see Figure 16.4).

To return to rape, what is striking about these two traditions of depictions of rape is that they are both products of medieval Christian society, though in one case, the rape is clothed in classical mythology and in the other in a contemporary romance setting. Why should the image of the abduction of a woman by a man crop up in both cases in spite of the fact that it was unlawful in both cases? Surely this phenomenon is related to the development of the medieval romance again, both in Byzantium and the West. The key here is to understand the imagery, as Cutler suggests, as intended more to amuse or delight than to edify or educate. That is, the imagery of rape, either as presented in relief on the sides of one of these caskets, or as related in medieval romances, does not instruct the viewer or reader in the virtues of rape, nor even warn the viewer or reader of its evils. The impact of this imagery was emotional and delivered in aesthetic terms. Rape, the message seems to be, is romantic.[21]

The notion of rape as romance is a ghastly one to modern sensibilities, though not, apparently, to medieval ones.[22] This disparity can be explained in two ways. First, the rapes depicted are really abductions, whether or not they include sexual assault. The words used for rape in both Latin and Greek carry connotations of abduction and violence respectively, rather than sexual assault; *raptus* deriving from *rapere*, to seize, and *biasmos* deriving from *biazo*, to do harm. In medieval law, the violence of rape seems to have been conceived of as violation not of the raped woman's personal rights but of her parent's proprietorial rights. Second, the late twentieth-century view of rape is completely conditioned by modern growing sensitivity to the woman, either the woman who is raped or the woman who reads of or views a rape. This was not, apparently, the case with these medieval images and some combination of a male-dominated society and a compliant female contingent allowed them to survive. Indeed, the complicity of the women in these reliefs parallels the complicity of heroines in medieval romances who are abducted by their heroes, not in violation of the moral milieu of the novels, but, among many other strands, as a demonstration

---

[20] R.H. Randall, 'Medieval Ivories in the Romance Tradition', *Gesta* 28 (1989), 30–40.

[21] On this theme in Classical Greece, see M.R. Lefkowitz, 'Seduction and Rape in Greek myth', in A.E. Laiou, ed., *Consent and Coercion to Sex and Marriage in Ancient and Medieval Societies* (Washington, 1993), 17–38.

[22] For Byzantine attitudes to rape and the legal position, see J. Beaucamp, 'La situation juridique de la femme à Byzance', *CahCM* 20 (1977), 153 ff., and, especially, A.E. Laiou, 'Sex, Consent and Coercion in Byzantium', in Laiou, ed., *Consent and Coercion*, 109–226.

Fig. 16.6. Ivory Mirror Cover, Baltimore, Walters Art Gallery, detail: *Attack on the Tower of Love* (photo: The Walters Art Gallery, Baltimore).

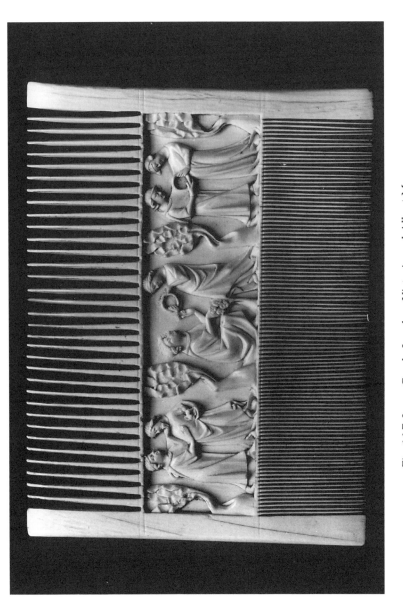

Fig. 16.7. Ivory Comb, London, Victoria and Albert Museum, detail: *Courtship Scenes* (photo: Victoria & Albert Museum).

of the inevitability of love conquering all, even the obstacles of parents who withhold consent; thus the romantic appeal of rape in a literary setting or in these exotic images.[23]

An interesting insight into this romantic colouring of rape from a male point of view is found in the *Progymnasmata* of Nicephoros Basilakes. In one section of this compendium of rhetorical exercises, there is a series of character studies, set pieces taking the form of monologues delivered by an assigned figure, whether biblical, mythological or literary, in a given situation. Of interest in the current context is one entitled 'What Danae would say after being deflowered by Zeus transformed into gold'.[24] The monologue begins with laments, mostly over her own avarice, but by the end she is won over by the formidable glories of the king of the gods, and lauds her conqueror in gratitude for honouring her as his choice. While this kind of reaction might make us at the end of the twentieth century cringe, it clearly spoke to the medieval Byzantine reader. Rape is permissible when perpetrated by the king of the gods or by the heroes of romances. They become, like our modern antiheroes, appealing, we are told, to the desire in all of us to break free from social constraints.

It is in this flaunting of the normal laws of behaviour that these images become enjoyable. Whereas in real life rape is illegal, in the myths of Zeus or the epic of Digenes Akrites, it is celebrated. Whereas in real life, arriving at an agreement to marry can be full of pitfalls, in the romantic world, the hero, by his valour, conquers all in his path. Whereas, for that matter, in real life, one might be a civil servant in Constantinople, in the romantic world, one is on the front lines, defeating Arabs, Persians, Canaanites, centaurs and beasts alike, and carrying off the girl at the end of it all.

Obviously, a different framework is required to understand the prevalence of Adam and Eve. It is, after all, a story with serious theological significance. Moreover, the appeal of the story is not based on the identification of the viewer with the protagonists, as in the rape scenes. What would have been the context in which the subject of Adam and Eve was brought before Byzantine ears most often? Quite likely it was the wedding ceremony.[25] The prayers of the Byzantine wedding rite, like the Roman, included rehearsals of the prehistory of marriage in the form of the Adam and Eve story. John Chrysostom goes into further detail in his homily on Ephesians, where he first indicates that God's creation of the human species was a single unit: 'He speaks of men and women as consisting of a single identity in these

---

[23] See R. Beaton, *The Medieval Greek Romance* (Cambridge, 1989), 31.

[24] A. Pignani, ed., *Niceforo Basilace, progimnasmi e monodie* (Naples, 1983), 343–4.

[25] For a quick introduction to Byzantine marriage practices, see *ODB*, 'Marriage' and 'Marriage Rites'.

words: *Male and female created he them*, and again, likewise: *There is neither male nor female.'*

Further on, Chrysostom relates sexual unions to the institution of marriage in Paradise:

> At the base of our nature is a hidden love which, by a secret instinct, works out this union of the sexes. This is why in the beginning, woman came out of man; and why since both man and woman proceed from the man and the woman. Do you see this perfect union; this intertwining by which God prevented any foreign nature from penetrating into ours? And look how careful he was: He allowed the man to marry his own sister, or, rather, his daughter, or rather again, his own flesh.[26]

Chrysostom expresses here the Byzantine celebration of sexual union as the sacrament of the unity and perfection of God's creation. Again, as with the rape imagery, the Adam and Eve imagery's best interpretation is a positive one, in terms of sexual union.

Given the positive – in medieval Byzantine terms – portrayal of sexuality on these caskets, it would appear that an equally positive model is required to frame this imagery. Graeven's model of voyeurism flies in the face of the sensually innocuous imagery, as does the model of the sublimation of sexual desires. It would not work any better, of course, to characterize the casket imagery as libertine, as free of sexual inhibitions as the erstwhile imagery on Greek vases.

The key is to understand medieval Christian culture, not as being hostile to sexual union, but as celebrating the spirit over the flesh in all things, including sexual unions. This truth lies behind both of the erotic themes on Byzantine caskets, the rape and the Adam and Eve, though each in a different way. In the first case, the ideal of rape, in a romantic sense, was that it was an adventurous illustration of the triumph of love over obstacles, even, in the literary imagination, legal ones. In a sense, the love of the hero for the heroine, the spiritual element in the story, gains ascendancy over the mundane aspects of the rights of the heroine's parents. As for the Adam and Eve caskets, the ideal of the sacramental interpretation of marriage equally allows a positive interpretation. In the context of common belief about the role of marriage righting the wrong of the Fall, the image of Adam and Eve becomes the prehistory of sexual union, placing emphasis on the spiritual, sacramental aspect of marriage over the corporeal.

Why have I bothered to resurrect Graeven's interpretation of the Adam and Eve imagery only to shoot it down? While I think his emphasis on nudity and the flesh is anachronistic, I am more optimistic about his linking of the Adam and Eve images to the mythological images by the common

---

[26] *In Eph.* 10.538, 539; *PG* 62, 135.

thread of sexuality. Too often the mythological past and the Old Testament traditions are sealed off from one another in our minds as discrete categories. They certainly mingled in a continuous narrative in Byzantine history writing – Malalas in the sixth century being a prime example of this tradition.[27] On the ivory caskets as well, they often blended quite effortlessly into one another in examples that combined biblical and mythological material.[28] In some cases, it is impossible to say whether the figures are nameless hunters and warriors from the pagan past or biblical warriors and hunters such as Joshua and his soldiers or David killing the lion and the bear and then Goliath.[29] This is the exciting possibility that Graeven was pointing to: the possibility that Zeus and Europa on the one hand, and Adam and Eve on the other, are not such strange bedfellows after all.

---

[27] As, for example, that of John Zonaras, *Epitome historiarum*, ed. L. Dindorff (Leipzig, 1868–75).

[28] Goldschmidt and Weitzmann, *Byzantinischen Elfenbeinskulpturen* I, nos 13–19, 28–9, pl. 7, and no. 84, 52, pl. 53.

[29] A case of ambiguity is the casket formerly in the Henry Oppenheimer Collection, Goldschmidt and Weitzmann, *Byzantinischen Elfenbeinskulpturen* I, no. 55, 44, pl. 35.

17. *Ostentatio genitalium*:
displays of nudity in Byzantium

Barbara Zeitler

My aim in this essay is to explore representations of nudity or semi-nudity in Byzantine art. In what follows I wish to make some tentative suggestions about ways in which Byzantine depictions of nudity or semi-nudity can be approached. For this purpose, occasional comparisons with material from western Europe will highlight similarities and differences between two separate, yet related, cultures. These remarks may be seen as prolegomena to the history of the body in Byzantium, an area which, in contrast to the western Middle Ages, is only beginning to be investigated.[1]

A sustained exploration of nudity in Byzantium requires an interdisciplinary effort. Images as much as texts enshrine perceptions of nudity, but the insights these two types of evidence provide are far from complementary. Texts express the prescriptions of a tiny élite, whereas most images had a much wider currency. But even though images had a potentially greater impact than texts, the extent to which images shaped the Byzantines' perception of their environment and to what extent they merely reflect it remains a moot point.

Texts, in tandem with images, can throw some light on the ways in which the Byzantine perceived nudity. This is illustrated by comparing texts referring to the Forty Martyrs of Sebasteia with images of the same subject. At first sight, the texts appear to present the martyrdom of the forty soldiers in the midst of a frozen lake in Armenia in a way that is more accurate than the pictures. The texts, among them a sermon by St Basil, refer

---

[1] On the body in the Western Middle Ages see, most recently, S. Kay and M. Rubin, eds, *Framing Medieval Bodies* (Manchester and New York, 1994). The article by M. Rubin, 'Medieval Bodies: Why Now, and How?', in M. Rubin ed., *The Work of Jacques Le Goff and the Challenges of Medieval History* (Woodbridge, 1997), 209–19 provides useful pointers for historians of Byzantine culture.

to the nudity of the soldiers.[2] This nudity is not depicted in the images: in Byzantine art, the Forty Martyrs, while still inadequately protected against the elements, are shown wearing loincloths. It is tempting to assume that the nudity of the Forty Martyrs is coyly veiled in Byzantine art because an image is more explicit than a text. Yet the texts and images relating to the martyrs may not in actual fact be at loggerheads with one another. The texts refer to the martyrs as being *gymnos* (γυμνός), but in Greek the adjective need not imply complete nudity and may merely mean lightly clad.[3] This suggests both that when Byzantines heard the word *gymnos* in the sermon of St Basil, they visualized the soldiers succumbing to death on a frozen lake whilst lightly clad, and, indeed, that Basil does not describe them as nude at all.

Byzantine texts and images relating to nudity, however, do not often parallel one another. Just like texts, Byzantine images do not necessarily provide evidence about perceptions and displays of nudity that is in any way comprehensive. An example is the practice of *anasyrma*, the display of female genitalia, a custom that finds its roots in ancient Greek culture.[4] According to textual evidence, such displays of genitalia not merely survived into the early Byzantine period; they were still performed in the last decades of the Byzantine Empire, as is suggested by a passage in the account by the Spanish traveller Pero Tafur who visited Constantinople in the first half of the fifteenth century.[5] In Byzantium, however, the significance of *anasyrma* was much altered. In the classical world, the display of female genitalia was seen as a fertility symbol, or it performed an apotropaic function. These meanings of *anasyrma* survived into the Byzantine period, but came to be replaced by obscene and downright demoniacal overtones in later periods.[6] Even though representations of *anasyrma* can be found in western European art, examples being the Irish Sheelagh-na-Gigs, such visual documentation is absent in Byzantium.[7] This is an instance where visual evidence from Byzantium does not complement the textual sources.

---

[2] *PG* 31, 516. On the Forty Martyrs in Byzantine art, see H. Maguire, *Art and Eloquence in Byzantium* (Princeton, 1981), 36–42.

[3] LSJ, entry for *gymnos*.

[4] M. Kilmer, 'Genital Phobia and Depilation', *Journal of Hellenic Studies* 102 (1982), 104–12.

[5] P. Tafur, *Travels and Adventures. 1435–1435*, tr. M. Letts (London, 1926), 143–4.

[6] E. Kislinger, 'Anasyrma. Notizen zur Geste des Schamwesens', in G. Blaschitz *et al.*, eds, *Symbole des Alltags. Alltag der Symbole. Festschrift für Harry Kühnel zum 65. Geburtstag* (Graz, 1992), 377–94. See, for instance, the passage in Psellos where he describes a chastity test, according to which a chaste woman can walk past a statue of Aphrodite, whereas a demon forces the unchaste woman to display her genitals on approaching the statue, cf. Kislinger, 384.

[7] Other western European depictions of anasyrma include the late twelfth-century sculpture from the Porta Tosa in Milan and a capital in the cloisters at Monreale in Sicily. See R. N. Bailey, 'Apotropaic Figures in Milan and North-West England', *Folklore* 94 (1983), 113–17; A. Weir and J. Jerman, *Images of Lust: Sexual Carvings on Medieval Churches* (London, 1986).

The absence of a Byzantine equivalent to the Sheelagh-na-Gig highlights a fundamental problem likely to prove counterproductive to the aims of this paper. There is not much relevant visual evidence from Byzantium, and it is unlikely, even considering the extensive losses of Byzantine secular art, that there ever were many depictions of nudity or semi-nudity. Judging by the surviving evidence, depictions of nudity are far less common than in western medieval art, a point to which I shall come back later.

With some determination, however, it is possible to find displays of nudity and its corollary, bodily desire, in Byzantine art. Such depictions range from males gazing at nude or semi-nude females, examples being the miniatures of David watching Bathsheba (II Sam. 11.2) and Susannah and the Elders (Daniel, 13.19–23) (Figure 17.1) in the well-known ninth-century manuscript of the *Sacra Parallela* (Paris, Bibliothèque Nationale, ms grec 923)[8] to depictions, in the same manuscript, of sexual congress, albeit with disastrous consequences, as in the miniature showing Phineas killing Zimri and Chosbi (Numbers 25.7–13).[9]

Apart from the dearth of suitable visual evidence, the interpretation of Byzantine images showing nude or semi-nude bodies is also dogged by fundamental methodological issues, which arise from the very nature of the material. Because the visual material dealt with here dates from an historically remote period, the nudity depicted and the Byzantine spectators' reactions to it may not necessarily coincide with modern depictions of nudity and contemporary interpretations.

Some of these methodological problems are highlighted by considering briefly one of the first works to investigate the nudity of Christ in art, Leo Steinberg's *The Sexuality of Christ and its Modern Oblivion*,[10] as well as the responses this book received. Apart from dealing with a neglected facet of Renaissance art, this study has raised the important issue of how to assess depictions of nudity from a period not our own. One of the fundamental criticisms levelled at this study was that it neglected to consider to what extent modern notions about sexuality can be projected on to the past, a concern that has also been raised in studies of sex and desire in the ancient world.[11] Indeed, the crux of the problem is whether nudity should automatically be associated with sexuality, a link commonly made in the

---

[8] K. Weitzmann, *Sacra Parallela* (Princeton,1979), figs 131 and 393.

[9] K. Weitzmann, *Sacra Parallela*, fig. 78.

[10] L. Steinberg, *The Sexuality of Christ and its Modern Oblivion* (New York, 1983; 2nd edn, Chicago, 1996).

[11] C.W. Bynum, 'The Body of Christ in the Late Middle Ages: A Reply to Leo Steinberg', in Bynum, *Fragmentation and Redemption. Essays on Gender and the Human Body in Medieval Religion* (New York, 1991), 79–117, esp. 85–7; see also M. Foucault, *A History of Sexuality* (New York, 1978); J. Winkler, *The Constraints of Desire. The Anthropology of Sex and Gender in Ancient Greece* (New York and London, 1990).

twentieth century. At the other end of the critical spectrum, Steinberg's presentation of Christ's nude body has been seen as far too cerebral and oblivious to the emotional and particularly the seductive potential of images depicting Christ.[12] Such diametrically opposed critical responses to Steinberg's study highlight the very different approaches that can be taken to the visual material. In the context of Byzantine art and culture, is it more appropriate to take an approach that stresses historical distance and cultural distinctness, or should visual material from Byzantium be seen as part of a common human experience that cuts across ages and societies?

A look at a Byzantine image allows us to raise these issues in a more concrete fashion. Would Byzantine viewers beholding the image of Susannah and the Elders in the *Sacra Parallela* have interpreted the Elders' feelings of desire in same way as we are inclined to do? And even if this feeling was experienced in the same way, would it have been understood in the same way? Can our notion of desire, with its heavy psychoanalytical baggage, be projected into the past? Is there a continuum of feelings that were experienced in the past as much as in the present?

Research into nudity in the western Middle Ages has shown not only that the extent to which nudity was tolerated in the medieval period was very different from the modern one, in the sense that it was bound to specific situations, but also that the perception and function of nudity was different in the Middle Ages.[13] This suggests that a view that emphasizes temporal and cultural distinctiveness is likely to provide profounder insights into pictorial evidence from Byzantium.

I wish to pursue some of these issues by focusing on different types of images from the Byzantine world. These are illustrations in medical manuscripts, depictions of classical myth and, finally, the treatment of the body in religious imagery.

Illustrations in Byzantine medical manuscripts require a great deal of further study. One of the few published examples is the tenth-century manuscript of Apollonius of Kition's *Commentary on Hippocrates' Treatise on Dislocations*. One miniature (fol. 200) from this manuscript shows patients being treated for dislocations of their limbs. They are shown naked on a rack (Figure 17.2), but even though one might expect anatomical exactness of an illustration in a medical manuscript, the naked patients are devoid of genitals.[14] We may contrast such anatomical incompleteness with a miniature from a western manuscript, dated to c.1300, containing Rolandus

---

[12] R.C. Trexler, 'Gendering Christ Crucified', in B. Cassidy, ed., *Iconography at the Crossroads* (Princeton, 1993), 107–21.

[13] R. Jütte, 'Der anstößige Körper. Anmerkungen zu einer Semiotik der Nacktheit', in K. Schreiner and N. Schnitzler, eds, *Gepeinigt, Begehrt, Vergessen. Symbolik und Sozialbezug des Körpers im späten Mittelalter und in der frühen Neuzeit* (Munich, 1992), 109–29.

[14] L. MacKinney, *Medical Illustrations in Medieval Manuscripts* (London, 1965), fig. 91A.

Parmensis's *Chirurgia* (Figure 17.3). This miniature depicts the treatment of an inguinal hernia.[15] Admittedly, this is a miniature illustrating a treatment in which the genital area was directly affected, but, bearing in mind that other western medical manuscripts tend to be more explicit in their depiction of genitalia, there is some evidence to suggest that Byzantine medical manuscripts tend to shun anatomical accuracy. The miniatures in Apollonius of Kition's *Commentary* show that Byzantine medical illustrations, that is illustrations most directly concerned with the body, epitomize what Jacques LeGoff has termed the medieval 'déroute doctrinale du corporel'.[16]

Another type of Byzantine imagery in which the representation of genitalia is all but absent is mythological representations. Depictions of anatomically correct figures in depictions of ancient myth do occur in Byzantine art, but they appear to have been rare. The nude figures disporting themselves on the tenth-century ivory box, the Veroli casket (London, Victoria and Albert Museum) are among the few Byzantine depictions of mythological subjects in which genitalia are represented. Indeed, the clear depiction of genitalia in mythological images tends to be confined largely to tenth-century ivories.[17] Other visual renderings of classical myth in Byzantium would suggest that representations of nude figures with clearly visible genitalia are an exception to the rule. The naked Curetes worshipping the statue of Rhea shown in a miniature (fol. 162v) in the twelfth-century manuscript containing the *Homilies* of Gregory of Nazianzos (Athos, Panteleimon, cod. 6) look like medieval precursors of Action Man, lacking, like the modern toy, any indication of genitalia (Figure 17.4).[18] Perhaps the comparison between the Veroli casket and the miniature in Gregory's homilies is not a fair one: the ivory box reflects a secular aesthetic of Constantinopolitan élite circles during the reign of the Macedonian dynasty, whereas the Curetes are shown in a religious manuscript. Anatomically incomplete figures, however, also occur in non-religious contexts. A good example is the miniature showing Herakles and the Cattle of Geryon (fol. 24r) in an eleventh-century manuscript of Pseudo-Oppian's *Cynegetica* (Venice, Marciana, gr. 479).[19] Here, Herakles striding through the countryside is shown semi-nude, wearing only a short toga which would reveal his genitals were they present.

The suppression of genitalia in many depictions of classical myth also raises the questions of how the Byzantines dealt with the many ancient

[15] MacKinney, *Medical Illustrations*, 78–9 and fig. 81B.

[16] J. LeGoff, *L'imaginaire médiévale* (Paris, 1985), 123.

[17] For other tenth-century ivories with mythological subject matter, see A. Goldschmidt and K. Weitzmann, *Die byzantinischen Elfenbeinskulpturen des X.–XIII. Jahrhunderts* I (Berlin, 1930).

[18] S. Pelekanidis *et al.*, *The Treasures of Mount Athos. Illuminated Manuscripts* 1 (Athens, 1975), fig. 311.

[19] K. Weitzmann, *Greek Mythology in Byzantine Art* (Princeton, 1951), 120–22, fig. 138.

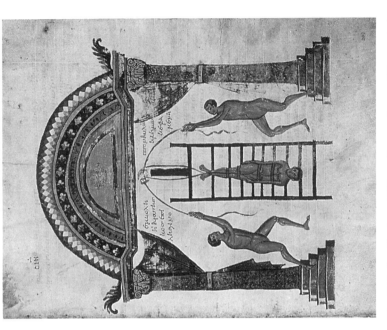

Fig. 17.2. Apollonios of Kition, *Commentary on Hippocrates' Treatise on Dislocations* (Florence, Laurenziana, ms 74.4): Treatment of Dislocated Vertebrae (fol. 200). With permission of the Ministero per i Beni Culturali ed Ambientali.

Fig. 17.1. *Sacra Parallela* (Paris, Bibliothèque Nationale, ms grec 923): Susannah and the Elders (fol. 373v). With permission of the Bibliothèque Nationale.

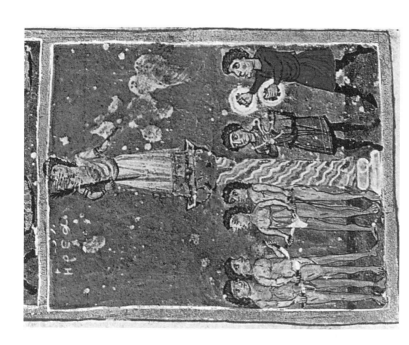

Fig. 17.4. *Homilies* of Gregory the Theologian (Mount Athos, Panteleimon, cod. 6): Curetes Worshipping a Statue of Rhea (fol. 162v). From *Treasures of Mount Athos* I (Athens, 1975), fig. 31.

Fig. 17.3. Rolandus Parmensis, *Chirurgia* (Rome, Biblioteca Casanatense): Treatment of Inguinal Hernia (fol. 24v). With permission of the Ministero per i Beni Culturali ed Ambientali.

statues, numbers of which were nude or semi-nude, surviving in Constantinople. Although this suggestion must, at present, be confined to the
realm of speculation, it is not impossible that the nakedness of these
statues was concealed by pieces of cloth. This is suggested by the ancient
Greek practice of clothing statues for ritual purposes.[20] Like *anasyrma*,
such a practice might have survived into the Byzantine period, albeit with
different motifs.

Secular images form a minority among the visual evidence surviving
from Byzantium. The remainder of this chapter will therefore be devoted
to the most common type of visual material that has come down to us from
Byzantium: religious imagery. Ostensibly, depictions of nudity in Byzantine
religious imagery, or their absence, offer themselves to very straightforward insights.

In Byzantine religious art nudity is often equated with evil and sin. This
equation is expressed in the depiction of naked women, probably prostitutes,
in the thrall of snakes in the Last Judgment fresco in the Church of the
Mavriotissa at Kastoria.[21] The all but full-frontal nudity of these bodies was
a powerful reminder of the consequence of lust to any Byzantine viewer
confronted with this fresco (Figure 17.5). This visual idea can also be found
in the sphere of Latin-rite Christianity, a particularly good example being
the sculpture of Luxuria being consumed by snakes in the south portal of
the church of Moissac in southern France.[22] If anything, however, western
medieval art tends to be more explicit in its equation of evil with nudity,
as is suggested by another sculpture from the south of France which shows
a female figure sporting a huge, snake-like penis, an image that is parallelled
in the hagiography of western saints.[23] This example and the Sheelagh-na-
Gigs indicate that depictions of nudity in general and of genitalia in
particular are more explicit in western medieval than in Byzantine art.

Another equation of nudity with evil can be found in depictions of
exorcisms. In fol. 35r of a thirteenth-century Gospel book (Mount Athos,
Iviron, cod. 5) the exorcism described in the Gospel of Matthew (Matthew
4.24) is shown (Figure 17.6).[24] In this miniature, two naked men with
dishevelled hair and broken chains round their neck are seen charging

---

[20] J. Pollard, *Seers, Shrines and Sirens* (New York, 1964), 44.

[21] S. Pelekanidis, *Kastoria*, 1 (Thessalonike, 1953), pl. 82b.

[22] M. Schapiro, *The Sculpture of Moissac* (London, 1985), 109.

[23] M. Camille, 'The Image and the Self: Unwriting Late Medieval Bodies', in Kay and
Rubin, *Framing Medieval Bodies*, p. 82, fig. 21. An example of western hagiography is St Bridget
who stated that: 'A serpent creepeth forth by the lower parts of my stomach unto the higher
parts, for my lust was inordinate; therefore now the serpent searcheth about my entrails without
comfort, gnawing and biting without mercy. My breast is open and gnawed with worms, for
I loved rotten things more than God.'

[24] Pelekanidis *et al.*, *Treasures of Mount Athos* 1, fig. 11.

towards Christ. The Gospel verse does not specify that those possessed by demons were naked. The nudity of the two figures in this miniature, together with the little black demons shown in the miniature, functions as a visual device expressing the state of mind of the two figures about to be cured by Christ. The crotch of the man closest to the front of the picture plane sports a lush growth of pubic hair, which forms a counterpart to his dishevelled hair. Even though the pubic hair entirely conceals the genitalia of the possessed, it serves to draw attention to his nudity, thus reinforcing the association of nudity with evil.

Some images from the Byzantine visual repertory, however, add a cautious note to the automatic equation of nudity with evil. An example can be found on fol. 272r of the *Sacra Parallela*, which shows St Basil between the chaste and the prurient woman (Figure 17.7).[25] In this miniature it is not the naked, but the clothed woman who is cast in a negative rôle. This identification is made not only in the text accompanying the miniature but also by the appearance of the woman: she is shown in luxurious, not to say extravagant, clothes and with the prominent earrings of a harlot. The good character of the nude female in this miniature is further emphasized by the gesture of blessing that the saint bestows upon her. The nudity of this woman, however, is of a special nature: the good nude is a prelapsarian one, lacking any indication of genitalia. Hers is a nudity of innocence. Even though the nude shown on fol. 272r of the *Sacra Parallela* is of a special nature, this example culled from the vast repertory of Byzantine religious art suggests caution in making blanket generalizations about the meaning of nudity in religious images.

In one of the very few studies of depictions of the body in Byzantium, it has been stated that the denial of the body was pronounced after iconoclasm.[26] This development is exemplified in depictions of Christ's baptism. The comparison between pre- and post-iconoclast depictions of Christ's baptism is instructive in this respect. In the Orthodox Baptistry in Ravenna, dated to the late fourth or early fifth century, and in the Arian Baptistry, which dates from the reign of Theoderic (493–526) and is modelled on the decoration in the Orthodox Baptistry, Christ is shown in the nude with his penis graphically depicted.[27] By contrast, the depiction of Christ without genitalia is standard in post-iconoclast representations of the

---

[25] Weitzmann, *Sacra Parallela*, 212–13 and fig. 567.

[26] I. Hutter, 'Das Bild der Frau in der byzantinischen Kunst', in W. Hörandner *et al.*, *Festschrift für Herbert Hunger zum 70. Geburtstag* (Vienna 1984), 163–70.

[27] Though there is, of course, an issue about restoration here. On the Orthodox Baptistry see A.J. Wharton, 'Ritual and Reconstructed Meaning: The Neonian Baptistry in Ravenna', *Art Bulletin* 69 (1987), 358–75.

Fig. 17.6. Gospel Book (Mount Athos, Iveron, cod. 5): Exorcism (fol. 35r). From *Treasures of Mount Athos* I (Athens, 1975), fig. 11.

Fig. 17.5. Kastoria, Church of the Mavriotissa: Last Judgement. From A. Moutsopoulos, *Kastoria* (Athens, 1967), fig. 110.

Fig. 17.8. Adam in Paradise, ivory (Florence, Bargello). Copyright © Hirmer Fotoarchiv.

Fig. 17.7. *Sacra Parallela* (Paris, Bibliothèque nationale, ms. 923): St Basil between the Chaste and Prurient Woman (fol. 272r). With permission of the Bibliothèque Nationale.

baptism.[28] The nudity of Christ in the Orthodox and the Arian Baptistries in Ravenna is likely to echo Early Christian baptismal practices. In baptismal rites of the Early Christian Church the nudity of the baptisands was associated with a state of innocence that contrasted with, and to some extent redeemed, Adam's state of shameful nudity after the Fall.[29] Later depictions of Christ's baptism suggest that this particular facet of nudity was no longer accepted in the post-iconoclast period and that Old Testament prohibitions of nudity (Exodus 20.26; Leviticus 18.6–19), echoed in some New Testament passages (Revelations 3.18 and 16.15), governed the making of images.

This point is also borne out by Old Testament images. Early Christian and post-iconoclast depictions of Adam and Eve in Paradise indicate that in the later period the genitalia of the First Beings were concealed or downright ignored. In an ivory dated to c.400 AD (Florence, Bargello Museum), Adam is shown in Paradise in full glorious nudity (Figure 17.8), whereas in an ivory dated to the first half of the eleventh century (Baltimore, Walters Art Gallery) the seated Adam is shown without any genitalia at all.

The later ivory would appear to conform quite closely with the views on Adam and Eve's nudity held by the early western Church Fathers. In the Christian West, Adam and Eve in their prelapsarian state were seen to be characterized by non-sexuality. The absence of Adam's genitalia in the Baltimore ivory can be seen to indicate that this image was intended to convey Adam's non-sexuality before the Fall. It was the Fall that, according to St Augustine of Hippo, marked the beginning of sinful carnal knowledge: 'Adam had defied God – and for every man born, the shame at the uncontrollable stirring of the genitals was a reminder of, and a fitting punishment for, the original crime of disobedience.'[30] The Early Christian ivory showing Christ in full nudity is less close to the spirit of St Augustine's views, even though it is much closer in date to his theological writings. This ivory, however, echoes the way in which the eastern Church Fathers interpreted the nudity of Adam. To them, his nudity was not worthy of condemnation. It was understood as a symbol not of sin but of human frailty.[31] This

---

[28] Examples are the Baptism of Christ in the two Athos manuscripts, the Homilies of Gregory the Theologian (Panteleimon, cod. 6) (fol. 161r) and the Gospels at the Iviron Monastery (Iviron, cod. 5) (fol. 138r). See Pelekanidis *et al.*, *Treasures of Mount Athos* 2, figs 309 and 22. In the depiction of the baptism in the Iviron manuscripts there is more of a hint of genitalia, but this may be a twentieth-century interpretation of the image.

[29] J.Z. Smith, 'The Garments of Shame', *History of Religions* 5 (1965/66), 217–38, repr. idem, *Map is Not Territory. Studies in the History of Religions* (Leiden, 1978), 1–23, see also S. Brock, 'Clothing Metaphors as a Means of Theological Expression in Syrian Tradition', in M. Schmidt, ed., *Typus, Symbol, Allegorie bei den östlichen Vätern* (Regensburg, 1982), 11–40.

[30] Augustine of Hippo, *Contra Julianum*, PL, 44, 648.

[31] M. Harl,'La prise de conscience de "la nudité" d'Adam. Une interprétation de Genèse 3,7 chez les Pères Grecs', *Studia Patristica* 7,1 (1966), 480–95.

disjuncture between the textual and the visual evidence may indicate that, by the time the ivory of Adam now in Baltimore was fashioned, the Byzantines interpreted the nudity of Adam in ways that approximated to the views of the Early Christian Fathers in the West.

This point is borne out further by an example from the late Byzantine period, the relief on the south portal of the Church of Hagia Sophia in Trebizond. Although much damaged, it is possible to discern that on this relief Adam and Eve appear respectably clothed in Paradise, but naked when expelled from the Garden of Eden.[32] This series of reliefs is based on the Orthodox Lenten Triodion recited in the week before Lent.[33] Clearly, this is not an image in which Adam and Eve's nudity was associated with innocence and frailty, as it had been in the view of the early Greek Fathers. At Trebizond, nudity is explicitly associated with shame and sinfulness.

Depictions of Adam and Eve in Byzantine art use the nudity of the First Beings in very complex ways. An early eleventh-century ivory casket in Cleveland serves to make this point: in the panel showing Adam and Eve in Paradise their genitalia are covered by large leaves emanating from a tree, whilst in the Expulsion scene Adam and Eve are shown with their crotches covered in identical hairy patches.[34] This is not a denial of the body as in both scenes the genitalia of Adam and Eve are acknowledged. Although hidden in the Paradise scene, the leaves refer to their presence, emphasizing that concealment is not the same absence. In the Expulsion scene the depiction of pubic hair draws attention to the genitalia of Adam and Eve and the sin they committed. Comparing the Early Christian ivory from Florence with the eleventh-century example from Cleveland, it is evident that there was no linear progression from a naturalist depiction of the nude body in the pre-iconoclast period to a denial of the body in the post-iconoclast period.

The depiction in art of a second Old Testament event allows us to explore further the complex meaning of nudity in Byzantine culture. This is the pictorial treatment of the Drunkenness of Noah. The rendering of this subject in the sixth-century Vienna Genesis is standard for this scene in Byzantine art. The illustrator has chosen to depict not the moment when Ham beholds his father lying naked in a drunken stupor, but the point in the story when Shem and Japheth cover their father, with averted eyes. The Genesis cycle at San Marco, which is based on the fifth- to early sixth-century Cotton Genesis, shows that, at any rate in the Early Christian period, other episodes of this Old Testament story could be depicted: at San Marco, the

---

[32] D. Talbot Rice, ed., *The Church of Hagia Sophia at Trebizond* (Edinburgh, 1968), pls 16–18.

[33] A. Eastmond, 'The Genesis Frieze at Hagia Sophia, Trebizond and Narratives of the Fall', *DOP* (forthcoming).

[34] Goldschmidt and Weitzmann, *Die byzantinischen Elfenbeinskulpturen* I (Berlin, 1930), pls XLVII b and d.

mosaicists have shown not only Shem and Japheth covering their father, but also Ham beholding his father's nakedness.[35] The thirteenth-century mosaicists at San Marco did not, contrary to artists in the East, refrain from depiction of what, at least from a modern perspective, appears to be a scene of same-sex voyeurism. The interpretation of this scene as having overtones of same-sex voyeurism is unlikely to be entirely anachronistic. Some of the vocabulary used in this Scriptural passage can indeed be read as having homoerotic overtones.[36]

Byzantine depictions of the Drunkenness of Noah concentrate on Shem and Japheth acting differently from their brother and avoiding his fate. The non-depiction of Noah's nakedness, however, not merely concerns Ham's more fortunate brothers, but also the viewer seeing this image. In most Byzantine renderings of Shem and Japheth covering their father, there is no need for them to avert their eyes because he is already covered. The cloth covering Noah's nakedness, it can be suggested, exists for the benefit of viewers. One way of explaining the fact that Noah is already covered is to see the cloth as a device that prevents viewers from succumbing, voluntarily or involuntarily, to either homosexual or heterosexual voyeurism and titillation. This is perhaps where some of the reasons for the incomplete, genitalia-free nudes in Byzantine imagery or, in the case of the Drunkenness of Noah, the conflation of different stages of the narrative in one image, lie: the effects of these images on viewers had to exclude dangerous forms of stimulation; viewers were meant to focus on more spiritual matters.[37]

Such an argument is not without its problems. These can be examined further by considering the image of Christ Crucified. Alongside the Old Testament subjects discussed above, the Crucified Christ is an image central to an understanding of nudity or semi-nudity in Byzantine art. Perhaps more so than the other images discussed here, it problematizes the relationship between spectators and the nude body.

Although the Scriptural passages state that Christ was crucified naked, it is unlikely that a person executed on the cross in the Late Roman period was stark naked. A person about to be executed at that period was likely to have worn a *subligaculum*, a Roman version of the G-string. In the earliest surviving depictions of the Crucifixion, examples being a fourth-century ivory plaque (London, British Museum) and the fifth-century wooden doors of the church of Sta Sabina in Rome, Christ is shown with such a cover concealing his genital area.[38] In Byzantine, as indeed in

---

[35] O. Demus, *The Mosaics of San Marco* (Chicago, 1984), 48

[36] Trexler, 'Gendering Christ', 115.

[37] Trexler, 'Gendering Christ', 111–13.

[38] P. Barbet, *La Passion de Notre-Seigneur Jésus Christ selon le chirurgien* (Paris, 1950), 77–83; P. Thoby, *Le Crucifix des origines au Concile de Trente* (Nantes, 1959), 22 and pl. IV, nos 9 and 10.

western medieval art, by contrast, Christ's genitalia are covered by a *perizonium*. Especially in the pre-iconoclast period, Christ may even be fully dressed in a *colobium*.[39]

It might be argued that the concealment of Christ's genitalia by a loincloth is an instance of prudery designed to protect the viewer, even though, as has already been indicated, it was unlikely that people executed on the cross in the Roman Empire were fully naked. Indeed, it has been suggested that Christ's genitalia were concealed to prevent viewers from using the image for purposes of sexual gratification.[40] Whether Christ's loincloth was designed to protect the faithful, especially women and young men, in the early Christian and medieval periods from the dangers of seduction – an argument that could also be applied to the Drunkenness of Noah – must, however, remain a moot point. Such a view would appear to be dangerously anachronistic, not least because it equates the depiction of the Crucifixion with a modern pornographic pin-up. At the same time, deliberations about Christ's loincloth can clearly benefit from a consideration of the rôle of the viewer. The concealment of Christ's manhood, it suggested here, can be viewed more profitably, not with regard to social control and attempts to suppress sexual gratification, but with reference to the way in which people in the Middle Ages dealt with shame.

Shame, a feeling or mental state, is often associated with nudity. Even though some people have argued that the concept of shame was only developed in the post-medieval period,[41] there is ample evidence to suggest that the feeling of shame was known to and experienced by people in the Middle Ages.[42] As with nudity, the experience of shame is not uniform over different periods of time. It has been suggested, for instance, that in the pre-modern period shame was felt not only by those being seen naked, but also by those seeing someone else naked.[43] Thus, the concealment of Christ's nudity, or even the avoidance of his semi-nudity, can be seen as a way of facilitating viewers' devotion by enabling them to ponder on the suffering body of Christ without experiencing shame. Christ's loincloth

---

[39] A representative pre-iconoclast example is a seventh- to eighth-century icon in the Monastery of St Catherine at Mount Sinai showing the crucified Christ wearing a *colobium*. See K. Weitzmann, *The Monastery of Saint Catherine at Mount Sinai. The Icons, vol.I: from the Sixth to the Tenth Century* (Princeton, 1976), 61–4 and plate XXV. On the Crucifixion of Christ in late western medieval art see J. Wirth, 'Sur l'évolution du crucifix à la fin du moyen âge', *Les ateliers des interprètes. Revue européenne pour étudiants en histoire de l'art* 2 (1989), 177ff.

[40] Trexler, 'Gendering Christ', 111–3.

[41] N. Elias, *Über den Prozess der Zivilisation* I (Basle, 1939), 222–4.

[42] H.P. Duerr, *Nacktheit und Scham* (Frankfurt, 1988); see also J.-C. Boulogne, *Histoire de la pudeur* (Paris, 1986).

[43] K. Schreiner, '"Si homo non pecasset..." Der Sündenfall Adams und Evas in seiner Bedeutung für die soziale, seelische und körperliche Verfaßtheit des Menschen', in Schreiner and Schnitzler, eds, *Gepeinigt, Begehrt, Vergessen*, 63.

made for a viewing experience that protected viewers from feelings of shame which would have been counterproductive to the exercises of meditation and devotion.

Bearing in mind the dangers of applying modern conceptual frameworks to depictions of the Crucified Christ, there is nevertheless evidence to suggest that the nudity of Christ on the cross was conceived of as a problem in the Middle Ages, at any rate in Latin-rite Christianity. Most famously, Gregory of Tours relates a miracle that involved an image of the Christ in Narbonne Cathedral, a picture described by Gregory as showing 'our Lord on the cross, girded as it were with linen.'[44] At one point a 'terrifying person appeared to the priest Basilius in a vision and said: "All of you are clothed in various garments, but you see me always naked. Come now, as quickly as possible cover me with a curtain."'[45] At first, Basilius did not react, but the man repeatedly appeared in visions and only vanished when Christ's body was hung with a curtain. This story finds echoes in Durandus's much later *Rationale Divinorum Officiorum* which he notes with approval that Greek artists not only avoided three-dimensional images, but painted all their icons 'only from the navel upwards that all occasion of vain thoughts be removed'.[46]

Byzantine depictions of the Crucifixion clearly do not accord with Durandus's characterization of Byzantine icons, at any rate those from the post-iconoclast period. It was in the wake of the iconoclast controversy that depictions of Christ dressed in a loincloth first co-existed with and then gradually replaced those showing Christ dressed in a colobium. Depictions of Christ wearing a perizonium became increasingly common after iconoclasm because the revealed body emphasizes Christ's suffering and his humanity.[47] Indeed, it is these post-iconoclast depictions of the Crucifixion that do not chime easily with the view, referred to earlier, that the body was comprehensively denied in post-iconoclast Byzantine imagery. The development of Crucifixion images in Byzantine art indicates that the renunciation of the body was not a straightforward and linear process.

The image of the Crucifixion, perhaps more so than any of the other images discussed in this preliminary assessment of depictions of nudity or semi-nudity in Byzantine art, also provides insights into perceptions of nudity. In the absence of equivalent Byzantine texts, Gregory of Tours' story of the Narbonne cross will have to serve as a way into this problem. According to Gregory's description of the cross, Christ Crucified was not

---

[44] Gregory of Tours, *Glory of the Martyrs*, tr. R. van Dam (Liverpool, 1988), 41.

[45] Gregory of Tours, *Glory of the Martyrs*, 41.

[46] G. Durandus, *Rationale Divinorum Officiorum*, eds A. Davil and T. M. Thibodeau (Turnhoult, 1995), 1.3.2.

[47] J.R. Martin, 'The Dead Christ on the Cross in Byzantine Art', *Late Classical and Medieval Studies in Honor of Albert Mathias Friend* (Princeton, 1955), 189–96.

naked, but his loins were shrouded in a cloth.[48] Yet the passage makes it quite clear that the image of the Crucified was considered to be naked. The perception of nudity enshrined in Gregory's account of the Narbonne cross is echoed in the Greek word for 'naked' or 'nude'. *Gymnos* not only means naked; it can also mean semi-nude, precisely the state Christ bemoans in the dream recounted by Gregory.

The semantic nuances of the word *gymnos* in ancient and Byzantine Greek have profound implications for an historically rooted understanding of nudity in Byzantium. The different shades of meaning provide one indicator that, in the pre-modern period, nudity was conceived in a manner that overlaps only partially with modern perceptions. At the very least then, the concern with reasons for the concealment or absence of genitalia in depictions of the Crucifixion or of other images whose textual sources imply nudity, says far more about modern than about Byzantine preoccupations.

---

[48] Gregory of Tours, *Glory of the Martyrs*, 41.

Section VI

Conclusion

18. Desire in Byzantium – the Ought and the Is

Averil Cameron

One of the main problems for a Byzantinist faced with a search for desire and denial lies in the nature of the material with which which he or she must work. Faced with the aim of finding examples of 'real' desire in Byzantium, the difficulty is the reverse of the standard philosophical dilemma about the logical status of general rules; rather, the problem for Byzantinists is how to get back from the 'Ought' (the prescriptive literature, the rules laid down in the canons and so on) to the real 'Is' of Byzantium. Many of the contributors have accordingly set out to persuade us that Byzantium was not really the repressed and ascetic society it liked sometimes to think it was, but, if anything, the reverse, a culture as much governed by desire as any other, a civilization in which people behaved much as they always have and always will, some following the rules, others, and probably the majority, lapsing from time to time, or even ignoring them altogether. A highly prescriptive society, organized along traditional lines, and with a highly prescriptive religion, does not necessarily guarantee uniformly conformist behaviour. If anything, it might be said on this view that an excess of the 'Ought' in fact produces and encourages its opposite. Taking the simplest definition of desire as sexual desire, it is probably true to say that a significant proportion of Byzantine men and women were committed to lives of celibacy. Yet the rules were probably not generally obeyed, and the real impact of denial, and the licence allowed to desire, in Byzantine society remain hard to grasp.

Thus in attempting to address the questions of desire and denial, Byzantinists are faced with many problems, first among which is the nature of the evidence. So much of the textual tradition is prescriptive. So much of it is either religious or else at least written by authors who are themselves clerics and monastics. The same problem is to be found in much of the surviving visual art, and many contributors have accordingly taken it as their first task to find evidence of the opposite, of sexual activity, or at least erotic interest. Furthermore, an ascetic discourse pervades many – even if admittedly not all – parts of Byzantine literature from the start to the end of the period. Does this make Byzantium an ascetic society?[1] Overtly, at least, it is the denial of desire, not its fulfilment, that confers power in Byzantium. Was Byzantium in fact pervaded by and organized round the principle of denial and restriction? Are those black-garbed nuns depicted in rows in the Lincoln College *typikon* in some way symbolic of Byzantine society as a whole? And do the persistence of heresy-hunting and the baroque variations manifested over centuries in the literature of heresiology indicate a genuinely repressive regime?

The professed objective of the Symposium which lies behind this volume was to concern itself with exploring 'Byzantine attitudes to their own humanity and the frailties of that humanity'. In the words of Liz James, 'it aims to look at the different ways in which Byzantine attitudes to corporeality affected their perceptions of themselves and of the world around them.' The public face of Byzantium was one either of denial, ascetic renunciation, the subjection of the body – which might involve rigours, discomfort, or even pain – or else at best one of respectability, the more domestic note attained by some kinds of hagiography such as the ninth-century *Life of St Philaretos*, or the maternal image of the Virgin cultivated after iconoclasm, or the eulogies of married love and family affection in the eleventh to thirteenth century literature recently discussed by Angeliki Laiou.[2] The body we hear most about in Byzantium is the ascetic body; yet the ascetic body is a a body unacknowledged, a body denied, a body submitted voluntarily to pain and discomfort. Asceticism also entails temptation, when the body is assailed by pangs of lust, or tempted by warmth and luxurious food; pleasure, even one of the ordinary pleasures of life, is symbolized as dangerous and evil. To the same sphere in the ideological sense belong all those categorized as the enemies of truth, so that in heresiology, as in religious art, the heretic, the Jew, the iconoclast 'other', is demonised, depicted as black and ugly, or presented as absurd. The opposite sphere ought logically to be the sphere of beauty and pleasure. Yet, as we have seen, there is little discourse of pleasure in Byzantium; indeed, pleasure is not regarded as a good, or as the object of human life, but rather as something illicit and potentially deceptive. Even Paradise is depicted in terms of a return to the virginal state of Adam and Eve before the Fall rather than, as it is for example in the Islamic tradition, as the location of pleasure. The just look pallid and uninteresting in Byzantine art

---

[1] The question is posed in A.M. Cameron, 'Ascetic Closure and the End of Antiquity', in V. Wimbush and R. Valantasis, eds, *Asceticism* (New York, 1995), 147–61.

[2] A. E. Laiou, *Mariage, amour et parenté à Byzance aux XIe–XIIIe siècles* (Paris, 1992).

in comparison with the vividly drawn sufferings of the wicked. The case is similar in the sphere of physical health during life itself: the sick body in Byzantium is the object of great attention, whether as the inmate of hospitals or such institutions, or as the recipient of charity from the more fortunate, or healing from the holy man. But the healthy body is not correspondingly celebrated.

The first question, then, must be how far this actually was the prevailing discourse in Byzantium, and if so, how representative it is of the society from which it springs; if it is not in fact wholly, or even partly, representative, then we must of course go on to ask why it is so prevalent. It is therefore not surprising if many of the contributions have chosen to focus on the task of discovering evidence of physical desire and erotic passion, in short, sex. Against the assumption that Byzantine society was undeveloped in its discourse of eroticism, let us show that real Byzantines lived and loved like us. We can certainly find such indications in many places. Alexander Kazhdan has done so in overtly ascetic saints' lives.[3] Another way of approach, followed in some of the papers included here, is to discuss the teachings of the religious texts on the body and the passions: Anastasios of Sinai on body and soul; Methodios on the nature of virginity; spiritual treatises on resisting the passions. A conspicuous absence in this Symposium has been medical evidence, in contrast with the extensive use made by writers about the body in earlier periods, like Michel Foucault or Aline Rousselle, of the Hippocratic corpus and the works of Galen. [4] It might be said that the many sets of miracle stories from the early Byzantine period which do seem to offer rich material for the topic are in practice mainly concerned to demonstrate the superiority of spiritual over scientific healing. Perhaps the Byzantines were more interested in the body as the locus for spiritual precepts, or for a theological anthropology, than as a real living organism subject to growth and decay.

The overall strategy adopted in this collection, however, is to seek to undermine the first impression of Byzantium as a culture in which desire is repressed and where denial prevails, and indeed one cannot help detecting a defensive tone in many of the papers, as though Byzantium needs to be claimed for the modern world of desire. Seen in this light, the historian's task is conceived as being that of digging out of this unpromising context the signs of sexual activity and sexual consciousness. Several contributors have therefore pointed to evidence of sexual themes in visual art, and we have been warned against essentialism, and taught to see the black and white language of the texts as standing in front of a grey and

---

[3] A. Kazhdan, 'Byzantine Hagiography and Sex in the Fifth to Twelfth Centuries', DOP 44 (1990), 131–43.

[4] See A. Rousselle, Porneia (Paris, 1983).

shifting background. A particularly good example of this strategy is provided by the contributions which tackle the question of same-sex love in Byzantium – just as it is a first strategy of feminist historians to try to 'find' women in the unpromising context of Byzantium, so we now look for same-sex love, or even, with John Boswell, same-sex marriage.[5] Queer theory, like women's history and gender studies, can probably uncover much that is relevant in Byzantium. [6] Indeed, the texts give us some encouragement, if only in their usual oblique way, through the persistent warnings in the ascetic literature against the dangers of consorting with 'beardless youths', and the licence allowed in some contexts to eunuchs. And whatever our own personal agenda, it seems only common sense to think that there must have been same-sex desire in Byzantium, just as it seems only common sense to want to show that the Byzantines were 'like us'.

Yet the concept of 'real life' or the everyday, in Byzantium as elsewhere, is highly problematic. The Byzantine man-in-the-street has been much sought, yet remains as elusive as ever, and the woman-in-the-street still more so.[7] Indeed, if we are to speak of the operation of desire, one might rather say that the saint, not the ordinary person, is the organizing figure in Byzantium.

Defined in Late Antiquity and regularly reinvented, the saint personified desire. Saints' lives, so fundamental to Byzantine writing, and the depictions of saints that are equally fundamental to Byzantine visual art, present a narration focused on the body; they are necessarily structured as stories of an individual who inhabits a human body. As such, discourse *about* the saint's body is to be found in every saint's life; how the saint inhabits and deals with his or her body is a main qualification for saintliness. It is equally essential to the narration that the saint's body is assailed – by temptation, in the form of demons, or passions – or by external factors such as weather, cold or sun.[8] The saintly body is the scene of trial and triumph, and Charles Barber has well shown the extent to which the body in these texts has become 'a battleground in the struggle over representation'. While ostensibly denying the importance of the body, the narrative in fact enhances its importance. In turn, visual depictions of saints by their very nature underscore the saint's physical being. The denial of the body is a trope

---

[5] J.Boswell, *The Marriage of Likeness. Same-Sex Unions in Pre-Modern Europe* (New York, 1995).

[6] For example see D. Bell and G. Valentine, eds, *Mapping Desire: Geographies of Sexuality* (London, 1995); J. Dollimore, *Sexual Dissidence: Augustine to Wilde, Freud to Foucault* (Oxford, 1993). There is food for thought, as well as much to criticize, in A. Betsky, *Queer Space. Architecture and Same-Sex Desire* (New York, 1997).

[7] Take for instance the problematic concept of *homo byzantinus*, raised by Kazhdan in A. Kazhdan and G. Constable, *People and Power in Byzantium* (Washington DC, 1983), and the various attempts to describe 'daily life' in Byzantium.

[8] See G. Harpham, *The Ascetic Imperative* (Chicago, 1987), chap. 3, 'The Signs of Temptation'.

which permits and requires a discourse that is in fact centred upon the very body it purports to deny. To return to desire: the saint in Byzantine saints' lives is also implicitly or explicitly suffused with *eros*, the desire or yearning for union with the divine. The saint's life is a journey led by this kind of desire, and beset with trials along the way. Theodoret of Cyrrhus in the fifth century writes of Syrian religious women as 'maddened' by yearning and desire. ... They see union with the Bridegroom in terms of love, which is 'like a firebrand' from the stimulus of their asceticism. One can only succeed in philosophy, says Theodoret, that is, the religious and ascetic life, if one is fervently enamoured of God. The apostles Peter and Paul were moved by desire; now, in Theodoret's own day, the ascetics in Syria are 'wounded by the sweet darts of love' and 'intoxicated with desire'.[9]

Four criteria have been said to determine the nature of saints' lives: 'narrativity, corporeality, textuality and historicality'.[10] All are present in the earliest classic saint's life of all, the fourth-century *Life of Antony*, which laid down a dominant pattern for the future.[11] The quality of corporeality, the intense focus on the physical and the symbolic body of the saint, gave rise, I would suggest, to certain real problems in Byzantine consciousness. In fact, I would argue, this very concentration on the body, and on the language of desire, at least during some periods of Byzantine culture, either affected or even prevented a discourse about the realities of human love. It called instead for a contrasting discourse of bodily failure, of temptation, of weakness or frailty.[12] Recent writers have studied the characteristic discourses of the body in early imperial Rome, and linked the sense of display, and of performance, and of suffering, in authors like Seneca, to the cultural spectacle of the Roman arena and theatre.[13] In Byzantium there was also a rhetoric of display and performance. But it was configured round the notion of the saint or ascetic, rising above the body through desire and amid pain and suffering. What this discourse did not do, any more than Seneca's *Letters*, was to offer a positive model in our terms for the human body, human passions or physical fulfilment. The ascetic discourse in fact paralleled the theological debate about the impassibility of God, whether

---

[9] See A.M. Cameron, 'Sacred and Profane Love: Thoughts on Byzantine Gender', in L. James, ed., *Women, Men and Eunuchs. Gender in Byzantium* (London, 1997), 1–23, at 13–14.

[10] E.Wyschogrod, *Saints and Postmodernism* (Chicago, 1990), 29.

[11] For interesting discussion of the problematization of the body in the *Life of Antony* and other such texts, see N. Kelsey, 'The Body as Desert in the *Life of St Anthony*', *Semeia* 57 (1992), 131–51; R. Valantasis, 'Daemons and the Perfecting of the Monk's Body: Monastic Anthropology, Daemonology and Asceticism', *Semeia* 58 (1992), 47–79.

[12] The inverse of the saint's life from this point of view (i.e. reversing the two aspects) is a work like J. Genet's *Our Lady of the Flowers* (for which see Wyschogrod, *Saints and Postmodernism*, 220).

[13] C. Barton, *The Sorrows of the Ancient Romans* (Princeton, 1993); E. Scarry, *The Body in Pain: the Making and Unmaking of the World* (Oxford, 1993).

Christ himself suffered in the flesh, that is, whether the divine could suffer; in this debate the extreme position, against which orthodox theologians had to argue with some vigour, and which also lay behind some aspects of the problems of images, was that Christ, being divine, could not really have suffered on the cross. The saint's imperviousness to suffering and discomfort is a theme in nearly all saints' lives, and one can read the ascetic aspiration in turn as an attempt, even if modified, to attain a similar degree of impassibility. There could hardly be a greater contrast between the Byzantine ideal and the postmodern experience, 'a discourse of limitless desire'.[14]

In Byzantium, *eros* was appropriated from Platonism into the sphere of Christian asceticism, and into the habitual language used of the relationship of the soul to God. Exegesis like that of Origen on the *Song of Songs* and the hierarchical schemas proposed in the writings of Pseudo-Dionysios the Areopagite, made desire, *eros*, and with it longing, *pothos,* the lynch-pins of religious experience. The soul longs for God, and God for the soul, like lovers thirsty for each other. Love's arrow, the wound of love, the darts which smite the lover – all these images of romantic love are to be found in the ascetic literature of early Byzantium, applied to the soul and its quest for God. The anthropology of mysticism was configured round *eros*, the passion which draws the soul ever towards God. It presents a grammar of desire, a pattern on which the soul aspires to heavenly truth, which has little to do with the everyday pragmatics of sexual or emotional experience. Yet this grammatology of desire, in which passion was taken from the human sphere and appropriated for the spiritual, consigned bodily passion, physical desire, to the lower and inferior rungs of the heavenly ladder. So powerful, I believe, was the model, and so strongly contrasted with the prevailing discourse of modern society, that it is hard for us to imagine the conflicts which it must have presented in relation to individual behaviour. The Byzantines were people like us, certainly, but in crucial ways their experience was not like ours at all.

Understandably, some of the contributors are at pains to read Byzantium differently by wresting it from its heavily Christian associations; indeed the old view of the Byzantine 'theocracy' makes it even more difficult to find ordinary life, let alone desire. However, not only the Byzantines themselves, but also some modern thinkers would locate desire exactly within theology: a female liberation theologian from Brazil has described women's theology as precisely 'the challenge to restore the primacy of desire within theological discourse', contrasting the warmth and passion which she demands with 'the cold circumspection of purely scientific inquiry'.[15]

---

[14] Wyschogrod, *Saints and Postmodernism*, 191.

[15] Maria Clara Bingemer, cited by U. King, *Christ in All Things* (Maryknoll, New York, 1997), 131. See Wyschogrod, *Saints and Postmodernism*, 144–5 on George Bataille.

In contrast, George Bataille differentiates Christianity from other religions precisely by its stress on love, seen as the means of achieving continuity and transcending violence.[16]

If then desire became problematic for ordinary Byzantines, what of love? The Byzantines on the whole had rather little to say about it. Some contributions have touched on the affective. But it is not very easy to write about the emotions, as distinct from the passions, in Byzantium. When Michel Foucault wrote *The Care of the Self*, in which he explored the greater emphasis placed on the regime of one's own body in the period roughly from the first century before to the first century after Christ – a book which lies behind a great deal of recent writing about the body – it was as part of a *History of Sexuality*. [17] In contrast, a book of Julia Kristeva's writings appeared at almost the same time with the title *Histoires d'amour*.[18] What then can be said about love in Byzantium? As we have seen, domestic love and conjugal affect are praised in the funerary and marriage orations of the eleventh to thirteenth centuries. But the stance of the writers is demanded by the social context and circumstances of the time, when dynastic marriages have become an important element in court and aristocratic life, and the literature praises the values and qualities claimed for such alliances. Eros is of course also an organizing principle in the romances of a similar period. In most other ways, though, the discourse of love in Byzantium is displaced from the human sphere. We encounter it not least in the homilies and visual art concerned with one of the most characteristic of Byzantine themes, that of the Mother of God. From the ninth century onwards, these representations draw to themselves the maternal, loving and affectionate qualities that are hard to find expressed in other Byzantine contexts.[19] Icons were themselves the objects of love, revered by the believer with kisses. And in the view of Julia Kristeva in her essay on the Virgin, 'Stabat Mater', the Virgin is above all the desiring subject: thus Mary, in the Deesis representation with the Virgin and St. John on either side of Christ on the Cross, is defined in relation to her Son by a relationship of desire.[20]

In Byzantium, I would argue, there was a constant dialectic between the language of denial and the language of desire. Its specific nature changed at different times, but the tension, the unease, remained. Most of the time we have more of the literature of condemnation and prohibition than of affirmation. A first problem, then, is indeed to excavate among all this the signs of actual sexual activity and sexual consciousness, and this problem

---

[16] See Wyschgogrod, *Saints and Postmodernism*, 144–5.
[17] M. Foucault, *The Care of the Self*, Eng. tr. (London and New York, 1986).
[18] J. Kristeva, *Histoires d'amour* (Paris, 1983).
[19] I. Kalavrezou, 'Images of the Mother: When the Virgin Mary became *Meter Theou*', DOP 44 (1990), 167–72.
[20] Eng. tr. in T.Moi, *The Kristeva Reader* (Oxford, 1986), 160–86.

AVERIL CAMERON

is itself concerned first and foremost with that of representation. Alexander Kazhdan's idea that there is a 'normal sexual activity' in every society, Byzantium included, has been challenged. Desire, on the contrary, is associated in Byzantium with danger, illusion and deception; whatever is going on, it is not straightforward. As Shaun Tougher memorably said during the Symposium, 'We as readers have our own part to play in the detection of desire and its denial.' Furthermore, desire in Byzantine texts is generally associated with women – women too are situated within the rhetoric of deceit, illusion and trickery. When we encounter desire, say, in the early Byzantine story of Pelagia the repentant prostitute, it is significantly in a theatrical context, the context of display, and therefore of falsity. Pelagia's beauty is central to the text, for unlike the representation of the Mother of God, it enables her to represent woman as both the object of desire and the source of illusion. She goes on to another illusion, the long disguise as a monk, and only death and the loss of her beauty can reveal the truth. Another story which turns on the matter of display is the slightly later *Life* of Symeon the Fool, in which Symeon's holiness is revealed by his displaying himself naked in the women's baths, in a deliberate negation of expected desire.[21]

As part of this process of metaphorically digging up the signs of desire in Byzantium, we have considered whether there is an archaeology of desire to balance Foucault's archaeology of knowledge. The anthropology of desire has been considered in relation to the writings of Anastasios of Sinai's views about body and soul, and in a sympathetic reading of Methodios. We have seen, in a very different connection, that the early monastic literature provided titillation as well as edification, peopled as it is with lapsed monks, nieces who turn out to be prostitutes, virtuous women who 'fall', and monks who leave their monasteries in order to rescue them. We have heard about desire in dreams and in erotic epigrams, lust on ivories, and romantic love in the novels.

Yet the Symposium left us, I suggest, with an intriguing view of Byzantium as a society officially and overtly 'in denial', where that very denial points to what was in fact a high awareness of sex and desire – of sex as dangerous, risky and important; of sex as a challenge to religion and the social order; of sex as a threat, and resistance to it as an achievement. On this reading Byzantium emerges not so much as a place of 'normal sexual activity', whatever that may be, but as a theatre of desire, where sex has been taken away from the everyday and located in a danger area hedged around with 'keep off' signs.

[21] For Pelagia, see conveniently B. Ward, *Harlots of the Desert. A Study of Repentance in Monastic Sources* (Kalamazoo, 1987); Leontius of Neapolis, *Life of Symeon the Fool*, ed. A.J. Festugière, (Paris, 1974); D. Krueger, *Symeon the Holy Fool. Leontius's* Life *and the Late Antique City* (Berkeley and Los Angeles, 1996).

This leaves precious little room for affection and emotion to come through in the sources, however much we would like to find them. When they do, as in the novels, or the letter collections, they surface generally in genres that are highly literary and highly artificial, and so difficult to interpret. And if sex and desire are fraught with tension in Byzantium, then it is going to be difficult even to find pleasure unalloyed. The most memorable result of the Symposium seems to me to be this very sense of constant dialectic between denial and desire. It seems appropriate to end with a passage from the conclusion of Gillian Rose's *Love's Work*, a book about all the kinds of eros which we have considered here:

> *L'amour se révèle en se retirer*. If the Lover retires too far, the light of love is extinguished and the Beloved dies; if the Lover approaches too near the Beloved, she is effaced by the love and ceases to have an independent existence. The Lovers must leave a distance, a boundary, for love; then they approach and retire so that love may suspire. This may be heard as the economics of Eros; but it may also be taken as the infinite passion of faith: *Dieu se révèle en se retirer*.[22]

---

[22] G. Rose, *Love's Work* (London, 1995), 133.

Index